THE JORDANIAN–PALESTINIAN–ISRAELI TRIANGLE
Smoothing the Path to Peace

The Late Prime Minister Yitzhak Rabin,
one of the architects of the peace process in the Middle East,
was assassinated because of his commitment to the peace process.
He succeeded in laying the foundation, but unfortunately was
deprived of the opportunity to complete the structure.
We dedicate this volume to his memory.

This book is sponsored by

The National Center for Human Resources Development, Amman

The Jewish-Arab Center, University of Haifa
The Gustav Heinemann Institute of Middle Eastern Studies
The Friedrich Ebert Stiftung
The Bertha Von Suttner Research Program

The Institute on Global Conflict and Cooperation,
University of California

THE Jordanian–Palestinian–Israeli TRIANGLE

Smoothing the Path to Peace

Forewords by
His Royal Highness Crown Prince El Hassan
Shimon Peres, MK

Edited by
Joseph Ginat
and
Onn Winckler

sussex
ACADEMIC
PRESS

2 4 6 8 10 9 7 5 3 1

First published 1998 in Great Britain by
SUSSEX ACADEMIC PRESS
Box 2950
Brighton BN2 5SP

and in the United States of America by
SUSSEX ACADEMIC PRESS
c/o International Specialized Book Services, Inc.
5804 N.E. Hassalo St.
Portland, Oregon 97213-3644

British Library Cataloguing in Publication Data
A CIP catalogue record for this book is available from the British Library.

Library of Congress Cataloging-in-Publication Data
The Jordanian–Palestinian–Israeli triangle : smoothing the path to peace : forewords by Crown Prince El Hassan, Shimon Peres / edited by Joseph Ginat and Onn Winckler.
p. cm.
Based on conferences held in Amman, Jordan and Haifa University, Israel.
Includes bibliographical references and index.
ISBN 1–898723–82–6 (hardcover : alk. paper). — ISBN 1–902210–03–4 (pbk. : alk. paper)
1. Arab-Israeli conflict—1993– —Peace—Congresses. 2. Israel—Foreign relations—Jordan—Congresses. 3. Jordan—Foreign relations—Israel—Congresses. 4. Palestinian Arabs—Politics and government—Congresses. 5. Israel—Foreign economic relations—Jordan—Congresses. 6. Jordan—Foreign economic relations—Israel—Congresses. 7. Palestinian Arabs—Economic conditions—Congresses. 8. Palestinian National Authority—Congresses. 9. Jerusalem—International status—Congresses. 10. Pacific settlement of international disputes—Congresses.
I. Ginat, J. II. Winckler, Onn.
DS119.76.J67 1998
956.05′3—dc21 98–14129
CIP

Printed by Biddles Ltd, Guildford and King's Lynn
This book is printed on acid-free paper

Contents

Foreword by His Royal Highness Crown Prince El Hassan

Two years ago, Palestinians, Jordanians and Israelis got together in Amman and Haifa to talk about the "special relationship" underlying their historic association with one another. They also discussed the ways that politics, culture and economics had shaped the context for this trilateral dialogue. Proceeding from the view that none of the "three legs to the table" could completely sever themselves from one another, even in the worst of times, the participants talked frankly about their expectations for peace, and offered practical solutions for concretizing it amidst the reality of constantly shifting political agendas in the "New Middle East."

I find their conversations stimulating and thought-provoking. Every participant at the conference must have felt that they were starting a new page, and that it was incumbent upon them to lay aside their historic grievances to reflect upon the demographic, economic and strategic alliances in the offing between three peoples at once very different from one another and yet very similar in so many ways.

It is true, as more than one participant observed, that Jordan's role has always been that of the median between two poles, in war or peace. We have always understood our strengths to be that of conciliation, moderation and centralism. This moderation has been used by my country to de-limit a space for discussion between former enemies, and to enter into a genuine dialogue between neighbors. It behooves us to use this once-in-a-lifetime opportunity well, to rationally and purposefully work out our many problems to the very best of our abilities.

Peace is a very long process. It entails not only shaking hands with a former opponent but engaging his mind and his heart as well. We cannot let hurdles in our way proscribe our march toward goals in common, such as reconciliation, understanding and rapprochement. We must not allow detours and circumventions in peace accords signed with the best of intentions.

Most of all, the realization that what unites us is far more than what divides us should be the central motif of all our endeavors.

It is with this spirit that I warmly recommend this book, and wish the contributors every success in their next trialogue.

Royal Palace
Amman, Jordan
20 December 1997

Foreword by Shimon Peres, MK

In the Israeli–Jordanian–Palestinian triangle, one side must be careful not to harm the other two sides. There are three entities involved here, whose geography and demography intermingle, and are sometimes confused. The long borderline, starting at the Yarmuk and ending at the Red Sea, is not incontestable. Two sections of it belong to Jordan–Israel relations, and one section belongs to Israel's relations with the Palestinians and the Jordanians. The residents of Jordan include many citizens of Palestinian origin, and for close to fifty years most Palestinians carried a Jordanian passport. Judea and Samaria, too, which are contiguous to the Jordanian border, do not constitute unequivocal demographic boxes. Any attempt to divide this triangle economically or politically means having to work out a difficult puzzle.

In those places where the ground alignments and settlement deployments do not enable unambiguous fencing, one must turn to the true alternative: the maintenance of good relations, which will compensate for the crazy borders.

It is clear that such relations are vital in the economic sphere. There must be an open economy among the three components of this triangle: something along the lines of Benelux. It is unthinkable to fill the West Bank and then scatter customs houses and transit arrangements along this border, so that the simple tomato would not be allowed to go from farmer to consumer without being squashed along the way. Most of the world is currently built on a market economy, not on a national economy. The economy of a still more open market is required even more within this triangle.

I, for one, think it possible to turn the border between us and the Jordanians into a geographical opportunity of cooperation. I believe that it is possible to tranform the length of the Arava into a region of joint tourist, agricultural, industrial, and scientific enterprises between us and our neighbors.

A border does not have to be a barbed-wire fence – it can be a bridge of understanding. My policy decision, and the name of "The Good

Fence," expresses my outlook on the potential of that border.

Constructing a joint airfield on Jordanian land north of Eilat and Aqaba, and possibly a canal and railway as well, would transform the whole of the northern Red Sea area – Taba, Eilat, and Aqaba – into a Riviera of tourism and a free trade zone. These proposals are currently in the hands of companies conducting feasibility studies. However, any feasibility in our lives is suffused with the cumulative fears of the past. Notwithstanding the importance of recognizing the past, the feasibility of new approaches relates to the future. And the future can herald not a continuation of the past, but a separation from it. The future heralds new beginnings. The possibilities are immense. Jordanians, Palestinians, and Israelis: These peoples do not have to hate one another, they can cooperate with each other.

As for permanent borders, one must make a distinction among three aspects – the political side, the security side, and the economic side. It is still too early to determine a final settlement, or even to go into details at this stage; however, there is one basic assumption – that the three parties in this triangle have been sentenced by nature and history to live together in peace, trust, and mutual cooperation.

Tel Aviv, 26 Iyyar 5757
2 June 1997

Acknowledgments

We are grateful to a number of people and institutes who have helped us with the preparation and production of this book. Our thanks and deepest appreciation to Crown Prince El Hassan of the Hashemite Kingdom of Jordan, who saw the importance of this conference and facilitated the accomplishment of its goals, as well as contributing to this volume by writing a Foreword.

A special word of thanks to Dr Abdallah Tuqan for his contribution to making the conference such a success. We also extend out thanks to Dr Taisier al-Nhar of the National Center for Human Resources Development (NCHRD) in Amman for coordinating the project together with the staff of the Jewish-Arab Center at the University of Haifa, and for supervising the conference in Amman. Our sincerest appreciation goes to Mr Khalil A. Adwan, director of Traveler's International in Amman, who was in charge of the organizational details of the conference and whose dedicated work undoubtedly contributed to its success.

Both the Freidrich-Ebert Stiftung and the Berta Von Suttner Research Programme of Germany provided financial assistance, for which we express our profound thanks. We are also indebted to the Institute on Global Conflict and Cooperation (IGCC), University of California, USA, for its financial support of the conference, as well as the publication of this book. We are especially grateful to Professor Steven L. Spiegel, who not only contributed an important article to the book, but also demonstrated an untiring commitment to organizing the conference, and to Ms Barbara Butterton, who provided administrative support.

Our heartfelt gratitude goes to Ms Zvia Haimovitz and Ms Rivka Fedder of the Jewish-Arab Center, who were responsible for the smooth running of the conference. We are grateful to the Directors of Sussex Academic Press for the prompt publication of this book, and their assistance and advice. We would like to thank Ms Sharon Woodrow for editing, Ms Nurit Litber for typing the manuscripts, and Mr Joshua Rubin for arranging the tables and figures.

Finally, our special thanks to Mr Shimon Peres for contributing a Foreword to this book. Shimon Peres was not only the Israeli Foreign Minister at the time that the Oslo Agreement and the Jordanian–Israeli Peace Treaty were signed, but he also played a key role in both of these agreements.

Joseph Ginat
Onn Winckler
University of Haifa
25 January 1998

Introduction

Joseph Ginat and Onn Winckler

The conference on which this book is based was unique. It was the first to take place both in Jordan and in Israel, beginning in Amman and moving to Haifa University three days later. It brought together Jordanian, Palestinian, and Israeli social scientists, who were joined by colleagues from Europe and America. The conference itself was considered by the participants to be a milestone on the road to Jordanian–Palestinian–Israeli cooperation. The peace agreements signed by the parties involved compromise. But it was only a cornerstone: the building itself has still to be erected by the three nations.

Peace is not an abstract concept. It is a living and breathing entity that has to be nurtured. Meeting and cooperation between farmers, between merchants, between industrialists, and between tourism professionals from the three sides of the triangle form the walls that hold up this building of peace. No less important are social and cultural meetings, as well as encounters between youth. Especially important in our minds is the academic encounter. The personal meetings among the participants of this conference helped to form enduring contacts between universities as well as research institutes. We have no doubt that academic relations, which set the stage for the Palestinian–Israeli Oslo agreement, will also contribute and encourage the process of peace between Jordanians, Palestinians, and Israelis in the future.

The sixteen chapters are based on the lectures of the participants at the conference. Some chapters deal with the historical perspectives of the peace agreements between the triangle, while others concentrate on ways in which to further promote the peace process, not only between the triangle, but also in the entire Middle East from various socioeconomic, cultural, and psychological perspectives.

Part I, The Political Aspects of the Triangle, gives a broad overview and analyzes the political perspective of Jordanian–Palestinian–Israeli relations. The main political issues and debates between the three parties of the triangle are evaluated.

Chapter 1, Joseph Nevo's "The Political Context of the Triangle: An Overview," surveys and analyzes the relationship between Jordan, the Palestinians and the Zionist movement (and later, after 1948, the state of Israel) from the late 1920s until the signing of the Oslo Agreement (September 1993). It shows that those relations have formed a "classical" triangle, "where each two legs cooperate, at a time, against the third one." The importance of the Arab-Israeli wars of 1948, June 1967, and October 1973 as turning points in the shaping of the relations between the legs of the triangle, in addition to King Hussein's decision of July 1988 to withdraw his claim of authority in the West Bank, are discussed. Nevo then goes on to analyze the process which led to the Oslo Agreement, as well as its impact on the peace negotiations between Jordan and Israel.

The author notes that: "The purpose of the current process is not necessarily an immediate full cooperation in all aspects of inter-state relations. One should not ignore the past histories of all parties involved. A peaceful coexistence in which each party reassesses the present situation and adapts its social and political values to the new reality – together with gradual cooperation – is the best prescription for a successful conclusion of the ongoing process and for a better future."

Chapter 2, Moshe Shemesh's "Bilateral and Trilateral Political Cooperation," argues that the best way to tackle the issue of political cooperation is to first examine the political reality with which the three parties are trying to come to terms, and then to evaluate the parties' own points of departure for such cooperation. Shemesh outlines seven fundamental premises pertaining to bilateral and trilateral political cooperation between the sides of the triangle, including: historical background, a permanent agreement, Jordan's national security, a confederation between Jordan and the Palestinians (after the establishment of an independent Palestinian state), the impact of the Arab arena, the Palestinian refugee problem, and the permanent status of Jerusalem.

Chapter 3, Menachem Klein's "Operating the Triangle by Bilateral Agreements," shows how the triangle has operated since 1993 by bilateral agreements and understandings regarding the core issues of the Middle East conflict, mainly, "the right of return" of the Palestinian refugees and the final status of East Jerusalem. The author claims that the bilateral framework of this triangle has two main effects: First, it allows political tensions among the three parties to curtail the full realization of the potential of this three-way relationship. Second, since the Palestinians are the weaker partner in this triangle, they are seeking help and support from other states and organizations, such as Egypt and the

Islamic Conference, regarding the final status of the holy places in East Jerusalem.

Chapter 4, Steven L. Spiegel's, "The Triangle Relationship: Three is not Better than Two," suggests that by using one set of political science themes, that of international relations systems analysis, we can shed light on the policies of these three parties. The basic assumption is that the tripolar system is particularly applicable to the Israeli–Jordanian–Palestinian relationship. In this system, Jordan is the most natural balancer and pivot, since it has maintained close contact with the Palestinians, and simultaneously its relations with the Zionist movement go back to the beginning of the 1920s. In this regard, the author argues that: "it is in Jordanian interest for a degree of tension to remain in the Palestinian–Israeli relations, since it forces Amman to the forefront. But if the conflict is too severe, then their maneuverability is destroyed."

Spiegel traces and examines the history of the triangle from the contacts between King Abdallah and the Zionist movement in the 1920s until the assassination of Prime Minister Rabin and the victory of the Likud party in the election of May 1996. From a historical perspective, Jordan has the most successful performance and the Palestinians the least. By failing to play triangular politics, the latter have lost a considerable number of opportunities.

During the past, the US often suggested a Jordanian–Palestinian confederation; however, the re-emergence of the Likud in the election of May 1996 seems to have diminished such a possibility. In any case, a confederation between the Jordanians and the Palestinians would replace tripolarity with bipolarity. The author concludes by stating that: "the best that the triangle parties might hope for would be to regularize their relations so that the triangular competition between them might be played out by non-violent means . . . Until that goal is achieved, the triangular pattern predicted by the systems theorists keeps reasserting itself to the consternation of all concerned."

Chapter 5, Moshe Ma'oz's "The Jerusalem Triangle," examines the positions and the attitudes of each party in the triangle regarding the question of the final status of East Jerusalem. In conclusion, the author notes that: "While the Jerusalem triangle will seek to safeguard the security and the strategic interests of the region and its peoples, it must not negate or threaten the interests of the neighboring Arab countries. This is particularly relevant to the case of Syria and Lebanon, which still have territorial conflicts with Israel . . . Failure to secure a Syrian–Israeli peace settlement is likely to entice Damascus to sabotage the Israeli–Jordanian–Palestinian triangular relations, particularly if they seem to be advancing toward an acceptable design by the three parties."

Part II, The Cultural-Sociopsychological Aspects of Making Peace, provides a broad overview of the various cultural-sociopsychological aspects of making peace within the triangle, mainly between the Palestinians and the Israelis. The longstanding Middle East conflict has produced much hate and prejudice between the Arabs and the Israelis. Thus, the main purpose of Part II is to trace these aspects of the conflict, as well as to suggest solutions and useful points of view regarding these issues in order to promote the understanding, the integration, and finally, the acceptance of the other side.

Chapter 6, Joseph Ginat's, "Building Up Peace," offers us a way of looking at the two other sides of each of the triangle parties. Ginat first traces the meaning of the "peace." The author then assesses the contacts and the relationships between the Jordanian Bedouin, the Israeli Bedouin, and the Bedouin in the area of the Palestinian Authority. The economic ties between Jordan and Israel, mainly in the tourism sector, are described, and the author concludes by saying that: "Peace between nations that for a very long time were enemies, cannot become manifest at the moment in which a peace agreement is signed. The agreement between the states is only the beginning."

Chapter 7, Aaron Ben-Ze'ev's, "The Emotional Aspects of the Path to Peace," begins with the argument that "a successful peace process requires a substantial change in the emotional attitudes of all parties concerned." However, such a change is not easy to achieve, as emotional attitudes express our most profound values and implicit knowledge. This chapter concentrates on two main aspects: The first is the emotions among enemies. In this respect, the author focuses the discussion on hate and anger, which are the major negative emotions involved in a relationship between enemies. The second aspect is the emotions among former enemies, in which case anger replaces hate as the main negative emotion in the transition from a relationship between enemies to one between former enemies. Awareness of the differences between the two types of negative emotions is of great importance for a successful peace process. The author concludes by emphasizing that the value of the peace process, from an emotional point of view, is that the proportion of positive emotions increases, making the negative emotions less destructive. Nevertheless, negative emotions do exist and can be more frequent and even more intense with increased interaction between the former enemies.

Chapter 8, Asher Susser's "The Cultural and Social Context of the Triangle," examines the cultural and social dimensions of the triangular relationship through two prisms: on the one hand, corporate identity, and on the other hand, the capacity to build peace via normal interaction and mutual political, cultural and social acceptance. Over the years, three distinct Israeli, Palestinian, and Jordanian identities have emerged in this region. However, at the same time, the Israeli–Jordanian–Palestinian triangle is not symmetrical. The author claims that, although all three identities are the product of their struggle for the land of Palestine, Israel does not share in the cultural, linguistic and religious affinity that links the Jordanians and the Palestinians, and that precisely because of these differences, the Arab-Israeli conflict has been so long and its solution so problematic. The author notes that hopefully, in the long run, the mutual fears will diminish over time and will pave the way for the development of mutual empathy between the three parties.

Chapter 9, "The Role of People in Building Peace," by *Fredrik Barth* and *Unni Wikan,* addresses the personal stakes of ordinary people in the condition of peace. Beyond the value to them of enhanced security, their personal stakes will increase if they have more economic or social links with the other side, or if they derive substantial economic benefits from the state of peace. The authors also provide some concrete suggestions on what this might entail, but note that the most critical issues are how to humanize the enemy, counteract gross stereotypes, and create space and tolerance for a greater diversity of social relationships between the parties. Most directly relevant to promoting peace between peoples are the conversations that will bridge the divisions between them. The authors ascribe great importance to academic and intellectual dialogue.

Chapter 10, Uri M. Kupferschmidt's "Some Social and Cultural Implications of the Triangle," suggests some practical ways to reduce the level of hate as well as the negative prejudices that prevail in order to promote the peace process between the triangle. The author argues that beyond the political triangular relationship, there is another triangle which has to be discussed: the relationship between political steps, economic cooperation and development, and the building of peace in social and cultural aspects. This is perhaps a more difficult side of the triangle, since the longstanding conflict has developed hate and dehumanization of the other side, and even under peaceful conditions, certain old feelings may still persist, which must be tackled rather than ignored.

The author indicates that President Sadat, and after him, King Hussein, have masterfully played on Israeli public opinion. The impact of their direct address to Israeli citizens may have been limited and short-lived, but at certain critical moments they were able to forge a change in Israeli public opinion, thereby promoting the peace negotiations between their countries and Israel. The author suggests several options and means for overcoming the cultural and other differences among the triangle, mainly between the Israelis and the two other parties.

Chapter 11, Musallam Abu-Helu's "The Cultural and Social Situation and the Peace Process," concentrates on several key issues that have had a clear effect on the peace process and may still exert a negative impact in the future: the educational dimension and its social results; general freedom rights and *de facto* policy; a comprehensive view of the social and cultural context; and lastly, social equality. The author notes the need to address: the role that individuals might play in designing the way to peace; the effect of the cultural and social habits of people as important factors in determining the best way to achieve peace; and lastly, planning as well as implementing projects which will contribute to creating an atmosphere of cooperation and peace between the parties involved.

Part III, The Economic Factor of the Peace Process, provides a broad overview of the economic factor in the Middle East peace process, especially regarding the Jordanian–Palestinian–Israeli triangle. The chapters in Part III deal both with the economic pressures (which are one of the major factors in the Middle East peace process), as well as the economic benefits that can be potentially reaped (some of which have already been realized).

Chapter 12, Mary E. Morris' "Regional Economic Cooperation in the Middle East: Prospects and Problems," presents the main economic problems and obstacles which face many Middle Eastern countries and are not necessarily involved with or derived from the Middle East conflict, such as the rapid population growth and its consequences, unemployment problems, and rapid urbanization. Morris also examines the economic costs of the military Middle Eastern conflict, as well as the necessity for regional economic cooperation among the countries in this region. Her primary conclusion is that "political stability must rest on stable economies." Thus, development of measures that can assist both economic as well as political stability are imperative. Steps toward economic cooperation will not only contribute to the peace process itself, but will also be a major tool in maintaining political stability in the region in the future. These include planning and conducting a massive national socioeconomic development campaign, with a focus on infrastructure development and the creation of a large number of work opportunities in order to narrow the high rates of unemployment, in parallel to targeting regional problems as well.

Chapter 13, Onn Winckler's "The Economic Factor of the Middle East Peace Process: The Jordanian Case," examines the major problems and obstacles that have faced the Jordanian economy since the mid-1980s, especially as a result of the Gulf crisis of 1990–1, and which constituted, according to the author, an important factor that led the Jordanian authorities to end the longstanding conflict with Israel. The most critical of them were as follows: The rapid population growth and its consequences, which were caused not only by the high rates of natural increase of the Jordanian society, but also as a result of massive migration of Palestinian migrants and refugees to the East Bank of the Jordan River between the 1948 war and the Gulf crisis; the presence of a large number of foreign workers, mainly Egyptians and Syrians; high rates of unemployment, mainly among educated manpower; increasing external debt; and lastly, the economic damage caused by the Jordanian support of Iraq during the Gulf crisis.

Winckler looks at the economic benefits to Jordan from the peace process, which include: a sharp reduction of the external debt, as well as rescheduling of large proportions of the rest of the debt; a sharp increase of foreign investment in the Jordanian economy; absorption of soft loans to support the economic reforms; and lastly, a sharp reduction in the unemployment rates. The author concludes that although many of the common Jordanian–Israeli economic projects which were planned have not yet been conducted, the contribution of the peace agreement has been substantial for the Jordanian economy.

Chapter 14, "The Development of the Jordanian Tourism Industry," by Onn Winckler and Gad G. Gilbar, examines one of the most, if not the most, important and profitable benefits for the Jordanian economy from the peace process, that is, the development of the tourism industry. During the past few decades, tourism has emerged as one of the world's major industries, exceeding many manufacturing industries and other services both in terms of number of employees and foreign currency earning. The article assesses and analyzes the development and the major trends of the tourism industry in Jordan after World War II, as well as the main advantages of the tourism industry to the development of the Jordanian economy. With respect to the main obstacles facing the tourism industry in Jordan, Gilbar and Winckler conclude by stating that with proper and wise investments, in parallel to political stability in the area, the tourism industry in Jordan can replace the Gulf oil-exporting countries as the major source, not only for employment, but also for hard currencies for the Jordanian economy in the coming years.

Chapter 15, Taisir I. Amre's "Opportunities in the Wind: Development and Cooperation in the Triangle," looks toward the basic assumption that there are five main imperatives in order to achieve comprehensive economic cooperation between the triangle parties. The first and the most important, according to the author, is the establishment of a just peace in the region. Such a peace is inconceivable without a political settlement between Israel and the Palestinians. The other imperatives include: the interface between cooperation and development; increasing and improving the economic independence of the Palestinians; reducing the economic disparities among the triangle; and the premise of Palestinian control over natural resources.

The author addresses and examines the existing economic barriers and obstacles in the areas under control of the Palestinian National Authority, which include: the limitations imposed by Israel on the Palestinians working in Israel; limitations on the movement of goods; and the economic damage of the long closures imposed by the Israeli army in the periods following the suicide bombs that occurred in February–March 1996. Finally, the author deals with the possible economic opportunities for the triangle parties within the framework of peace.

Part IV, Concluding Remarks, *Dale F. Eickelman*'s *"The Importance of Timing and Momentum,"* discusses the importance of operationalizing the signed peace agreements so that they will affect all levels of society in each party of the triangle, including "ordinary people" who often have no direct political voice. Our task as educators, argues Eickelman, "is to pay attention to the timing and sequencing of events intended to demonstrate that the peace agreement has practical and immediate implications."

Eickelman also emphasizes the role of educators in implementing the peace agreements. He points out that they have to understand what the younger generations are thinking and what the prevailing stereotypes are in each of the triangle's societies that have to be overcome. In this respect, the curricula of the students, their textbooks, and the mass media have an important role to play. Eickelman concludes by stating that: "Such initiatives must be started now so that all parties concerned can see practical effects and benefits within a reasonable period of time."

Part I

The Political Aspects of the Triangle

1

The Political Context of the Triangle: An Overview

Joseph Nevo

Jordanian–Palestinian relations were once described as "a love-hate affair extending over two generations."[1] Like in any love story (or love-hate story), the adding of a third party to a given bilateral equation might stir up the plot, create tension, change the equilibrium and lead to frequent formation of new coalitions. That has indeed been the case since the Jordanian–Palestinian–Israeli(Zionist) triangle came into being.

The foundations of the ties between Palestine and Jordan (Transjordan) in the modern history of the region were laid throughout the nineteenth century when familial and commercial connections were established between individuals in Nablus, Nazereth, Jerusalem and Hebron, and inhabitants of Salt and Karak.[2] Yet they were enhanced, consolidated and eventually formalized in the 1920s, 1930s and 1940s, following the introduction of the British mandate and the arrival of Amir (later King) Abdallah in Amman. Abdallah was not too happy with the desolated realm that Colonial Secretary Winston Churchill allotted to him under the emerging post-World War I *Pax Britanica*. From the beginning of his sojourn in Transjordan, Abdallah sought to enlarge his domain, particularly coveting the greener grass on the other side of the river. The fact that the same mandate was imposed on the whole territory between the Mediterranean and Iraq, encouraged Abdallah in directing his expansionist endeavors toward Palestine. Moreover, Palestine was already the battlefield between two national movements: the Jewish one (Zionism) and the Palestinian Arab one. The Amir soon became a latent factor within the bilateral relations of the two communities in Palestine. From the early 1920s onward, he occasionally suggested Palestine's unification with Transjordan under his throne as the best, if not the only, solution for the Arab-Jewish conflict therein. It would appear that already then, Abdallah subscribed to the idea that if an Arab ruler was appointed to the unified Transjordan and Palestine, then the Palestinian Arabs would feel less threatened. They might acquiesce to the implementation of the Balfour Declaration in certain parts of Palestine, once they realized that the Jews were to occupy only a small percentage, in terms of both land and population, of the proposed United Kingdom.[3]

In pursuing various schemes to incorporate Palestine in his Amirate, Abdallah regarded the Jews as potential allies against the militant Palestinian nationalists, who rejected any notion of Transjordanian control over their homeland.[4] To the Jews he offered regional autonomy in certain parts of the designated enlarged Kingdom with the right to emigrate and to purchase land in their territories. The Jews, on their part, were reluctant to comply, as all those plans left them devoid of sovereignty and national independence. Abdallah, nevertheless, took pains in his efforts to persuade them to accept it. Indeed, he was also ready to discuss the partitioning of Palestine into Arab and Jewish states, in the spirit of the 1937 and 1947 proposals, but only as a fall-back position and providing that the former would be incorporated into Transjordan.

During the British mandate, Abdallah enjoyed cordial relations with the Jews as well as with the Arabs of Palestine. The Amir had meticulously cultivated those ties not only to create the impression of the friendly neighbor who undertook to mediate between the adversaries in the Holy Land, but also to promote his own territorial and political interests. The Jews appreciated his friendship and cooperation, but were not too enthusiastic about his territorial ambitions in Palestine and advised him to direct them elsewhere (Syria, for example). The Arabs of Palestine usually sought his support and assistance, but this time suspected his intentions. Mistrust between the Amir and the leading Palestinian faction, the Husaynis, was mutual. Abdallah therefore inclined to lean mainly on the Nashashibis, the Husaynis' life-long rivals and contenders for national leadership.[5]

During most of the mandatory period, the conflicting parties in Palestine maintained good working relations and even friendly ties with the ruler of Transjordan. Yet, no practical cooperation between two of the actors against the third one transpired, as Abdallah endeavored to attract the attention of both parties to his unification plans. It was only in the wake of World War II and particularly in 1947–8 (following the UN resolution on the partition of Palestine) that the oral understanding between Abdallah and the Jewish agency (later, Israel's Provisional

Government) to let Jordan have the Arab parts of Palestine and thus to foil the creation of a Palestinian Arab state, was shaped.

In November 1947, the representative of the Jewish agency, Mrs Golda Mayerson, complied with the King's proposal that his army would take over those parts of Palestine allotted to the Arabs by the UN. In return, she demanded that Abdallah refrain from crossing the partition line, from entering the Jewish areas, and from interfering with the establishment of their own state therein. Even though in their second meeting in May 1948, Abdallah retracted his previous proposals, due to the intensive military and political changes of recent months, one may speculate that it was probably tacitly understood that, developments in the battlefield permitting, the November understanding might serve as a basis for a postwar agreement.[6]

In this period, nevertheless, during the first months of the 1948 war, when no definite conclusion with Abdallah was reached, and in the absence of any concrete knowledge regarding the King's genuine intentions, Israel contemplated, for the first time, cooperation with the Arabs of Palestine on the possible creation of a Palestinian Arab state. The idea was cultivated in July 1948 by officials of Israel's Foreign Ministry, some of whom believed that a small and dependable state on Israel's eastern border would serve its interests better than a stronger enlarged Transjordan. Others favored the idea only on tactical ground: to put indirect pressure on King Abdallah and to spur him into entering practical negotiations with Israel.[7] Either due to this "encouragement" or because of other considerations, Israeli-Jordanian negotiations were soon precipitated.

In the wake of the British mandate when the Arab armies invaded Palestine, Abdallah's Arab Legion indeed took over those parts of Arab Palestine that bordered Transjordan (i.e., the future West Bank). Most of this area was devoid of any Jewish presence, and the local Arab population basically welcomed the Jordanian troops. Hence, in the first four weeks of fighting in Palestine, Abdallah's army took control of most of those Palestinian territories coveted by the King.

Abdallah did not settle, however, for a *de facto* annexation, but wanted the population to legitimate his moves. Ever since his plans toward Palestine were crystallized, after World War II, he endeavored to persuade the Arab population on the wisdom of cooperation with Jordan, as only he and his army could and would save their homeland (or at least part of it) from the Jews. Events since late 1947 had partially proven his point. In December 1948, when the state of Israel was a *fait accompli*, with the Arab Legion controlling most of Arab Palestine and with the other Arab armies there performing rather poorly, the Palestinian Arabs had not much choice. With Abdallah's encouragement, their leaders and notables convened in Jericho, acclaimed him as King of Palestine and Transjordan, and provided him with a power of attorney to solve the Palestine problem as he saw fit.

After Jordan had incorporated Arab Palestine, King Abdallah believed that only Israel or the neighboring Arab states would be able to jeopardize his country's position in the newly acquired West Bank. He sought to secure at least the acquiescence of one party to the new territorial reality. The Arab states' reluctance to comply was the main reason that Abdallah entered into peace negotiations with Israel. Once the Arab League agreed, in the spring of 1950, to a temporary *de facto* recognition of Jordan's control over the West Bank, then peace with Israel was promptly regarded as less essential and negotiations were duly curtailed.[8]

In the following decade and a half, Israel hardly played any role in the shaping of Jordanian-Palestinian relations on both banks of the river. In Jordan, however, those years constituted a formative period. During the trials and tribulations of the 1950s and the early 1960s, a new Jordanian-Palestinian entity began to emerge, mainly in the East Bank, to which many West Bankers migrated. The Palestinians were gradually integrated into Jordan's political and economic systems, and played a growing role in the various sectors, including the army. External Arab attempts to foil this crystallizing coexistence intensified around 1960. The rulers of Iraq and Egypt, who traditionally vied over the hegemony of the Arab world, did not leave a stone unturned in their efforts to look for a winning card, which they thought they found in the Palestinian issue. Both Abd Al-Karim Qassim and Gamal Abd Al-Nasser advocated that the Palestinians in Jordan form their own entity, thus embarrassing and agitating King Hussein. Fortunately for the Jordanian regime, those endeavors went almost unheeded and failed to attract the attention of the West Bankers. A more serious threat to the integration of the two Banks emerged in 1964 when the PLO was founded and began to compete with Jordan over the representation of the Palestinians. As the new organization came into being by a resolution of the first Arab summit meeting, Jordan was in no position to ignore or disobey it. The King, to his chagrin, was forced to host the PLO's official founding in East Jerusalem. The PLO's vibrant chairman, Ahmad Shuqairi, took advantage of Jordan's limited freedom of action *vis-à-vis* the Arab League and seriously tried to exercise his authority over the Palestinians in Jordan, particularly in the West Bank. This conflict of interest soon turned into an inevitable confrontation, and the authorities eventually placed severe restrictions on the PLO's activity in Jordan.

Only at this stage did Israel become involved in Jordanian-PLO relations, as the Palestinian reawakening of the early 1960s led to the resumption of the armed struggle against Israel. This campaign, partly launched from the West Bank (even though most of it was carried out by *Al-Fatah*, which was operated by the Syrians and not by the PLO), resulted, in 1965–6, in Israeli retaliations against Jordanian targets. The last one, in Samu'a (in southern Mount Hebron) in November 1966, had a shocking impact on the Palestinians and was followed by violent demonstrations and riots throughout the West Bank.[9]

The June 1967 war and its consequences created a new reality in the Middle East whose impact on the triangle was unprecedented. The postwar situation also opened entirely new avenues for all three parties. Israel reemerged as a main player; with much of the political future of Jordan and the Palestinians, willy-nilly, now dependent on it. The takeover of the West Bank gave Israel three possible courses of action from which to choose: annex the newly acquired territories or keep them permanently; promote the creation of a Palestinian state or an entity therein; or hand the territories back to Jordan, in return for an appropriate *quid pro quo.*

Jordan, from the outset, was ready to consider only one eventuality, taking pains and investing ceaseless efforts in order to retrieve the West Bank under its sovereignty. This was attempted both by bringing international pressure on Israel to withdraw and by holding direct secret meetings between the King and Israeli leaders. In the meantime, Jordan tried to maintain its presence and influence there, as it regarded the West Bank to be an undisputable Jordanian territory. This was accomplished, *inter alia,* by continuing to pay the salaries of its former civil servants, teachers and lawyers there. Israel did not interfere in these actions and even encouraged such dependence of the population on Jordan, as this kept all the options open. Government departments in Amman continued to issue licenses, permits, loans, and grants in order to aid private and public organizations in the West Bank.[10]

The Palestinians, the indigenous population of this area, also faced three options: remain loyal to Jordan and support its efforts to retrieve to the West Bank; cast their lot on the PLO that was just gaining power and influence; or work for an independent Palestinian entity either in coordination with Israel or under its auspices. As the last one soon proved to be a non-viable option (both as far as Israel and most Palestinians were concerned), the populace had to choose between Jordan and the PLO. The latter had, after the 1967 war, undergone a salient change: It was no longer a conservative political organization under Ahmad Shuqairi, but – since early 1969 – had now become a militant framework for the various *Fida'i* groups under Yassir Arafat. From the late 1960s onward, Jordan and the PLO were no longer merely political adversaries, each one insisting on being the legitimate representative of the Palestinians. They were now competitors over the future of the West Bank, both claiming to be its lawful owner, entitled to control it if and when Israel were to withdraw.

The Palestinians' dilemma, brought forth by the new reality, put to test not only their loyalty to the Jordanian regime, but also the input of 19 years of a formal as well as a practical integration. Here was a policy that offered the Palestinians an alternative national identity: a Jordanian-Palestinian one. This dilemma had to be negotiated by the Palestinians residing on both banks of the Jordan. In the West Bank, with its monolithic and exclusively Palestinian population, their choice would not produce a direct and immediate impact on the Jordanian regime, as they were then living under Israeli occupation. In the East Bank, on the other hand, where a sort of Jordanian-Palestinian entity was indeed gradually crystallizing,[11] the presence and activity of the armed organizations, representatives of the new form of Palestinian nationalism, had somewhat damaged the delicate balance of bi-communal relations. Moreover, their confrontation with the regime and the eventual showdown in September 1970, threatened not only an ethnic or a national integration, but the Hashemite regime and the whole structure of the Jordanian state itself.

The process that came to transpire in the West Bank was the gradual shift of the population's loyalty from Jordan to the *Fida'i* organizations and to the PLO, and the simultaneous transformation of their collective identity. By the end of 1968, King Hussein had realized that even if Israel were to hand him back the West Bank, it would not be the same place that he had lost 18 months earlier. He felt that he could no longer take the West Bankers' support for granted and that they would no longer be willing to settle for either his pre-1967 Palestinian policy or for the unwritten social charter that regulated the bi-communal relations. Therefore, the King had to contemplate autonomy for the West Bank or at least a more decentralized regime there, should it ever be returned to his possession. Such views were indeed acceptable to pro-Jordanian local leaders in the West Bank.[12]

In early 1972, Hussein became aware that the problem was exacerbating. The bad blood with the Palestinians following the encounters of September 1970 and July 1971 still prevailed. Jordan's government resumed the payments to its former employees in the West Bank (suspended in June 1971),[13] but had little hope regarding the prospects of blocking the erosion of its position there. On the other hand, Israel then announced its intent to hold municipal elections in the West Bank (according to Jordanian law) that were postponed because of the 1967 war. The King feared that the ballots would tip the scale in favor of the PLO's candidates and that the transformation of loyalty would be publicly demonstrated. He also suspected that the idea of the election indicated an Israeli plot to either annex the West Bank or to encourage the formation of an independent entity there under Israeli aegis. Therefore, in March 1972, Hussein issued a new Federal Plan designed to redefine the ties and the nature of relations between the two Banks under his throne, once Israel would withdraw from the occupied territories.

Under this plan, Jordan was to be reorganized as the "United Arab Kingdom," with two autonomous provinces under a single executive authority (King and government), a single legislative authority, and one army. Each province, however, would have its own executive and legislative authority and would enjoy vast local autonomy. The concept of integration of the Palestinians in the Kingdom, which was Jordan's guideline hitherto, was giving way to a concept of Palestinian autonomy in a specific territory which was to exceed the West Bank.[14]

The Federal Plan was flatly rejected by all the parties concerned: the West Bank Palestinians, the PLO, the Arab states, and Israel.[15] Nevertheless, Hussein's apprehension about the municipal elections proved to be groundless. Many of Jordan's loyalists were elected as mayors and councillors, while candidates affiliated to the PLO did rather poorly. It took another four years before Hussein's fears materialized. Only in the second (and last) municipal elections held in 1976, did pro-Jordanian candidates lose many seats and mayorships to PLO's protégés and other "nationalistic" candidates.[16] During those years, however, tremendous changes took place in the PLO's regional and international position. The Arab summit conference in Rabat, in October 1974, recognized it as "the sole legitimate representative of the Palestinians" and acknowledged its right to form a "national authority" in any available Palestinian territory. A month later, the organization acclaimed worldwide recognition when its chairman, Yassir Arafat, was invited to speak at the UN General Assembly.

Israel, too, was indirectly involved in the ensuing conflict between Jordan and the PLO, taking a definite side and politically cultivating Jordan's senior position in the territories by advocating the *Jordanian Option*, which meant recognition of Jordan (and not of the PLO) as a natural partner for a political settlement. This inclination crystallized in the summer of 1970 and reached its prime after the October 1973 war. The practical aspect of this option did not rule out a territorial compromise, according to the lines of the Allon Plan (Israel's unofficial guide for settlements under Labor governments between 1967 and 1977) or other plans, in which those parts of the West Bank that would not be annexed or attached to Israel would be returned to Jordan.[17] Israel provided Jordan with incentives to pursue an opposing policy to the

PLO and to become a partner for bilateral negotiations.

King Hussein was infuriated by the Rabat resolution's wording that recognized the PLO as "the *sole* legitimate representative of the Palestinians," suggesting that the King was denied representation of even those one million Palestinians who lived in the East Bank and constituted an integral and indispensable part of the population and civic society there. Publicly, Jordan adhered to that resolution and henceforward expressed its support for the Palestinians' right to self-determination. Practically, however, Hussein adopted a series of measures designed to prove that the PLO alone was incapable of regaining the West Bank and that any viable solution to the "Palestinian problem" should include Jordan.

Shortly after the Rabat meeting, King Hussein summoned a special session of the parliament in order to amend the constitution and remove the Palestinians from the parliament. This was duly endorsed, and the 60-seat national assembly (half of which was made up of Palestinians) was dissolved. Simultaneously, the Jordanian cabinet resigned and was promptly superseded by a new one, in which the Palestinians were very poorly represented. Those measures were construed as a general reorganization initiated by Hussein, ostensibly in order to "Jordanize" his kingdom.[18] Nevertheless, the King contended that those moves were in compliance with the Rabat resolutions which deprived him of any representation of the Palestinians whatsoever and crowned the PLO as their sole and legitimate representative.

Hussein's point was eventually taken. The notion that Jordan should be involved in the efforts to regain the West Bank and hence should participate in the shaping of its future became acceptable to many Palestinian and non-Palestinian Arabs alike. President Sadat suggested that the West Bank and the Gaza Strip be connected institutionally or confederally to Jordan. Those ideas were also accepted by President Assad of Syria. Even in Israel, a more favorable attitude to the idea was heard, particularly from Deputy Prime Minister Yigal Allon.[19] In parallel, a cautious dialogue was initiated between the Jordanian government and the PLO, for the first time since 1971. President Sadat's pioneering trip to Jerusalem and the peace process it inaugurated, precipitated this *rapprochement*, as they both suspected that the Egyptian-Israeli deal was on their account. Jordan, however, taking advantage of the PLO's plight following its violent encounter with the Syrians in Lebanon, resumed its efforts in early 1977 to regain greater influence in the West Bank by once again advocating a Jordanian-Palestinian federal framework. Jordan also endeavored to gain the PLO's recognition and acquiescence to its activities and interests in the West Bank.[20]

The coming to power in 1977 of a right-wing government in Israel for the first time, also contributed to improving ties between Jordan and the PLO. The platform, as well as the practical policy, of the new government rejected any notion of territorial concessions in the West Bank. The Likud governments since 1977 have taken great pains to destroy the influence of the PLO in the West Bank (and elsewhere, as was manifested in Operation Peace for the Galilee). This has been done not only by dissolving bodies affiliated with the organization and deporting its leading supporters, but also by attempts to develop and promote an alternative leadership to the PLO. Toward this end, the *Village Leagues* were formed in the late 1970s. These were district-wide organizations ostensibly set up to foster rural development. In the early 1980s, several *"Leagues"* were active in Hebron, Ramallah, Bethlehem, and Jenin. The *Village Leagues* failed to deliver the expected goods and to produce an alternative leadership. On the other hand, opposition to their activity drove Jordan and the PLO to closer cooperation. PLO agents made several attempts on the life of League members, and at least one succeeded. Jordan, on its part, classified them as collaborators who were engaged in treason punishable by the death penalty.[21]

Moreover, a few leading Likud members publicly advocated regarding Jordan (namely, the East Bank) as *the* "natural" Palestinian state, given the fact that about half of the country's population consisted of Palestinians, and encouraged the Palestinians (with varying degrees of explicitness) to topple the regime and to turn it into their own homeland.[22]

Not only was that an appalling idea as far as the Hashemite establishment was concerned, but the various components of the PLO, including those organizations who ideologically opposed the Jordanian monarchy, would not consider the East Bank as an alternative to the desired homeland between the Jordan River and the Mediterranean Sea (i.e., instead of Israel).

Israel also sought to diminish the PLO's influence in the occupied territories through its acquiescence to (if not by tacit encouragement of) the emergence of radical Islamic movements (predominantly the *Hamas*), hoping that they would undermine the PLO's prestige and popularity.

Israel's policy, albeit not the exclusive factor that promoted the bilateral *rapprochement,* did contribute to the increasing Jordanian-PLO cooperation and coordination in the 1980s (even Jordan's willingness to improve relations with the PLO following the Peace for the Galilee operation in 1982 was alleviated by the weakening of this organization by Israel).

Throughout the 1980s, Jordan took increasing initiative *vis-à-vis* both the Palestinians and Israel. King Hussein realized that the only way to regain any foothold in the West Bank (despite the Rabat resolution, the PLO's popularity, and Israel's reluctance to withdraw) was to exhort for the political option. If he could manage to mastermind an elaborate move to persuade Israel to withdraw, or at least to discuss such an eventuality, even in principle, by making the Arab world and the PLO meet some of Israel's demands, then he might earn, as a commission, the right of involvement in the future of the West Bank. That line of thinking was encouraged by the resolutions of the recent conventions of the Palestinian National Council (PNC), which did not ignore Jordan, but rather considered it as a partner for close cooperation and even for confederal ties with the future independent Palestinian state.[23] Arafat, on his part, being afraid of an Israeli-Jordanian agreement (under US auspices) on the future of the West Bank, which might leave the PLO out of the picture, felt obliged to meet Hussein halfway.[24]

In April 1983, King Hussein and Yassir Arafat issued a joint Declaration of Intent to form a confederation between the Jordanian and the Palestinian states. Two years later, in February 1985, they took a further step and concluded an agreement for political coordination, based on the understanding reached in 1983 on future confederal links. Arafat, reservedly and indirectly, recognized UN Resolution 242 of November 1967, which constituted one of the American administration's preconditions to recognizing the PLO. The contracting parties undertook to negotiate with Israel on the various aspects of the Arab-Israeli conflict, through a joint Jordanian-Palestinian delegation under the umbrella of an international conference.[25] Even though the proposed guiding principles for the convening of such a conference (UN resolutions regarding Palestine, total withdrawal, and the establishment of a Palestinian state) had been utterly rejected by Israel,[26] King Hussein succeeded at this point in offering a mechanism that might create a future common ground for cooperation between all parties involved and to bypass the traditional obstacles. The proposed joint Arab delegation was designated to meet Israel's insistence on direct negotiations, on the one hand, and to overcome both Israel's and the PLO's reluctance for mutual recognition, on the other hand.

As it turned out, however, Arafat could not or would not ratify the agreement (in view of mounting opposition within the PLO and accusations that the agreement best served Jordan's and Israel's interests rather than those of the Palestinians). A year later, therefore, King Hussein unilaterally suspended cooperation with Arafat, but, almost immediately, initiated a series of steps to enhance Jordan's position and influence in the West Bank.[27] In the spring of 1987, King Hussein endeavored one last time to bring together the three sides of the triangle.

He clandestinely met in London with Shimon Peres, who was then the Foreign Minister of Israel's national coalition government under Itzhak Shamir (Peres himself was the Prime Minister through the first two years of this government). They drafted an agreement on Israeli–Jordanian–Palestinian negotiations within an international framework, in order to terminate the Middle East conflict. It was, more or less, along the same lines of the February 1985 agreement but devoid of preconditions and declared principles that Israel could not tolerate. Jordan was faced with the Sisyphean duty to persuade Arafat to join in a process similar to an even more favorable one which he had failed to accept two years earlier. Nevertheless, it was the Israeli government which rejected the agreement, as the notion of an international conference contradicted the steadfast Israeli demand for direct negotiations with the Arabs.[28]

Following this failure, the respective positions of the three parties seemed further away from each other than ever before. Jordan realized that even its meagre prospects of achieving any influential position regarding the future of the West Bank was quickly dwindling. Hussein's feeling that his traditional policy *vis-à-vis* the Palestinians and Israel required a reassessment, was strengthened by the outbreak of the *Intifada* in the Gaza Strip and the West Bank in December 1987. Of the three parties concerned, all taken by surprise when the uprising broke out, King Hussein was the first one to regain his senses and to realize its real meaning. Fear of the impact of the *Intifada* on the Palestinians in the East Bank and apprehension that their loyalty might be put to test, was the ultimate incentive for his historic decision to give up Jordan's claim to the West Bank. Hussein's speech of July 31, 1988, harbingering the severing of Jordan's legal and administrative ties with the West Bank, symbolized Jordan's *real politik:* its recognition of the inclination of the Arab world and the general public to support the Palestinian claim to this territory, and its recognition of the PLO as the legitimate representative of the Palestinians. Hussein's move, however, also forced the other parties concerned to adapt themselves to the new reality.

On November 15 of the same year, at the conclusion of the PNC's 19th session in Algiers, the organization declared the establishment of a Palestinian state with Jerusalem as its capital. That statement indirectly implied a recognition of Israel, as it referred to UN Resolution 181 of November 1947 that called for the partitioning of Palestine into an Arab and a Jewish state. Additional statements by Yassir Arafat in Stockholm and Geneva more explicitly interpreted the Declaration of Independence in a way that would meet the US conditions for recognizing the PLO (recognition of Israel's right to exist, recognition of UN Resolution 242, and denouncement of terrorism). Jordan was hardly mentioned at all in those statements, save for reaffirmation of the PNC's previous decisions that "the future relationship between the State of Palestine and the Hashemite Kingdom of Jordan will be established on a confederal basis of a voluntary and free choice of the two fraternal peoples . . . ".[29]

Israel's response to Jordan's retirement from the struggle over the West Bank and to the PLO's revised strategy (as well as to the ensuing *Intifada*) was the issue of a new peace initiative in May 1989. It resembled an ameliorated version of the Camp David accord whose gist was general elections to be held in the West Bank and the Gaza Strip. The elected body would represent the Palestinians, administrate those territories under a Home Rule and negotiate with Israel an interim agreement and later a permanent settlement. Jordan was to participate in the advanced stage of the negotiations during which a Jordanian-Israeli peace treaty would also be discussed. Even though the plan was publicly rejected by the PLO, Jordan and the West Bankers as a "farce" and "a waste of time," the proposal for general elections was acceptable, providing it would undergo certain modifications. They wanted assurance that the elections would be held under international supervision with PLO consent, and that at the end of the day, they would bring about Palestinian independence. Yassir Arafat also resented Israel's utter disregard of the PLO and its refusal to participate in any negotiations regarding the future of the West Bank.[30]

Even though neither Israel nor the PLO perceived a clear future Jordanian presence in the West Bank (be it an independent state or an autonomous entity), Jordan did not entirely detach itself from the area, despite Hussein's disengagement speech. That statement was indeed followed by practical measures, such as the retirement of most Jordanian civil servants in the West Bank, the abolition of the Supreme Committee for West Bank Affairs, and the abolition of the Ministry for the Occupied Territories. Yet, over 3,000 employees of the religious establishment remained on the government's payroll, and the parliament resolution of April 1950 on the unification of the East and the West Bank, as well as the 1952 Jordanian constitution (that underlined Jordan's territorial integrity) were not amended.[31]

Post factum, as it turned out, Jordan's decision to give up the West Bank not only improved its relations with the PLO, but also removed the major bone of contention between Jordan and Israel. Since 1967, Jordan had made it clear that in return for the West Bank it would be ready for a political settlement with Israel – within the appropriate Arab or international context. This intention was well reflected in Jordan's endeavors to formalize UN Resolution 242. When the issue of the West Bank was no longer relevant as far as Jordan was concerned, most territorial claims were removed from the bilateral relations, and the way was paved to a future Jordanian-Israeli peace accord. Indeed, such a move was possible only following an Israeli-Palestinian appeasement and after Jordan's commitments and moral obligations to the Palestinian cause were satisfied. Even a potential Israeli-Palestinian peace process would be easier if Israel had to discuss the future of the West Bank *vis-à-vis* only one contender rather than two.

The Gulf crisis of 1990–1 found Jordan and the PLO in the same camp. They both supported Saddam Hussein against the international coalition, albeit for different reasons and with different levels of enthusiasm and commitment. The US, Israel and, to a certain degree, even Egypt were ready to understand the domestic and regional constraints that drove King Hussein onto the Iraqi side and thus to forgive him. Arafat, on the other hand, seemed to deliberately support Saddam out of ideological conviction, and that was less tolerated by the international community. Arafat's pick proved to be a bet on the wrong horse from another aspect as well: Kuwait and Saudi Arabia, Saddam's victim and potential victim, were among the major financiers of the PLO. Not only were their contributions suspended, but the PLO also lost the financial support of the hundreds of thousands of Palestinian expatriates who were then deported from Kuwait. However, it was the PLO's financial and political weakness in the wake of the Gulf crisis that contributed, *inter alia*, to Arafat's decision in favor of negotiations with Israel.

The direct result of the Gulf crisis, in terms of the triangle (and the Arab-Israeli conflict in general), was the Madrid conference of October 1991. The US *quid pro quo* for the Arab states' joining in the coalition against Iraq was pressure on Israel to be more flexible *vis-à-vis* the Palestinians and to partake in a peace conference under an international sponsorship. The Madrid process was a major victory for King Hussein, as it adopted the course he had been advocating since the mid-1980s: a joint Jordanian-Palestinian delegation (as well as other Arab ones) to negotiate a political settlement with Israel under international aegis. This was not only an acknowledgment that the King's idea to level the playing field and to enable an Israeli-Palestinian dialogue was the most realistic one, but it also recognized Jordan's right to discuss the future of the West Bank.

Unfortunately, the Madrid process soon deteriorated into endless rhetoric, primarily due to media exposure and its portrayal of the conference as a public relations exercise rather than a real attempt at peacemaking. Simultaneously, however, a direct clandestine Israeli-Palestinian channel of negotiations was opened in early 1993. This became possible not only, as noted, because of the inherent weakness of the PLO, but also due to the change in the political landscape in Israel.

The general elections in the summer of 1992 brought the Labor party back to power. The new Prime Minister, Itzhak Rabin, was determined to negotiate a political settlement with the Arab world, the Palestinians included, and was ready for a *quid pro quo*, offering a new dimension to the old Labor concept of ***peace for territories*** and taking the place of the Likud's ***peace for peace*** formula.

The first indication of Labor's intentions was the annulment in late 1992 of the law enacted during the term of a Likud government that prohibited Israelis from meeting with PLO members. Rabin's transformation and Arafat's weakness enabled the secret Israeli-Palestinian channel in Oslo that yielded the joint Declaration of Principles (August 1993) and the ongoing Israeli-Palestinian peace process. It also precipitated, as indicated, a Jordanian-Israeli peace treaty. As the solution of the "Palestinian problem" was a declared all-Arab precondition to any contact with Israel, the PLO-Israeli negotiations constituted a sufficient alibi for Jordan to pursue its own political arrangement with Israel.

Moreover, Jordan was also worried at the unveiling of the Israeli-Palestinian negotiations, lest it might be at the expense of its own interests. King Hussein duly summoned Prime Minister Rabin to Aqaba in October 1993, and the latter had to allay the King's apprehension. Nevertheless, in early November, Israeli Foreign Minister Shimon Peres arrived in Amman to discuss the formal *rapprochement* between the two countries. Intensive negotiations that followed this visit yielded, in July 1994, a joint declaration signed by Prime Minister Rabin and King Hussein in Washington, formally ending the state of conflict between Jordan and Israel. In October of the same year, a peace treaty was concluded.

The fear of an Israeli agreement with another side of the triangle that might jeopardize the interests of the third party, turned out to be advantageous to Israel. It not only speeded up negotiations with Jordan, but also with the Palestinians. Those achievements, however, have not yet tied together all the loose ends of the triangle. The attitude of a zero-sum-game still prevails with certain aspects of the trilateral relations. The Palestinians were not too happy with the special position accorded Jordan in the Islamic holy places in Jerusalem, as recognized by Israel and guaranteed by the Israeli-Jordanian peace treaty of October 1994. Jordan, nevertheless, undertook to relinquish all its rights and privileges there to the future independent Palestinian state.

On the other hand, Jordan and the PLO have coordinated their policies *vis-à-vis* Israel, mainly regarding the economic ones. In May 1994, they held a joint conference to discuss economic cooperation in various fields. Moreover, Jordan backed the PLO (as the other Arab states have done) in the debate with Israel (particularly after the May 1996 general elections that brought a Likud government back to power) over the implementation of their interim agreement and over the advancement toward discussions on a permanent settlement. It seems, however, that all three parties identify the mutual benefits hidden in their potential cooperation. They still have not made this realization the guiding principle of their respective policies due to political constraints and mutual suspicions.

One may say that the trilateral relations have just completed a full circle and entered a new era, in which the Palestinians, who lost their territory to Jordan in 1948, are getting it back from Israel, who took it from Jordan in 1967.

The purpose of the current process is not necessarily an immediate full cooperation in all aspects of inter-state relations. One should not ignore the past histories of all parties involved. A peaceful coexistence in which each party reassesses the present situation and adapts its social and political values to the new reality – together with gradual cooperation – is the best prescription for a successful conclusion of the ongoing process and for a better future. There is still a long way to go. The following chapters suggest ways, methods and ideas on how to make such a future possible and how to achieve it most effectively.

Notes

1 Joseph Nevo, "The Jordanian–Palestinian Pendulum," *Middle East Focus*, Vol. 9, No. 5 (Summer 1987), p. 4.

2 Eugene L. Rogan, "Bringing the State Back: The Limits of Ottoman Rule in Jordan 1840–1910," in Eugene L. Rogan and Tariq Tell (eds), *Village Steppe and State, The Social Origins of Modern Jordan* (London: British Academic Press, 1994), pp. 51–3.

3 Joseph Nevo, *King Abdallah and Palestine: A Territorial Ambition* (London: Macmillan, 1996), p. 6.

4 Ibid., pp. 12–15.

5 Mary C. Wilson, *King Abdullah, Britain and the Making of Jordan* (Cambridge: Cambridge University Press, 1987), pp. 103–28.

6 Nevo, *King Abdallah*, p. 121.

7 Israel State Archive, *Documents on Israel Foreign Policy*, Vol. I, 14 May–30 September 1948 (Jerusalem, 1981), No. 381; Vol. II, October 1948–April 1949 (Jerusalem, 1984), Nos. 4, 20, 36.

8 Hussein H. Hassouna, *The League of the Arab States and Regional Disputes: A Study of Middle East Conflicts* (New York: Oceana Publication, 1975), p. 40; Wilson, p. 204; Robert B. Satloff, *From Abdullah to Hussein, Jordan in Transition* (Oxford and New York: Oxford University Press, 1994), p. 9.

9 Asher Susser, *On Both Banks of the Jordan, A Political Biography of Wasfi al-Tall* (London: Frank Cass, 1994), pp. 102–22.

10 Zvi Elpeleg, "Hussein's Federation Plan; Causes and Comments" *Occasional Papers* (The Shiloah Center, Tel Aviv University, 1977), p. 14 (in Hebrew).

11 In 1967, about 35–45 percent of the population in the East Bank were of Palestinian origin.

12 Elpeleg, "Hussein's Federation Plan," p. 7; Moshe Ma'oz, *Palestinian Leadership on the West Bank* (London: Frank Cass, 1984), pp. 100–2.

13 Elpeleg, "Hussein's Federation Plan," p. 13.

14 Ibid., p. 1. Article 2 of the plan stated that the proposed Palestinian province would consist of the West Bank and "any other Palestinian territories". Later on Hussein claimed that by "any other Palestinian territories" he meant the Gaza Strip. *The Times*, 2 March 1973. In this regard see also: Asher Susser "Jordan, the PLO and the Palestine Question," in Joseph Nevo and Ilan Pappe (eds), *Jordan in the Middle East 1948–1988, The Making of A Pivotal State* (London: Frank Cass, 1994), p. 213.

15 Elpeleg, "Hussein's Federation Plan,"pp. 17–29.

16 Ma'oz, *Palestinian Leadership on the West Bank*, pp. 105–6, 136–9.

17 Dan Schueftan, *A Jordanian Option* (Ef'al: Yad Tabenkin, 1986), pp. 300–4, 334–5 (in Hebrew); Geoffrey Aronson, *Israel, Palestinians and the Intifada* (London and New York: Kegan Paul International, 1987), pp. 14–16, 50.

18 *Middle East Journal*, Vol. 29, No. 1 (Winter 1975), pp. 67, 74; *Middle East Monitor*, Vol. 4, Nos 21, 15 (November, 1974).

19 *Middle East Contemporary Survey* Vol. I, 1976/7, p. 479; *Newsweek*, 13 December 1976; *Washington Post*, 30 December 1976; *Time* 24 January 1977; Elpeleg, "Hussein's Federation Plan," p. 32; Ma'oz, *Palestinian Leadership on the West Ban*, pp. 143–4, 153; Clinton Bailey, *Jordan's Palestinian Challenge 1948–1983, A Political History* (Boulder and London: Westview Press, 1984), p. 84.

20 *Middle East Monitor*, Vol. VII, No. 5 (1 March 1977); *Middle East Contemporary Survey* (MECS), Vol. I, 1976/7, p. 480; Ma'oz, *Palestinian Leadership on the West Bank*, pp., 147, 171.

21 Ma'oz, *Palestinian Leadership on the West Bank*, pp. 200–1; Aronson, *Israel, Palestinians and the Intifada*, pp. 248–9.

22 Bailey, *Jordan's Palestinian Challenge*, pp. 106–7; Kamal Salibi, *The Modern History of Jordan* (London and New York: I.B. Tauris, 1993), p. 261.

23 For the resolutions of the 16th meeting of the PNC in Algiers in 1983 see: *Haaretz*, 25 February 1983; for those of the 17th meeting in Amman, 1984 see: *Middle East Contemporary Survey* Vol. IX, 1984/5, pp. 224–6; for the resolutions of the 18th meeting in Algiers, 1987, see Congressional Research Service, Library of Congress, *Documents on the Middle East Peace, 1982–88* (For the use of the Committee of Foreign Affairs, U.S. House of Representatives), U.S. Government Printing Office, Washington, D.C., 1989, pp. 40–1.

24 Schueftan, *A Jordanian Option*, p. 472.

25 Moshe Gabai (ed.), *Declarations and Resolutions on the Palestine Question 1950–1989* (Efal: Yad Tabenkin, 1990), pp. 167–71 (in Hebrew); *Documents on the Middle East Peace*, p. 21; Susser, *On Both Banks of the Jordan*, p. 215.

26 *Jerusalem Post*, 13 February 1985; *Haaretz*, 13, 14, 18, 19, 21, 25 February, 1985.
27 Susser, *On Both Banks of the Jordan*, p. 215.
28 *Documents on the Middle East Peace*, p. 39
29 Ibid., pp. 81–8.
30 Gabai, *Declarations and Resolutions on the Palestine Question*, pp. 267–8; *Jerusalem Post*, 16, 17, 18 May, 1989; *Haaretz*, 15, 17, 19, 22 May 1989.
31 Susser, *On Both Banks of the Jordan*, pp. 218–20.

2

Bilateral and Trilateral Political Cooperation

Moshe Shemesh

Discussing steps to political cooperation between Jordan, Israel, and the Palestinians presents a dilemma. It is pertinent to ask: What do we mean by political steps? We are in a post-Cold War era in which the world turns out to be a "global village." Grand strategy has become a key word in Middle East regional politics, while financial assistance is envisaged as an incentive for political steps designed to maintain regimes' democracy and stability. And indeed, Israel, under the Rabin and Peres governments, has endeavored to muster financial and economic assistance for the Palestinian Authority in order to strengthen Arafat's position and to stabilize the internal political situation of the Palestinian Authority. Shimon Peres spoke about "the new Middle East." It is a remarkable phenomenon, however, that in this "new Middle East" the steps to economic cooperation preceded the pure political steps.

We are in an era in which Arab local patriotism (*wataniya*), rather than pan-Arab nationalism (*qawmiya*), has become dominant in inter-Arab politics. Inter-state relations are being conducted largely by direct personal communications, like those between Shimon Peres, King Hussein, and Yasir Arafat. These three leaders personally directed the peace process and promoted political cooperation. Even in inter-Arab relations, we witness such personal contacts between the Presidents Mubarak and Asad, and King Hussein.

In such an era, one may ask whether it is practicable to separate the discussion on the political, economic, social, and cultural cooperation between Israel, Jordan and the Palestinians. From the Palestinian point of view, the four spheres are intertwined and mobilized for the national interest. Hence, I would suggest that political cooperation be seen as encompassing the steps taken by these parties in all four spheres.

The aim of this chapter is to outline the fundamental premises concerning bilateral and trilateral political cooperation between Jordan, Israel, and the Palestinians. These premises may serve as a framework for the discussion in this volume. The best way to tackle the issue of political cooperation is to first examine the political reality with which the three parties are trying to come to terms, and to study the parties' own point of departure for such cooperation. Such an approach is indispensable for assessing the prospects of progress along the path to peace. When I refer to the Palestinians, I relate primarily to the Palestinian leadership of the PLO, the Palestinian Authority or, to be precise, the Fatah leadership, which has been leading the Palestinian National Movement since 1968.

The Historical Background

There is an asymmetry which exists between two or three systems of political cooperation among the three parties. In one domain are the cordial and intimate historic relations, whose roots are to be found in the pre-1948 period, between the Hashemite Kingdom of Jordan and the Jewish leadership. This special relationship translated, since the signing of the peace agreement between Jordan and Israel, into close, friendly and personal contacts between the leaders of the two countries. On both sides, the political will to speed up the normalization process has been remarkable.

By contrast, violent enmity and lack of confidence have characterized the relations between the Jewish Yishuv, the State of Israel, and the Palestinians since the early 1920s. The repercussions of the 1948 war, the "armed struggle" which the Palestinian *Fidai* organizations have waged against Israel since 1965, and Israel's retaliations against the Palestinians, all deepened the bitter enmity on both sides. The continuing acts of violence by the Palestinian Islamic fundamentalists against the Israelis, even after the signing of the peace agreement between Israel and the PLO, have added another layer to the Israeli public's lack of confidence in the Palestinians' commitment to peace. Yossi Beilin, one of the architects of the Oslo Accord, observed in early November 1995 that:

> In the past, we (the Palestinians and Israel) were enemies, but now we are strangers. Every side goes his (own separate) way. Cooperation exists only in indispensable spheres.[1]

The third bilateral relationship is that between the Palestinians and the Hashemite Kingdom of Jordan. This relationship has been characterized by deep enmity and armed confrontation. The struggle for survival between the Palestinian entity and the Jordanian entity reached its climax in "Black September" in September 1970.[2]

One may discern five turning points in the relations between Jordan and the Palestinians since 1948:

1 "The unity of the two Banks of the Jordan River," which was approved by the Jordanian Parliament in April 1950, creating a Palestinian majority among the population of the "new" Jordanian state.
2 The establishment of the PLO in June 1964, which symbolized the revival of the Palestinian Entity as the institution representing the Palestinian people. Thus began an era of struggle between the PLO and Jordan over the political allegiance of the Palestinians.
3 The June 1967 war and its repercussions: Jordan shrunk back to its 1949 size, and the *Fidai* organizations became "a state within a state" in Jordan and a substitute for the Jordanian national movement, thereby endangering the stability of the regime.
4 The Rabat Summit's resolutions (October 1974), which recognized the PLO as "the sole legitimate representative of the Palestinian people." The Rabat Summit defined the tenets of "Palestinian national rights," that is, the territorial and national (ruling) elements of the future "Palestinian State."
5 The disengagement of Jordan's administrative and legal ties to the West Bank on 31July 1988.[3] These ties were the last vestige of Jordan's connections with the West Bank. On 1August 1988 the King stated that "Jordan has no sovereignty over the West Bank, which belongs to the Palestinians in the occupied territories."[4]

Since the Oslo Agreement in September 1993 and the Israel-Jordan peace treaty in October 1994, Israel has become a decisive factor in the trilateral relations between the Palestinians, Jordan and Israel. The Palestinians are perturbed that the developing of relations between Israel and Jordan might be at the expense of their own interests. Thus, since the Madrid peace conference in October 1991, there has been no serious and meaningful political coordination between the Palestinians and Jordan. Instead, their relations have been characterized by mutual suspicion and persistent rivalry.

Such asymmetry also exists in the economic relations among the three parties. To begin with, the dependence of the Palestinian economy on Israel and, to a lesser degree, on Jordan's market, is conspicuous. Ten of thousands of Palestinian workers seek employment in Israel. The Gaza Strip suffers a high rate of unemployment, in fact, one of the highest all over the Middle East region. Most of what Palestinians consume is either produced in Israel or imported by Israelis. Israel is seen by the Palestinians as the most profitable market for selling their consumer goods.[5] Israel, on the other hand, is dependent on cheap Palestinian labor for agricultural production and for the construction industry. The balance of trade of the West Bank and the Gaza Strip in 1987 is set out in table 2.1.[6]

Table 2.1 Balance of Trade of the West Bank and Gaza Strip, 1987 (in millions of US dollars)

	Israel	Jordan	Other Countries	Total
West Bank				
Import	580.7	9.4	49.0	639.1
Export	160.5	66.4	1.3	228.2
Balance	–420.2	57.0	–47.7	410.9
Gaza Strip				
Import	380.5	0.0	31.6	412.1
Export	143.2	11.8	2.1	157.1
Balance	–237.3	11.8	–29.5	–255.0
Total WB and GS				
Import	961.2	9.4	80.7	1,051.2
Export	303.7	87.2	3.4	385.3
Balance	–657.5	77.8	–77.3	–665.9

Source: State of Israel, Central Bureau of Statistics, *Statistical Abstract of Israel* – 1988 (Jerusalem, 1989), p. 715.

Jordan, on the other hand, expects to reap great benefits from developing its economic relations with Israel. While Jordanian citizens were expecting a "better life" in the wake of the peace agreement, the reality has not yet lived up to these expectations. In spite of the substantial improvement in the Jordanian economy since the sign of the peace treaty with Israel, many problems and obstacles must be overcome before the Jordanians can take full advantage of the peace, a result which might encourage them to develop their relations with Israel to the extent that the Israelis would like to see. Consequently, disappointment and frustrated hopes among the Jordanians have made them more cautious in their relations with Israel.[7]

Thus, the Palestinians are the weak link in this political and economic chain of relationships. They are economically dependent on both Jordan and Israel, whereas Jordan and Israel complement one another economically. Dr Hisham 'Awartani, a Palestinian economist, envisages that:

Notwithstanding the sensitivities and the psychological and political barriers, which one may not underestimate, it is preferable for us to admit that releasing the trade between Filastin and Israel (free trade) within a framework of many detailed bases agreed upon between both sides, is the Palestinian preferable option.[8]

A Permanent Agreement

The first and foremost objective of the Palestinians at this stage is to achieve a permanent agreement with Israel which would lead to the establishment of a Palestinian state. As long as a permanent solution has not been achieved, political cooperation between Israel and the Palestinians is restricted to steps that both sides consider indispensable.

One may discern three principles which have been guiding the Palestinians in their negotiations with Israel and Jordan: equality, mutuality, and independent Palestinian decision making. These principles are designed to overcome their inferior position *vis-à-vis* the other two parties. They are the result of the lessons derived from their struggle for survival over the last two decades. Being in a transitional period, in which they lack sovereignty and full political independence, they will adhere to these three principles so that their rights, as they conceive them, will not be jeopardized.

Arafat, in his speech at the Amman Economic Conference held in Amman in October 1995, outlined four prerequisites for economic cooperation with the states of the region:

1 Equality between the parties, recognizing the fact that economically, the parties are not in an equal situation.
2 Freedom of movement of people, transportation, and services, leading Arafat to criticize the closure of the territories by Israel.
3 Economic cooperation that is fruitful and useful, bringing relief for all the parties, and not just for one of them.
4 Regional cooperation compatible with the participants' national plans.[9]

It may be recalled that before the Oslo Agreement, the PLO called for the convening of an international conference with the participation of the PLO on an equal footing with the other participants. The Palestinian leadership is concerned lest the strengthening of the political cooperation with Israel during this transitional period be perceived by the Palestinian public as succumbing to Israeli demands, as in the case of cancelling those articles of the Palestinian Charter which contradict the peace agreement between the PLO and Israel. For the Palestinians, it is essential that the advancement of their political cooperation with Israel be compatible with the progress achieved toward a permanent agreement.

Jordan's National Security

Preserving Jordan's national security, namely, Jordan's territorial integrity and the stability of the Kingdom as a unified society, is the prime goal of the Hashemite regime. Within this context, the following factors are decisive in determining Jordan's political cooperation with both Israel and the Palestinians.

The first factor is that in many areas the process of "Jordanization" of the Palestinians, since the unification of the two Banks in April 1950 (until June 1967) has not been fully accomplished and, in some aspects, even failed. Since the June 1967 war, Jordanian society has remained divided into two sectors: the Jordanians and the Palestinians. This division, comprising social, economic and political arenas, creates an undercurrent of tension between them. In many circles of the Palestinian sector, or as the official term defines it, "the Jordanians of Palestinian origin," there exists a strong Palestinian consciousness and sense of Palestinian identity. Hence, within the context of a future Palestinian state, the questions pertaining to the dual loyalty of those Palestinians, namely, political affiliation to both the Palestinian and the Jordanian regimes, might arise again. The regime's concern is that the establishment of Palestinian autonomy at the first stage and, at a later stage, an independent Palestinian state, would precipitate the "Palestinization" process of the East Bank Palestinians and, in the long term, strengthen their affiliation to the Palestinian state on the West Bank.

Ahmad 'Ubeidat, Jordan's former Prime Minister, addressed this complex issue by making the following points:

1 One has to admit that indeed there exists a historical crisis of confidence between the Jordanian leadership and the Palestinian leadership. Internal and external factors, in addition to personal and ideological attitudes of the official and popular Palestinian and Jordanian prominent figures, have caused a division between the two camps among Jordan's citizens.
2 Since the union of the two Banks in 1950, Jordanian society has been growing in such a way that the Palestinian capital has been historically controlling the economy of the country by means of the

banking and business communities as well as through industrial and trade projects. On the other hand, the Jordanian element has been controlling the armed forces and the security apparatus, as well as occupying the high administrative functions in the Jordanian regime.

3 As a result of this situation, especially since the declaration of the establishment of "the State of Filastin" and Jordan's disengagement from the West Bank, a political vacuum has existed in Jordan. Consequently, a "Jordanian nuclear" has been created, calling for the "Jordanization" of Jordan in order to withstand the growth of the Palestinians' economic and financial influence in Jordan.[10]

There is a difference between the Palestinian and Jordanian positions concerning the attitude of the Palestinian sector toward Palestinian-Jordanian relations. Jordan claims that the approach of the "Jordanians of Palestinian origin" differs from that of the inhabitants and the leadership of the West Bank. The Palestinians minimize and even deny the difference. The Jordanian point of departure is the situation before the June 1967 war, when both banks were united under the Hashemite crown. Under these circumstances, the attitude of the Jordanians and that of the Palestinians of the East Bank (or the Jordanians of Palestinian origin) were essentially the same regarding Palestinian-Jordanian relations. Accordingly, the real distinction should be made between the inhabitants of Jordan "as one united people," on the one hand, and the Palestinians of the West Bank, on the other.[11]

The Palestinians claim that behind the official declarations and what is written in newspapers, the Jordanians of the East Bank have begun to see the Palestinian-Jordanians (the Jordanians of Palestinian origin) through the same glasses with which they see the Palestinians of the West Bank. The Palestinians of the West Bank, on the other hand, view the Jordanians and the Palestinians of the East Bank in different ways. Their conclusion is that there is a convergence in views of the Palestinians of the East Bank and the West Bank. This means that the views of the Jordanian sector and those of the Palestinian sector of Jordan's population, concerning Jordanian-Palestinian relations, are basically incongruent.[12]

There is no doubt that King Hussein's efforts, during the last two decades, to ease his relationship with the PLO and to maintain the dialogue with the Palestinian leadership, had a positive impact on the relationship between the regime and the Palestinian sector of his people. His policy was also aimed to prevent Palestinian activities against his regime.

Both Jordan and the Palestinian leadership are concerned that Israel may try in the future to turn Jordan into a Palestinian state and thereby secure control over the West Bank. This would be an implementation of the notion of a Palestinian "substitute homeland" (*al-watan al-badil*). They envisage that Israel would, in this way, solve its future demographic predicament, namely, by another Palestinian emigration to the East Bank. In July 1986, King Hussein expressed this concern by stating that:

> The high rate of birth of the Palestinians in Israel and the territories might bring about an attempt to expel them . . . This (possibility) stands at the top of my concerns because of the danger which it might create for the Kingdom's security . . . If we look at this issue through Jordanian's eyes, our national security, even in the narrowest framework, compels us to strengthen our people in the occupied territories; otherwise if they (the Israelis) expel them, this would be done to our direction here (Jordan).[13]

Against this background, one may understand the Jordanian apprehension about the situation in the West Bank and the Gaza Strip, and consequently, King Hussein's efforts to bring about an agreement between the Palestinian Authority and Israel pertaining issues on their agenda. Jordan is concerned that further deterioration of the situation in the West Bank might serve as an incentive for Palestinians to emigrate to Jordan, *inter alia*, to find employment there. In that case, the notion of a Palestinian "substitute homeland" would be raised in the Palestinian arena. Thus, Jordan considers the establishment of new Jewish settlements in the West Bank as a danger to the peace process and as a threat to its national security. Moreover, Jordan views the expansion of the Jewish settlements as a reason for violent outbursts in the West Bank which would encourage Palestinians to emigrate to Jordan. This emigration would, in turn, create political problems for the Jordanian regime.

Thus, it is imperative for Jordan's national security to fully support the PLO, Arafat, and the Palestinian Authority in their efforts to achieve self-determination for the Palestinians and establishment of an independent Palestinian state in the West Bank and the Gaza Strip. On the other hand, Arafat and the Palestinian Authority, being very keen to prevent the creation of a Palestinian "substitute homeland" in Jordan, have great interest in preserving Jordan's independence.[14]

Another factor that plays a major role in Jordan's political affiliations is its geopolitical location, having borders with Syria, Iraq and Saudi Arabia. Jordan has the longest frontier with Israel. Hence, on the one hand are Jordan's adherence to pan-Arab consensus pertaining to solving the Arab-Israeli conflict, its joining the June 1967 war, and its signing of the Rabat Summit resolutions in October 1974 which recognized the PLO as: "the sole legitimate representative of the Palestinian people."[15] On the other hand are the liquidation of the Palestinian organization's strongholds in Jordan in the wake of what the Palestinians called "Black September" (September 1970) and Hussein's secret meeting with Israeli leaders.

King Hussein only signed his peace treaty with Israel after the PLO had done so first. Just as the peace treaty between Israel and Egypt (March 1979) paved the way for the Oslo agreement, so did the Oslo agreement pave the way for the Jordan-Israel peace treaty. Adnan Abu-Odeh, former Minister of the Royal Court, admitted that:

> Two constraints prevented Jordan from reaching a peace agreement with Israel earlier: the Arab and the Palestinian. The first was blown up in 1991 on the beach of Kuwait, when Iraq invaded the country and Syria joined the American coalition. The Palestinian constraint disappeared on September 13, 1993 when Arafat signed the Oslo agreement.[16]

A Confederation between Jordan and the Palestinians

Under these circumstances, one may dare to suggest that a confederation between the Palestinians and Jordan is not feasible in the short and medium range. In my view, such a confederation has become a "vision" for the long range. My impression is that King Hussein is no longer as enthusiastic about the idea as he used to be due to the recent political developments in the region. The idea of a confederation was originally raised in order to bypass Israel's objection to the PLO's participation in the peace process. In this respect, the idea has outlived its usefulness.

Indeed, the 18th Palestinian National Congress (PNC) resolved that: "the future relations with Jordan would be based on confederal bases between two independent states," namely between "the State of Filastin" and Jordan.[17] Thus, from the Palestinian point of view, the issue should be discussed only after the establishment of the Palestinian state. Then, the Palestinian state's institutions would determine whether or not to approve a confederation with Jordan.

Neither Jordan nor the Palestinians reveal any interest of any kind in a substantial political connection between them. Both are eager to act separately and independently: Jordan to advance the peace process and its relations with Israel, and the Palestinians to achieve a permanent agreement with Israel that would lead to a Palestinian state. Jordan considers that its interests would best be served if the Palestinians themselves conduct the negotiations leading to self-determination in their own way.[18] Both acknowledge that the moment Israel recognized the

PLO, a confederation between Jordan and the Palestinians became unnecessary.

Jordan raised another reason, unrelated to the conflict, for its denying the notion of a confederation, at least for the short range: establishing such a joint political framework might undermine the internal security and "the delicate balance" of Jordanian society, "which since 1989 has been experiencing a new political system of political pluralism." Jordan claims that this system is based upon the commitment by all the political parties not to practice violence to achieve political aims. Jordan is concerned lest the Palestinian experience develop in a way that would not be compatible with the new Jordanian political system. This new system, Jordan emphasized, "could not endure any intervention by unstable elements which would create conflict with the Palestinians and others, and shake the internal stability and the delicate balance established in Jordan."[19] Another interesting argument raised by Jordan for not imposing a confederation was that it would mean the resolution of the refugee problem at its expense, namely, that Palestinian refugees would stay in Jordan as part of the confederal Jordanian-Palestinian state.

The Impact of the Arab Arena

The fact that both Arafat and the King Hussein signed their peace agreements with Israel without prior coordination with the other Arab states, does not necessarily imply the lack of Arab arena impact on their policy pertaining to political cooperation with Israel, or the lack of Arab impact on Palestinian and Jordanian public opinion. Arab writers and intellectuals are continuing to preach to the Arab masses about Israel's alleged aspirations for economic and cultural domination of the Arab world. Large-scale opposition to the state of peace with Israel still exists in Egypt, Jordan, and among the Palestinians.

Jordan has in fact openly admitted that it cannot neglect the "Arab depth" of its foreign policy. In the wake of the peace agreement with Israel, Jordan made a strategic decision to improve its relations with the other Arab states, claiming that enhancing its relations with Israel would not be at the expense of its relations with the rest of the Arab world. On the contrary, Jordan suggested that good relations with the Arab states would strengthen its position *vis-à-vis* Israel. As proof, Jordan emphasizes the improvement of its relations with Egypt, Bahrain, the Gulf Emirates, and Saudi Arabia.[20]

Marwan Al-Mu'ashar, Jordan's former Minister of Information, stated in Washington (after the election of Benyamin Netanyahu) that:

> Jordan cannot accept a situation in which she has peace relations with Israel, whereas at the same time there is no progress in Israel's relations with the Palestinians and Syria. . . . Negative trends in Israel-Palestinian relations might isolate Jordan in the Arab world. On the other hand, positive developments in the West Bank and the Gaza Strip would contribute to enhancing the relations between Israel and Jordan.[21]

Amru Musa, Egypt's Foreign Minister, expressed the impact of the Arab arena when he claimed, at the Economic Conference held in Amman in October 1995, that:

> Some Arab states were in a hurry to sign a peace agreement with Israel, and it was preferable for them to coordinate their policy in order to achieve a comprehensive solution of the Arab-Israeli conflict.[22]

The implication was that they should not have moved ahead of Syria. King Hussein responded instantly:

> To those who say that Jordan was the first who hastily signed a peace agreement with Israel, I remind that Egypt has already done so 17 years before. If we take into account the necessity to compensate for the time which has been lost for the Egyptians, the Jordanians, the Syrians and the Lebanese, then we have not only to hasten, but actually to run.[23]

Moreover, an Egyptian economist, Sa'id Al-Najar, who supported the notion of "the new international order," wrote in 1994 as follows:

> Any settlement in the Middle East, in which Israel is a party, should not be made at the expense of inter-Arab relations. We have fifty years of inter-Arab cooperation which is embodied in inter-Arab agreements. These agreements must not be negatively influenced by any agreement within the framework of Middle Eastern cooperation.[24]

In this context, one may add the impact of Egypt's political involvement in solving problems arising between the Palestinian Authority and Israel. Since the signing of the Camp David Accord in August 1978, the relations between Israel and Egypt have been strongly influenced by the progress which has been achieved in solving the Palestinian issue. Egypt still sees the advancement in implementing the Oslo Agreement as a precondition for warming the "cold peace" between the two countries. Egypt, of all the Arab states, continues to be the most involved in the Palestinian national issue and has a great impact on the Palestinian Authority. Thus, its influence is paramount in Palestinian decision making, and Arafat and Fatah's leaders, who are well aware of this important role, are trying to make the most of it.

The Palestinian Refugee Problem

Jordan claims that it is unquestionable as to who represents Jordanian citizens – both those from Palestine and the East Bank – namely, the Hashemite Kingdom of Jordan. The PLO represents the Palestinian refugees who are living outside Jordan – a fact, Jordan claims, that is agreed upon with the PLO. Therefore, from the Jordanian point of view, the refugee problem relates not only to Palestinian refugees all over the world, but also to the Jordanian citizens of Palestinian origin. It is a Jordanian problem because a great number of Jordanian citizens are refugees, and as such, have rights which are protected by the Jordanian government representing them.[25]

The Palestinians demanded that Jordan not negotiate separately with Israel on this issue before May 1996 and, in any case, coordinate its approach with them. They objected to the negotiation on the refugee problem between Jordan and Israel on the grounds that if Jordan did so before May 1996, some agreements might be reached with Israel, which the Palestinians would be committed to implement in the future. They emphasized that they had already arranged to deal with Israel on the refugee problem only in May 1996, when the negotiations on the final status were due to start.[26] Thus, the Palestinians and Jordan agreed to simultaneously discuss the issue with Israel.

The Permanent Status of Jerusalem

Each of the three parties claims historic, emotional and religious ties with Jerusalem, which has deep meaning for the whole Arab and Muslim world. It is significant that King Hussein began his memoirs (1962) by telling us how Jerusalem was very important for him:

> When I was a boy, my grandfather, King Abdullah, used to tell me that Jerusalem was one of the most beautiful cities in the world. His first love, it is true, was the Hijaz where he was born. . . . But, as the years passed and he settled in the north and his wise rule brought peace and independence to the country that is now Jordan, he grew to love Jerusalem more and more. He was deeply religious and could never enter the city without being aware of its spiritual significance. And as a boy, I used to see it through his eyes.[27]

King Hussein still sees Jerusalem through his grandfather's eyes. Before 1967, Hussein was proud that his grandfather had returned the holy places to the Arabs. Following the June 1967 war, he saw himself as responsible for its having fallen to the occupation of Israel. Since then, it is his aspiration that the holy places be again under Jordanian or Arab authority. Jordan's official and clear attitude on Jerusalem is: "East Jerusalem is part of the Arab occupied land and should be returned to the Palestinians and be their capital."[28] It is noteworthy that at the same time, Jordan did not refrain from declaring its intention to have some role in controlling or directing the Muslim (and Christian) holy places in Jerusalem, especially the al-Aqsa Mosque.

Hussein's aspirations to have some responsibility or influence upon the Islamic holy places in Jerusalem is well exemplified by his continued financial support to the Islamic religious system in Jerusalem in spite of Jordan's disengagement from the West Bank in July 1988. In his speech on 31 July 1988, Hussein announced the official disengagement of Jordan's administrative and legal ties to the West Bank.[29] The decision affected 18,000 government-employees in various departments and institutions. However, the decision did not apply to the employees of the Ministry of Awqaf (religious endowment) and Religious Affairs, including the Islamic Religious Court system. They were exempted because, according to the government statement, they embodied "the Islamic cultural presence in the occupied territories."[30] The Jordanian Minister of Awqaf stated (September 1988) that his office continued to spend four million JD (Jordanian Dinars) on religious institutions and mosques in the West Bank. This included the upkeep of 750 mosques (the most important of these being the al-Aqsa mosque in Jerusalem) and the payments of salaries to about 3,500 workers in the ministry (1,800 in the Awqaf, 200 in religious courts, 420 teachers, and the rest functionaries in various Islamic institutions).[31]

On another occasion (July 9, 1994), King Hussein stated as follows:

> Jerusalem is above all other consideration. It is in our hearts and minds. Concerning our Islamic holy places in Jerusalem, sovereignty must be for the Islamic nation.[32]

Jordan's higher interest in the Muslim holy shrines in Jerusalem is clearly expressed in two documents signed between Jordan and Israel. The first was Article 3 of the Washington Declaration (25 July 1994) which stated that: "Israel respects the present special role of Jordan in Muslim holy shrines in Jerusalem. When negotiations on the permanent status will take place, Israel will give high priority to the Jordanian historic role in these shrines." The second was Article 9.2 of the Israel-

Jordan Treaty of Peace (26 July 1994) which reiterated Article 3.[33]

It was apparent that Article 3 would provoke the PLO's suspicions about Jordan's political aspirations in Jerusalem. Protesting against this article, the PLO claimed that it reduced Palestinian chances of gaining political sovereignty over East Jerusalem. Jordan found it necessary to illuminate its position on this issue. In an official announcement published on 28 July 1994, the Jordanian government responded to "various media organs reported stands and statements on the third clause of the Washington Declaration." It distinguished between the political aspect and the religious aspect of the issue stating, *inter alia*, that:

1 "Jerusalem is a Muslim and Arab territory that was occupied in 1967 as part of the territories of the Hashemite Kingdom of Jordan. What applies to Jerusalem would also apply to the occupied Arab territories included in UN Security Council Resolutions 242 and 338.

2 In 1974, Jordan accepted the Rabat Summit resolution which considers the PLO as the sole legitimate representative of the Palestinian Arab people. In order to enable the Palestinian people to establish their independent state on their soil, Jordan in 1988 decided to sever its legal and administrative links with the West Bank. The decision excluded the Awqaf, Islamic and holy affairs, as well as Islamic shari'a courts, in recognition of the Hashemite role in taking care of these holy shrines and in order to protect them from falling directly under occupation and foreign control. The PLO blessed and approved this decision, which continues to be valid until now.

3 There is no contradiction between restoring political sovereignty over Arab Jerusalem through Palestinian-Israeli negotiations and the continuance of Jordan's role in practicing its religious custody over the holy shrines in Jerusalem.

4 The Washington Declaration is only a reiteration of the Hashemite Kingdom of Jordan's role and that of the Hashemites during their long history of working to achieve the Islamic and Arab interest, including the Palestinian interest. Thus, the Washington Declaration recognizes the Hashemites' right to take care of the holy shrines and does not establish their right to that. This was clear throughout the stages of Hashemite reconstruction of the Holy al-Aqsa Mosque and the blessed Dome of the Rock in 1924, 1944, 1952, and 1994."[34]

The Palestinians, on the other side, emphasize their own political aspirations, claiming that Jerusalem should be the capital of the future Palestinian state. One should keep in mind that the Palestinians refer to East Jerusalem when they relate to the city, as does the rest of the Arab world. The Palestinian leaders, having the support of the Arab world, have been endeavoring to instill this into the minds of their people and to mobilize the support of the international community for their cause. Thus, they are very sensitive to any move or sign by Jordan or Israel concerning the present or future status of Jerusalem. Article V3 of the Israel-PLO Declaration of Principles (13 September 1993) should be considered within this context. It states that:

> It is understood that these negotiations (on the permanent status) shall cover remaining issues, including Jerusalem, refugees, settlements, security arrangements, border relations and cooperation with other neighbors, and other issues of common interest.[35]

Following the Oslo Agreement, the Revolutionary Council of Fatah clearly defined the organization's (and in fact the PLO's) attitude pertaining this issue, stating in a "political statement" (15 November 1993) that: "Holy Jerusalem is the eternal capital of Filastin and it is an inseparable part of our Filastin and Arab territory which was occupied in 1967. UN Resolution 242 applies to it as it applies to all the occupied territories." The Revolutionary Council stresses the Fatah Movement's commitment to the Arab nature of Jerusalem in accordance with the UN Security Council and General Assembly resolutions which have rejected the annexation decision (by Israel).[36]

The importance of Jerusalem for Israel and the Jewish people needs no elaboration. Israel proclaimed in 1967 its sovereignty over Jerusalem as the united and eternal capital of Israel. For the Palestinians, the resolution of this intricate issue is a *sine qua non* not only for a permanent agreement, but also for any significant political cooperation with Israel. It is reasonable to assume that King Hussein and the Arab world would accept any solution approved by the Palestinians regarding this issue.

Arafat's Leadership

Since the establishment of the Palestinian Authority, there has been a question as to whether Arafat has the ability to lead his people to peace with Israel. This issue is important not only for the Palestinians, but also for the Israelis as well as the Jordanians. I would say that in comparing the composition of today's leadership of Fatah, namely the Palestinian Authority, with that of 1974 when Fatah led the change in PLO's strategy, the picture seems less promising for Arafat, although Fatah achieved overwhelming victory in the first elections to the Palestinian Assembly and Arafat himself was elected by a vast majority as the president of the Palestinian Authority. Today Arafat is surrounded mostly by Fatah's second-echelon leaders, except for Abu-Mazin (Mahmoud Abbas) and Abu Al-Lutuf (Faruq Al-Qaddumi). Qaddumi, who is not considered as a charismatic leader, opposed the Oslo agreement, preferring to stay in Tunis. Arafat lost his two charismatic lieutenants, Abu-Jihad (Khalil Al-Wazir) and Abu-Iyad (Salah Khalaf), some years ago. Nevertheless, Arafat retains power and authority in the eyes of the Palestinians as the symbol of the "Palestinian Revolution" and the veteran leader of Fatah and the PLO. The fact is that there is no alternative to his leadership of the Palestinian people, nor a substitute for his dominant presence in the quest for attaining a permanent agreement with Israel.

To conclude: The impression is that in a situation of protracted lack of advancement in the implementation of the Oslo Agreement and the interim agreements, both the Jordanians and the Palestinians prefer a "slow motion" process in developing their political cooperation with Israel. They are still not prepared for an accelerated process. Moreover, progress in the negotiations on the final permanent agreement between the Palestinian Authority and Israel is crucial for further enhancing such cooperation. Netanyahu's election as Israel's Prime Minister gives credence to all the above premises.

Notes

1 *Haaretz*, 1 November 1995.

2 For the Palestinian–Jordan relations between 1964 and 1974 see: Moshe Shemesh, *The Palestinian Entity 1959–1974: Arab Politics and the PLO* (London, 1988).

3 Hussein's speech, see: *al-Dustur*, Amman, 1 August 1988.

4 King Hussein in a press conference (7 August 1988), see: *Journal of Palestine Studies*, No. 69 (Winter 1988), pp. 290–300.

5 Khalil Shikaki, "The Peace Process, National Reconstruction, and the Transition to Democracy in Palestine," *Journal of Palestine Studies*, No. 2 (Winter 1995), pp. 2– 20.

6 See also: Hisham 'Awartani, al-'Ulaqat al-Tijariyya al-Filastiniyya- al-Isra'iliyya: al-Waqi' wa al-Mustaqbal, in a*l-Siyasa al-Falastiniyya*, Vol. 1, Nos 1–2, Winter–Spring 1994.

7 Marwan al-Mu'ashar, Jordan's Minister of Information, former Jordan's Ambassador to Israel and Minister of Information, in a debate with Palestinian scholars, on 16 July 1995, sponsored by the Center For Palestine

Research and Studies of Economy, Nablus, the West Bank, *al-Siyasa al-Filastinyya*, Vol. 2, Nos 7–8 (Summer and Fall 1995), pp. 163–80.

8 Awartani, "al-Ulaqat al-Tijariyya al-Filastiniyya"; Dr Hisham 'Awartani is a lecturer on economics and Head of the Department of Economics at al-Najah University, Nablus, and is a member of the Palestinian delegation to bilateral economic negotiations with Israel.

9 *Haaretz*, 30 October 1995.

10 Ahmad 'Ubeidat, *al-Dirast al-Filastiniyya*, No. 24 (Winter 1995), pp. 90–100.

11 See, Marwan al-Mu'ashar, note 7.

12 See Palestinian scholars' attitudes in the debate with Marwan al-Mu'ashar: Khalil Shikaki, Mamduh al-'Aker, Mahir al-Masri, Muhammad Jad-Alla, Amin Maqbul, Raji al-Surani, Mundhir Salah, Samir 'Abdulla, and Jamal Mansur, see note 7 above.

13 *al-Ra'y* (Amman), 13 July 1986; see also: Hussein's speech following the breakdown of the Joint Palestinian-Jordanian peace initiative, *al-Ra'y*, 20 February 1986.

14 For the PLO's attitude see: Khalid al-Hasan, *al-Ittifaq al-Urduni al-Filastini lil Taharruk al-Mushtarak* (Amman, 11 February 1985).

15 See the text of the Rabat secret resolutions in: *al-Safir*, Beirut, 30 November 1977. For an analysis of the Rabat summit resolutions see: Shemesh, *The Palestinian Entity 1959–1974*, pp. 306–15.

16 *Haaretz*, 6 May 1996.

17 See resolutions of the 18th PNC (20–26 April 1987): *Shuun Filastiyyia*, Nos 170–1 (May–June 1987), pp. 166–70.

18 See: al-Mu'ashar, *al-Siyasa al-Filastinyya*, Vol. 2, Nos 7–8 (Summer and Fall 1995), pp. 163–80.

19 Ibid.

20 Ibid.

21 *Haaretz*, 16 June 1996.

22 *Haaretz*, 29–30 October 1995.

23 *Haaretz*, 30 October 1995.

24 Sa'id al-Najar, *Toward An Arab Peace Strategy* (Tel Aviv, 1994) (in Hebrew).

25 Al-Mu'ashar, *al-Siyasa al-Filastinyya*, Vol. 2, Nos 7–8 (Summer and Fall 1995), pp. 163–80.

26 See note 12.

27 King Hussein of Jordan, *Uneasy Lies The Head* (London, 1962), p. 1.

28 al-Mu'ashar, *al-Siyasa al-Filastinyya*, Vol. 2, Nos 7–8 (Summer and Fall 1995), pp. 163–80.

29 See: Hussein's speech, *al-Dustur*, Amman, 1 August 1988.

30 See: Hani al-Khasawna, Information Minister, Interview (3 August 1988) *Journal of Palestine Studies*, No. 69 (Autumn 1988), p. 285; see also: *Shuun Filstiniyya*, No. 185 (August 1988), p. 138; No. 186 (September 1988), pp. 103–4.

31 Ibid.

32 King Hussein's speech to members of Parliament, *Jordan Television*, 9 July 1994.

33 See the Washington Declaration, Washington, D.C., 25 July 1994, Israel-

Jordan and the United States, in *Journal of Palestine Studies*, No. 89 (Autumn 1993), pp. 115–18. See also: Treaty of Peace Between the State of Israel and the Hashemite Kingdom of Jordan, signed on the Israeli-Jordanian border, 26 October 1994, in *Journal of Palestine Studies*, No. 94 (Winter 1994), pp. 126–43.

34 *Radio Amman*, 29 July 1994; also in: *Journal of Palestine Studies*, No. 93 (Autumn 1994), p. 136. See also: Jordanian Council of Ministers, decision on Jordan's role in Jerusalem, *Jordan Television*, 27 September 1994 ; and also in: *Journal of Palestine Studies*, No. 94 (Winter 1995), p. 146.

35 See Israel-PLO Declaration of Principles, Washington, D.C., 13 September 1993, in *Journal of Palestine Studies*, No. 89 (Autumn, 1993), pp. 115–18.

36 See Revolutionary Council of Fatah 'political statement', Tunis, 15 November 1993, in *Journal of Palestine Studies*, No. 89 (Autumn, 1993), pp. 133–6.

3

Operating the Triangle by Bilateral Agreements

Menachem Klein

I shall argue in this chapter that the Israeli–Jordanian–Palestinian peace triangle has been simplified regarding the two themes considered by many to be the core issues and most troublesome points of the Israeli-Palestinian conflict: the question of the Palestinian refugees (the right of return, in the PLO's terminology) and the future of Jerusalem. According to my perception, Israel, Jordan and the Palestinian Authority have already begun their give-and-take over Jerusalem and the right of return and have even reached several agreements on these subjects. The bilateral framework of the Israeli-Palestinian-Jordanian negotiations – between Israel and the Palestinians; Israel and Jordan; and the Palestinian Authority and the Hashemite Kingdom – allowed political tensions and differences between the three parties to curtail the full realization of the potential of this tripartite relationship. Historical reasons and divided interests and perceptions led to higher levels of understanding and tighter agreements between Israel and Jordan than those concluded between them and the Palestinian Authority. This lack of clarity on the Palestinian track was reinforced by the Palestinian Authority's status as a state in creation; its power and status were weaker than those of Jordan and Israel. As a result, and in order to improve its position, the Palestinian Authority approached the Islamic Conference for help in its debate with Jordan over Jerusalem's Islamic holy places and delayed its negotiations with Jordan over the return of displaced persons in 1967, until the founding of a Palestinian state or, at least, until the legitimacy of a future Palestinian state, was accepted by Israel.

The Palestinian Refugees

Until the Israeli-Palestinian Declaration of Principles was signed in September 1993 (The Oslo Agreement), the PLO viewed the right of return as a principle rather than a policy or program. Indeed, the PLO has never described in detail how this right is to be realized,[1] even though the PLO leadership's view of its conflict with Israel has changed from an existential zero-sum game to one over equality of rights and borders. Ironically, though, this lack of specificity over the right of return, coupled with the PLO's 1974 policy of linking the right of return to self-determination and the demand for official recognition as the sole legitimate representative of the Palestinian people, helped the organization reach an interim agreement with Israel.[2]

In the absence of any concrete program for actualizing the right of return, the PLO and Israel agreed, within the framework of the Declaration of Principles, to divide the issue into two parts. Israel agreed in principle to the return of those displaced from the West Bank and Gaza Strip in 1967, while delaying the resolution of the problem of the 1948 refugees until the final status negotiations. According to the Declaration of Principles, a standing committee encompassing the Palestinian Authority, Israel, Egypt, and Jordan was to be formed in order to decide "on the modalities of admission of persons displaced from the West Bank and Gaza Strip in 1967, together with necessary measures to prevent disruption and disorder."[3]

Working without a reliable database, the PLO is conscious of the need to define who and how many such refugees there are. The Palestinians, though, are not alone in this regard, as there is significant disagreement among other international agencies and countries as to the numbers of refugees and displaced persons. In 1995, the UN Relief and Works Agency (UNRWA) presented to its contributor states a five-year program for providing education, relief, and employment services to 1.19 million Palestinian refugees who reside in Jordan, 340,000 in Lebanon, 330,000 in Syria, 640,000 in the Gaza Strip, and 500,000 in the West Bank.[4] According to UNRWA's 1995 registrations, the number of people displaced in 1967 totals 856,228.[5] However, according to American and Jordanian data, in 1991 there were 430,083 refugees from 1948 and 530,129 displaced persons in Jordan. Since the Iraqi invasion of Kuwait in August 1990 and the war against Iraq in January 1991, between 230,000 to 300,000 Jordanians were deported or returned to the Hashemite Kingdom of Jordan, most of them Palestinians.[6] Several PLO spokesmen have claimed that the number of Palestinians who returned to Jordan after the Gulf War was as high as 800,000,[7] but the heads of the PLO concur that this estimate remains to be documented.

The PLO and the governments of Egypt and Jordan have agreed to register the 1967 displaced persons, although work on the census has yet to begin. This notwithstanding, the bilateral Jordanian-Palestinian committee has agreed on the definition of "a displaced person" as anyone who, on 4 June 1967, was officially registered as a resident of the West Bank, or their descendants were so registered. Both sides were also able to concur on the formulation of the census questions.[8]

Palestinian leaders have expressed their awareness of the need to coordinate the return of 1967 displaced persons with the building of the Palestinian Authority's infrastructure, lest systems and public services, such as education, health and housing, collapse. Indeed, Abu-Mazin, a key member in the executive committee of the PLO, declared, "The only consideration that may suspend this return is the problem of capacity," while Dr Elias Sanbar, the head of the Palestinian delegation to the multilateral workshop on the refugee problem of the Madrid peace conference, suggested that the quota and rate of return be determined by the quadralateral committee (the Palestinian Authority, Israel, Egypt, and Jordan), as agreed upon in the Declaration of Principles.[9] However, other than acknowledging their awareness of the current limited abilities of the Palestinian Authority, PLO leaders have taken no additional steps nor suggested any policies for absorbing the displaced. Dr Sanbar raised the issue at the heart of the refugee and displaced persons problem by saying that before dealing with housing or economic possibilities, there is a need to assure acknowledgment of the very existence of the right of return itself.[10]

The PLO's agreement with Israel has raised the question of Jordan's policy toward the Palestinians living in Jordan. By cutting off legal and administrative relations with the West Bank in July 1988, the Kingdom explicitly demanded that Palestinians in Jordan consider themselves as Jordanians, while the PLO regarded them as Palestinian nationals. Thus, subsequent to the Declaration of Principles, the question arose: Do those Palestinians holding Jordanian citizenship or passports also need to carry a visa-passport document of the Palestinian Authority? PLO leaders suggested that Jordan allow the refugees from 1948 and the displaced persons from 1967 to hold both documents, but the Kingdom refused. It did signal, however, its readiness to consider changing its citizenship law in order to offer citizenship to 1967 refugees who prefer not to return to the West Bank. No conclusion has been reached on this problem of two conflicting nationality models – the territorial Jordanian citizenship *vis-à-vis* the Palestinian ethnic identity – nor has any conclusion been reached regarding Jordan's quest to receive compensation for absorbing those 1967 displaced persons willing to remain in Jordan and for accommodating the returnees. Similarly, it is as yet unclear whether

Jordan's citizenship offer is conditioned upon fulfillment of the demands for compensation.[11]

These different points of view were expressed in two working papers presented at the bilateral Jordanian-Palestinian committee assembled in January 1994. The Jordanian paper declared that the refugee problem "influences Jordan directly" and therefore the joint committee should: "(1) decide upon a common strategy of stages in order to cooperate on this sensitive subject within the framework of the bilateral and the multilateral negotiations; (2) unify figures, data, and information concerning the refugees and the displaced and also establish a database in order to create a reliable [information] source for both sides; (3) conduct specific studies on the current situation of the refugees and the displaced, wherever they are, including the economic, demographic and social dimensions, and on the appropriate permanent solution that the two sides will make every effort to implement; (4) decide on different models of mutual activity regarding this problem [of the refugees and the displaced] so that their rights will be kept in accordance with common political rights of both the Jordanian and the Palestinian sides."

The Palestinian paper read: "Taking into consideration that the problem of the refugees and the displaced is first and foremost a Palestinian problem, each decision or direction may have a direct impact on Jordan and other Arab sister countries accommodating some of the Palestinian refugees. This determines that the committee will act as follows: (1) To decide upon a common strategy based on UN resolutions 194 and 237 [UN Resolution 194 proclaimed the right of each individual refugee to choose between return or compensation and conditioned his return on living at peace with his neighbors in Israel; UN Security Council Resolution 237 called all sides involved in the June 1967 war to safeguard the human rights of prisoners-of-war and civilians] for cooperation in this issue within the framework of the bilateral and the multilateral negotiations . . . (4) to decide on different models of activity regarding this problem so that the rights of the Palestinian refugees will be kept in accordance with the shared political guidelines of both the Palestinian and the Jordanian sides, and in accordance with an act to unify Arab attitudes on this subject."[12]

Thus, while Jordan stressed that it is directly influenced by the problem of the refugees and the displaced, the PLO emphasized that it is first and foremost a Palestinian problem influencing not only Jordan, but other Arab countries as well. Consequently, the PLO included Resolution 194, while the Jordanian document disregarded it. Finally, while the Jordanians mentioned the "common political rights of both the Jordanian and the Palestinian sides," the PLO, afraid of Jordanian intervention in Palestinian affairs, narrowed the Jordanian role to coordinating policy and stressed the need to cooperate with other Arab states.

In January 1995, a detailed agreement ("Memorandum of Understanding and Cooperation") regarding the fields of education, culture and information, monetary issues and banking, trade issues, postal delivery and communications, transportation, and administration was signed by Jordan and the Palestinian Authority. However, the Palestinians and the Jordanians could reach only a very loose agreement on the problems of the 1948 refugees and 1967 displaced persons. The two entities concluded that:

> The agreement that Jordan signed with Israel on October 26, 1994, constitutes an important step toward restoration of Jordan's rights on its land, water, and borders, and toward securing the rights of the (Palestinian) refugees and the displaced in accordance with international laws and resolutions.[13]

As both sides could not bridge their differences, including the issues of Palestinian refugees and displaced persons, they agreed "to reactivate the Jordanian-Palestinian higher committee to follow up mutual issues of concern, and provide an appropriate mechanism that would ensure the realization of the two people's interests through constant and direct contacts."[14]

Thus, although not coming to a resolution of the refugee issue, a mechanism for further discussion was developed. Similarly, although the PLO leadership has not yet developed any detailed program for realizing the right of return, they do now have the political means to negotiate over the issue with Jordan and Israel. By transferring the PLO's infrastructure and personnel to the Gaza Strip, the Palestinian Authority leaders succeeded in building their political institutions and developing power bases to balance the power of Jordan and Israel. This preference for political foundation building meant that the first meeting of the four-sided committee did not convene until March 1995, fully 30 months after signing the Declaration of Principles. No conclusion was reached at that first meeting. However, the four sides decided to continue their discussions over the return of 1967 displaced persons in a technical subcommittee, which would convene once a month, as well as in meetings between the four heads of the delegations, which would take place every two or three months. Since then, very few meetings have been arranged and no substantial conclusions have been reached.[15]

Doubts arose among Palestinians living in Jordan about their return, either as 1948 refugees or 1967 displaced persons. An indication of these sentiments can be found in the results of a poll conducted by Dr Mustafa Hamarnha (from the Center for Strategic Studies at the University of Jordan). Although the poll did not specify results for the Palestinian citizens or residents of Jordan from among the total population, one may learn about their attitudes from answers by Amman and Al-Zarqa residents, the cities where most of the Palestinians live. While 76.9 percent in Amman and 75.8 percent in Al-Zarqa supported the Washington Declaration, signed between Israel and Jordan on 25 July 1994, only 54.5 percent in Amman and 66.7 percent in Al-Zarqa expected Jordan to achieve a peace agreement with Israel which would completely realize the right of return for the 1967 displaced persons and arrange for their compensation, while 25.1 percent and 18.3 percent, respectively had no such expectations at all. Moreover, fewer than that expected Jordan to reach an agreement with Israel which would completely resolve the issue of the right of return for the 1948 refugees or arrange for their compensation: only 38.8 percent in Amman and 49.2 percent in Al-Zarqa, while 41.8 percent and 37.5 percent, respectively, had no such expectations at all.

However, the expectations regarding Jordan's ability to achieve other goals were much higher: 68.9 percent in Amman and 80.8 percent in Al-Zarqa expected Jordan to gain Israel's full recognition for Jordanian claims regarding water sources in the Arava desert, and only 21.1 percent in Amman and 13.3 percent in Al-Zarqa said that they did not have such an expectation. Furthermore, 64.5 percent in Amman and 70.8 percent in Al-Zarqa answered affirmatively to the same question regarding Jordan's security interests, while 24.4 percent in Amman and 20.8 percent in Al-Zarqa answered negatively.[16]

In sum, the give-and-take over the question of the Palestinian refugees has begun. Questions and doubts over the capabilities of the three sides to reach a comprehensive solution to the problem abound; however, movement has taken place within the Israeli–Jordanian–Palestinian triangle which suggests that there is at least a remote possibility that future agreements can be reached. At the present time, though, the Palestinians have not done much in the way of translating their claim to the right of return into actual policy. Indeed, the PLO seems to be in a holding pattern: waiting for the founding of an independent Palestinian state, or at least until Israel officially recognizes the Palestinian right to found such a state.

The Jerusalem Question

Within a relatively short period of time – from summer 1994 until midwinter 1995 – the Islamic holy sites became a card played in the Israel-Jordan-Palestinian Authority game. Israel and Jordan – each for its own reasons – tried to weaken the Palestinian position. In response, the Palestinian Authority mobilized Arab states which sought to weaken Jordan and prevent it from having sole (or preferential) authority over the holy shrines on the Temple Mount. Such states included Egypt, Saudi Arabia, and Morocco. Their involvement has manifested itself in the framework of the Islamic Conference Organization. Through their backing of the Palestinian Authority, the bilateral relations between Palestinian Authority and Jordan have been reshaped.

The Israeli-Jordanian peace talks resulted in the Washington Declaration, signed by Prime Minister Rabin and King Hussein on 25 July 1994. One of its clauses relates to the holy sites in Jerusalem. Later copied verbatim into the Israeli-Jordanian peace treaty of October 1994, this clause confirmed Palestinian apprehensions from 1993 about Israeli activities in Jerusalem and rekindled the discord between the Palestinian Authority and Jordan. The Washington Declaration states as follow:

> Israel respects the present special role of the Hashemite Kingdom of Jordan in Islamic holy shrines in Jerusalem. When negotiations on the permanent status will take place, Israel will give high priority to the historic Jordanian role in these shrines. In addition, the two sides have agreed to act together to promote inter-faith relations among the three monotheistic religions.[17]

Thus, Israel has taken upon itself in the Washington Declaration an initial commitment regarding the permanent status of Jerusalem. As I view the Washington Declaration, Israel has relinquished any claim to actualize sovereignty over the Islamic holy shrines in Jerusalem, including the *Haram Al-Sharif*. Israel claims that its paramount interest is to guarantee its political sovereignty over the eastern city, and that the management of the Islamic holy shrines is not included in this intention. The Washington Declaration represents the first time that Israel officially recognized Jordan's special status regarding the Islamic holy shrines in Jerusalem.

The administration of the Islamic *Waqf* (religious endowment) has been historically and traditionally responsible for these holy sites. The *Waqf* of Jerusalem remained subordinate to Jordan even after the Israeli conquest of 1967; and even the severance of Jordan's legal and administrative ties to the West Bank in July 1988 did not alter this condition. As a rule, the Hashemites have a special attachment to the Islamic holy shrines in Jerusalem. They have gained legitimacy for their rule from this connection, as well as their own political survival. (Within the framework of this commitment, King Hussein refurbished the golden dome of the Dome of the Rock in 1994.) Until the Israeli-Jordanian treaty, Jordan's control over the *Waqf* was maintained by virtue of the continuation of the past state of affairs, rather than by choice or conscious preference about the future. The Washington Declaration opens the possibility for the future application of the option that the holy sites in Jerusalem be expropriated from any religious sovereignty.

Since 1967, then, Israel has aspired to retain its political sovereignty over East Jerusalem and to gain pan-Arab, pan-Islamic and international legitimacy for its actions there. In return for Jordan's agreement to separate the political and religious questions regarding Jerusalem, Prime Minister Rabin was ready to uphold Jordan's special religious status over the city's Islamic sites.[18] Accordingly, Jordan gained a foothold in the Islamic holy sites in Jerusalem, while Israel strengthened its position that the existence of Islamic shrines in East Jerusalem does not in itself prevent Israeli political sovereignty over the city. One must emphasize that in the Washington Declaration, there was the expression of Jordanian-Israeli cooperation, clearly weakening the Palestinian position in their struggle for making East Jerusalem their capital.

Prime Minister Rabin and King Hussein worded the paragraph about East Jerusalem in the Washington Declaration in such a way that the Palestinians could not legally claim that it counters any Israeli commitment toward them, and at the same time that it would be seen as an indirect acceptance by Jordan of Israel's political sovereignty over East Jerusalem.[19] Indeed, from a legal and literal point of view, it is possible to say that Israel did not violate its agreement with the Palestinian Authority; but this is not the case politically. Israel did not act in good faith with the direction indicated in its Declaration of Principles with the PLO. Israel wanted to exploit its contacts with Jordan in order to influence the permanent status of Jerusalem and thus weaken Palestinian claims over East Jerusalem.

Naturally, the Washington Declaration incensed the Palestinians. They understood it as an Israeli attempt to push them into a corner. According to the Palestinian Authority, political sovereignty over the eastern part of the city is a Palestinian right, and it is they who will decide the future of the Islamic holy sites in Jerusalem. They do not deem it possible to separate political and religious sovereignty over the Islamic holy sites, especially since a large part of Palestinian claims to political sovereignty in East Jerusalem is based on the religious status of the *Haram Al-Sharif* in Islam. Therefore, the Palestinian Authority viewed the treaty between Israel and Jordan as an attempt to excise the Palestinian Authority from Jerusalem. Arafat commented, "No Arab or

Israeli leader controls the holy shrines in East Jerusalem. This right is the Palestinians' alone."[20] Reacting to Israel's invitation of King Hussein to pray in Jerusalem, Arafat declared that he alone was entitled to invite King Hussein to pray there. Indeed, Arafat mobilized the Supreme Islamic Council, headed by Hasan Tahbub, which announced that this council was the only body responsible for the Islamic holy shrines in Jerusalem.[21]

In early December 1994, Feisal Husseini, who negotiates on the issue of Jerusalem for the Palestinian Authority, visited Jordan in order to settle some differences about the issue and to prepare the ground for an official visit by Arafat to Jordan. At the end of his visit he stated:

> We know full well that the holy places have been placed under Jordanian administrative guardianship. This situation has been recognized and accepted by Israel since 1967. We are not interested now in changing this situation. We agreed to discuss the status of Jerusalem with Israel in the second stage. We are not ready to open this file before the beginning of the official talks. Therefore, we believe that Jordan considers the holy places a trust that will be turned over to the Palestinians when they become capable of shouldering this responsibility. We agreed to maintain the situation as it is and to hold further coordination so that we will not make any wrong moves . . . The matter is not one of sensitivities toward the Jordanian stand. However, in the absence of coordination, even the steps that are taken with good intentions might be misinterpreted by this or that party.[22]

In other words, both sides agreed that the Palestinian Authority will recognize the *status quo* that has existed in Jerusalem since 1967, namely, Jordanian guardianship over the Islamic holy places in the city. In return, the Jordanian authorities will undertake to regard this guardianship as a trust that will be transferred to the Palestinians when the latter is able to accept the responsibility. It is not clear whether, and if at all, Feisal Husseini received a mandate from Arafat to reach this agreement, which seems closer to the Jordanian position (as we have seen above) than to the Palestinian one. In any case, Arafat did not ratify this agreement, and his visit to Jordan did not take place in early December 1994 as planned. Alternately, Arafat moved the arbitration between himself and the King Hussein to a new arena, the Islamic Conference Organization.

The Islamic Conference Organization met in Casablanca in December 1994. The discussion between Jordan and the Palestinian Authority over the holy sites in Jerusalem erupted forcefully. Jordan – supported by Qattar, Oman, and Yemen – demanded that the closing statement of the Conference extol its role as guardian of the holy sites, and congratulate King Hussein on his interest in the holy sites in Jerusalem. In his effort to mobilize the heads of Islamic countries, King Hussein claimed that as soon as a final agreement is reached between Israel and the Palestinians about the permanent status of Jerusalem, Jordan would relinquish to them the guardianship over the holy sites in the city. But the Palestinian Authority – supported by Saudi Arabia, Egypt, and Morocco – recognized Jordan's political intent and adamantly refused. The Palestinians claimed that the clause dealing with this issue in the Jordan-Israel treaty is a stumbling block to their achieving sovereignty in East Jerusalem and Israel's withdrawal from it. Morocco, Saudi Arabia, Egypt, and the Palestinian Authority even tried to convince the assembly to form a committee on behalf of the Islamic Conference Organization, which would take over from Jordan the guardianship over the holy sites until the Palestinian Authority gains full responsibility over East Jerusalem. Upon realizing that he could not achieve a majority behind the Jordanian position, King Hussein left the Conference before it ended. For the first time since the founding of this organization in 1972, there was no consensus over its resolutions, which were ultimately forced upon Jordan.[23]

The closing statement of the conference emphasized "again that the problem of Palestine and of Honorable Jerusalem is the fundamental problem for all Muslims, and they identify with the PLO in its just struggle for the removal of every vestige of Israeli occupation and building Palestinian institutions on Palestinian land." It goes on to say that the members of the Islamic Conference Organization "must assist the PLO in its future negotiations, until all authority and sovereignty in the occupied territories – including Honorable Jerusalem – will be transferred to the hands of the Palestinian Authority, and to ensure the return of Jerusalem to Palestinian sovereignty . . . as Honorable Jerusalem is an inseparable part of the Palestinian territories occupied by Israel in 1967 and is subject to the same laws as the other occupied territories. Jerusalem must be returned to Palestinian sovereignty as it is the capital of Palestine." Moreover, the statement stipulates that responsibilities over Jerusalem in the interim period must be handed over to the Palestinian Authority, and completely disregards Jordan's role in the holy sites. King Hussein felt this drift before he left the Conference and said to the assembly: "If you believe that Jordan's role in Jerusalem is harmful and you prefer Islamic guardianship, be it so. But you must then take responsibility for your decision."[24]

The statement highlights the political aspect of sovereignty over the Islamic sites. It was not the preferential religious status accorded to Jordan that aroused the strongest Muslim countries in the Middle East, but the political meaning couched in the Washington Declaration: the indirect recognition given by Jordan to the annexation of East Jerusalem by Israel. Saudi Arabia, Egypt, Morocco, and the PLO believe that the status of the holy sites in Jerusalem is derived from political sovereignty over it. Therefore, if political sovereignty remains with Israel, then the holy sites are not freed from occupation. Saudi Arabia even added to this argument that separation between religion and politics, as condoned by King Hussein with regard to Jerusalem, is foreign to Islam.

On 16 January 1995, the Jerusalem Committee of the Islamic Conference Organization was convened in Morocco in its new composition – as initiated by Morocco, Saudi Arabia, Egypt, and the Palestinian Authority – and in this framework the controlling members of the Conference finalized what they had begun in the plenary session the month before. The concluding statement of the Jerusalem Committee states that: "The holy city of Jerusalem is an indivisible part of the Palestinian land occupied in 1967, and it underlines the need for it to return to Palestinian sovereignty as capital of the state of Palestine." The Jerusalem Committee called for urging "the Islamic nation to join efforts to support the Palestinian right to the holy city of Jerusalem, and to back by various means the positions of the PLO for the transfer of all authority and responsibilities in the Palestinian occupied land, including Jerusalem, to the Palestinian national authority."[25]

After the issue of the holy sites was settled in favor of the Palestinians, the door was open for Arafat to visit Jordan. On 25 January 1995 Arafat arrived in Jordan to sign a memorandum of understanding and cooperation between the Palestinian Authority and the Hashemite Kingdom of Jordan in the areas of communications, passage of goods and people, banking, postal delivery, culture, education, and local administration. The signing of these agreements was delayed until the establishment of the Palestinian Authority and the signing of separate and detailed agreements with Israel by Jordan and the Palestinian Authority. Nevertheless, the signing of the agreements between Jordan and the Palestinian Authority came to regulate the bilateral relations between the Palestinian Authority and the Kingdom. Following this, Jordan established a liaison office in Gaza. As an introduction to the series of agreements mentioned above, a political document was signed ("the Agreement for Cooperation and Coordination"), which states:

> The Hashemite Kingdom of Jordan reiterated its constant and continuous support for the Palestinian people, under the leadership of the PLO, to attain their right to self-determination on their national soil and to establish an independent Palestinian state, and to support the Palestinian quest to implement the Palestinian-Israeli Declaration of Principles as a step

> toward the realization of the Palestinian people's national rights. The Hashemite Kingdom of Jordan will cooperate with the Palestinian Authority in all fields, and will provide all the needed expertise to build national institutions capable of assuming their responsibilities and tasks in the interests of the Palestinian people . . . The agreement that Jordan signed with Israel on October 26, 1994 constitutes an important step toward the restoration of Jordan's sovereign rights over its land, water, and borders and toward securing the rights of the [Palestinian] refugees displaced in 1948 and 1967 in accordance with international laws and resolutions. The agreement also enhances the other tracks of negotiations in a way that secures the attainment of Arab legitimate rights. In order to complement all aspects of coordination and consultation and to serve the interests of the two peoples, the two sides believe it is crucial to reactivate the Jordanian-Palestinian higher committee to follow up mutual issues of concern, and provide an appropriate mechanism that would ensure the realization of the two peoples' interests through constant and direct contacts.[26]

This document does not indicate Jordan's special status in Jerusalem nor does it deal directly with the Islamic holy sites in the city; at the same time, it states clearly the political sovereignty of the Palestinian people over Jerusalem. The spirit of this document is one of an agreement between two political entities of equal national status. The Palestinian side views favorably the peace treaty between Jordan and Israel and states – as opposed to the Syrian position – that this treaty does not harm the other tracks of negotiations between Israel and its neighbors (i.e., Syria's efforts to regain sovereignty over the whole of the Golan Heights).

The Jordan-Israel peace treaty is presented in this document as ensuring Jordan's rights "over its land, water, and borders and toward securing the rights of the refugees"; as such, it does not contradict the rights of the Palestinians. Jordan pledges, therefore, to assist the Palestinian people and the PLO in realizing their right for self-determination and for the establishment of an independent state whose capital is Jerusalem. It can be deduced that Jordan is not free to deter the Palestinians by differentiating between political sovereignty over Jerusalem and religious sovereignty over the holy sites within it. This may also be deduced from the clause in which Jordan pledges to cooperate with the Palestinian Authority and to assist it in establishing its national institutions. Thus, there is nothing in the Jordanian-Palestinian agreement confirming Jordan's preferential status over the holy sites in Jerusalem. Therefore, one of the outstanding clauses in the Jordan-Israel peace treaty disappeared completely in the agreement between the

Palestinian Authority and the Kingdom of Jordan.

This new situation, created by the Islamic Conference Organization and later by the agreement with the Palestinian Authority, was forced upon King Hussein and has been difficult for him to accept. As he knows that the issue of Jerusalem will only be fully settled with the finalizing of an Israeli-Palestinian peace accord, he hopes to reverse the recent decisions with regard to Jerusalem. In the signing ceremony of the agreement with the Palestinian Authority, King Hussein said that his country would continue to fulfill its duties and to give its auspices to the holy sites in Jerusalem "as it did in the past." Jordan would do this "out of its diligence to cherish these holy sites and as a fulfillment of its obligation to guard Jerusalem and preserve its Arab and Muslim identity."[27]

Israel thought it could outflank the PLO politically by playing the religious card, but the Islamic states saw the move and trumped Israel's attempt. In 1974, the Arab Summit meeting held in Rabat removed Jordan from its position as the legitimate representative of the Palestinian people; then 20 years later, the Islamic countries removed Jordan from its preferential position regarding Jerusalem's Islamic holy sites. In essence, the debate among the Islamic states was between two political alternatives. Jordan was extremely skeptical about the Palestinians' prospects of extracting an agreement from Israel that would turn the Palestinian Authority into an independent state, and thought it even less likely that Israel would agree to forgo sovereignty over East Jerusalem. Therefore, the Jordanians felt that at the very least, Israel should be deprived of its religious hold over the Islamic holy sites in the city, by separating political from religious sovereignty. Naturally, this would entail strengthening Jordan's religious status in the city.

However, the majority of Arab and Islamic states thought that this would be tantamount to implicit recognition of Israel's political annexation of East Jerusalem. They insisted that the termination of Israel's religious hold over Jerusalem's Islamic sites was inseparably bound to the termination of the occupation itself. It followed that the optimal course of action would be to strengthen the Palestinians and reject Jordan's preferential status. In comparison to Jordan, the Arab and Islamic states are certain that they will be able to obtain Israel's agreement to the transformation of the Palestinian Authority into an independent state, hence their decision to counter Israel's consent to Jordan's special status.

The fact that the disagreement between Jordan and the Islamic states was fundamentally political is of significance with regard to the future administration of the Islamic holy places. It is far from certain that the Islamic states will agree to exclusive Palestinian administration. The Islamic states, according to the above interpretation, want to end the

Israeli occupation of East Jerusalem and therefore supported the Palestinian demand. However, they have not yet decided who will administer the holy places after Israel transfers East Jerusalem to Palestinian sovereignty. The option of joint religious administration of the Islamic holy places in Jerusalem under the political auspices of the Palestinian regime has not been ruled out for the time being.

Toward Conclusion

Indication of the progress which has thus far been achieved in the peace process can be found in a "non-paper" agreed upon by delegations headed by Minister Yossi Beilin and Abu-Mazin. Following extensive negotiations, in November 1995 the two sides agreed upon a framework for the resolution of the permanent statues issues, negotiations which are scheduled to begin in May 1996. Although Arafat and Prime Minister Peres did not accept the Beilin–Abu-Mazin document, it is clear that this "non-paper" represents a significant breakthrough. Regarding Jerusalem, both sides agreed that the city's boundaries would be greatly expanded and that a super-municipality of "Greater Jerusalem" would be set up. The eastern part would include areas now under the Palestinian Authority, like Al-'Azariyah and Abu-Dis, and would be called Al-Quds. The other part, the Israeli Jerusalem, would include settlements near Jerusalem, such as Ma'ale Adumim and Giv'at Ze'ev and the new Jewish neighborhoods of Jerusalem built since 1967. The *Haram Al-Sharif* would be declared extraterritorial and would be controlled by the Palestinians, while the Church of the Holy Sepulchre would also fall under Palestinian jurisdiction, although without extraterritorial status. However, no agreements were made on the status of the rest of the Old City, which remains open for further negotiations.[28]

On the subject of the refugees, both sides agreed that Israel would assist financially in the efforts to absorb Palestinian refugees outside its borders. At the same time, Israel would allow the unification of families on its territory in accordance with its obligations from 1948–9. In addition, both sides agreed that the Palestinians could maintain the right of return for all the refugees, although Israel need not accept that position.[29]

The comprehensiveness of the "non-paper" could not have been achieved without an Israeli acceptance of the establishment of an independent Palestinian state, as the Beilin–Abu-Mazin document states in its first clause.[30] Thus, while the Palestinians stress their fundamental goal of establishing a state, they are now more flexible on the issues of Jerusalem and the refugees, as is Israel. Hence, it seems that all players in the Israeli–Jordanian–Palestinian triangle have accepted that the triangle should be operated by bilateral agreements, steps which are necessary for ultimate three-party cooperation.

Notes

1 Rashid I. Khalidi, "Observations on the Right of Return, *Journal of Palestine Studies*, Vol. 21 (Winter 1992), pp. 29–40.
2 For further discussion in this regard, see: Menachem Klein, "Between Right and Realization: The PLO Dialectics of 'The Right of Rerurn'," *Journal of Refugee Studies* (December 1997, forthcoming).
3 Israel, Ministry of Foreign Affairs, *Declaration of Principles on Interim Self-Government Arrangements* (Jerusalem, September 1993).
4 UNRWA, *Palestine Refugees Today* (January 1994), pp. 6–7. *Haaretz*, 7 March, 1995.
5 *Haaretz*, 5 March 1995.
6 On the Palestinian population of Jordan see: Asher Susser, "Demography and Politics in Jordan," in Ami Ayalon and Gad Gilbar (eds), *Demography and Politics in the Arab States* (Tel Aviv: Moshe Dayan Center, Tel Aviv University and Hakibbutz Hameuhad, 1995), pp. 131–52.
7 *al-Dustur*, 27 January 1994. Abu-Mazin in *al-Quds* 1 July 1994. *Filastin al-Thawra*, 13 February 1994. Dr Elias Sanbar, Ibid., 1 May 1994.
8 *Saut al-Sh'ab*, 27 January 1994.
9 Abu Mazin in *al-Quds*, 7 January 1994. Sanbar in *Filastin al-Thawra*, 1 May 1994. See also: *al-Sharq al-Awsat*, 8 February 1994; *al-Dustur*, 27 January 1994; *Saut al-Sha'b*, 27 January 1994.
10 *Monte Carlo Radio*, 16 January 1993, according to FBIS *Daily Report* and Israeli News Agency, 16 January 1993.
11 *Haaretz*, 16 December 1994, 2 January, 1995. *al-Hayat* (London), 25 January 1995. On the PLO–Jordan debate see: Susser, "Demography and Politics in Jordan."
12 Paragraphs 2 and 3 were the same as in the Jordanian paper. *Saut al-Sh'ab*, 27 January 1994.
13 *al-Sharq al-Awsat*, 27 January 1995.
14 Ibid.
15 *Haaretz*, 5 March; 8 March 1995, and *Davar* (Tel aviv), 10 March 1995.
16 Mustafa Hamarnha, "Taqrir: Dirasat Istitla Lilrai Hawul al-mufawadat al-Urduniyya al-Israeliyya," *al-Siyasa al-Filastiniyya*, Vol. 1, No. 3–4 (Summer–Fall 1994), pp. 91–105. On claims among Palestinians living in Lebanon see: A'bd Al-Slam A'ql, "Al-Falastinyun Fi Lubnan Dahaya al-Harb w-al-Salam," *Majalat al-Dirasat al-Falastiniyya*,Vol. 17 (Winter 1994), pp. 170–82. See also: Zvi Barel, "Be'od Shlosh Meot Shana Yahzeru Kulam – After 300 Years Everyone Will Return", *Haaretz*, 21 July 1995; Edward Said, *Haaretz*, 28 January 1994; Khalid al-Hasan, *Al-Hawadith*, 18 March and 15 April 1994, and *Haaretz*, 9 January 1995. On the PLO since Oslo agree-

ment see: Menachem Klein, "Quo Vadis? Palestinian Dilemmas of Ruling Authority – Building Since 1993," *Middle Eastern Studies*, (forthcoming).

17 *Haaretz*, 26 July 1994; and FBIS, *Daily Report*, 26 July 1994. For a furthere discussion see: Menachem Klein, "The Islamic Holy Sites as a Political Bargaining Card (1993–1995)," *Law Review*, The Catholic University of America, Vol. 25, No. 3 (Spring 1996), pp. 745–63.

18 This, in spite of the fact that Rabin unofficially expressed his wish to discuss the future of the Islamic holy sites in Jerusalem with more than one Arab partner. Rabin in a background interview, *Haaretz*, 27 July 1994.

19 *Haaretz*, 27 July; 4 August 1994.

20 *Haaretz*, 23 November 1994.

21 *Haaretz*, 25 July 1994.

22 *Haaretz*, 5 December 1994; and FBIS, 5 December 1994.

23 *al-Quds*, 15 December 1994; *al-Wassat*, 19 December 1994.

24 *al-Quds*, 16 December 1994; *Haaretz*, 22 December 1994, 2 January 1995.

25 *al-Quds*, 18 January 1995 and FBIS 18 January 1995.

26 *al-Shark al-Aussat*, 27 January 1995; *al-Hayat*, 24 January 1995; see also: *Haaretz*, 27 January 1995 and FBIS, 25 January 1995.

27 *al-Hayat*, 27 January 1995; *al-Shark al-Aussat*, 27 January 1995. See also: FBIS, 26 January 1995.

28 *Haaretz*, 22 February 1996; and FBIS, 22 February 1996.

29 Ibid.

30 Ibid.

4

The Triangle Relationship: Three is not Better than Two

Steven L. Spiegel

There are endless analyses of the Arab-Israeli conflict, but rarely as Israeli–Jordanian–Palestinian relations viewed in isolation. By using one set of political science themes, that of international relations systems analysis, we can shed light on the policies of these three parties. We can then gain a better understanding of the pressures on each, their historical records, their relatives successes, and the challenges each face.[1]

The Concept of Tripolarity

In Jean Paul Sartre's famous play, *No Exit*, hell is defined as a relationship of three players. As international relations theorists have long recognized, in a relationship between three states there are three connections. This compares with only one relationship between two states, six between four, and ten between five. International relations systems theorists have long debated comparative stability induced by the number of states in a particular international or regional system. Some believe that bipolarity induces clarity by forcing the two major states to focus on each other and thereby preventing outright war, as occurred in the Cold War between 1945 and 1990. Others believe that there are great advantages in multipolarity because the lack of clarity induces caution caused by confusion. Some assert that the nuclear era really prevented war between the superpowers, not bipolarity itself.

In the bipolar–multipolar debate, there is a clear trade-off in the virtues and vices of both systems. In bipolar systems, wars between superpowers are less likely to occur, but because of the intense competition and antagonism that exists within that system, war is likely to be more violent and costly when it occurs. In a multipolar system, great power wars are more likely to occur, but tend to be less violent. In other words, there will be more brushfire wars, but they will be less likely to burn out of control. States will have an incentive to moderate their behavior and not threaten defeated states too harshly, since today's enemy might be tomorrow's ally.[2]

A three-power world is generally regarded as multipolar, but less attention has been paid to this particular phenomenon.[3] The tripolar world, however, is particularly applicable to the Israeli-Palestinian-Jordanian relationship. Of course, there are other regional countries that have a major impact on this relationship, such as Egypt and Syria, and many external states with an influence, such as the United States, Britain, France, Russia, Germany, China, and Japan. But it is intriguing to look at the relationship in isolation.

What is distinctive of a tripolar relationship? First, all states want to be the pivot or balancer and avoid the position of pariah. A pivot state is the one with which the other two seek to ally. This is the enviable position in a tripolar connection because it is highly unlikely that the other two will gang up against the pivot. Indeed, the pivot usually emerges in that position because of unresolvable antagonism between the other two. A similar position, but not necessarily identical, is the balancer – the state that is equally acceptable to the other two parties and is strong enough to throw its weight to either side. In that case, the position of the third, the pariah, is in jeopardy if it alienates the balancer – encouraging the latter to ally with the second state.

In the Soviet-Chinese-American triangle in the 1970s, for example, the United States emerged as the pivot state sought by both parties to align against the third. Since Sino-Soviet antagonism appeared unresolvable, both feared an American alliance with the third. Although not strictly a tripolar situation, Britain in Europe during the eighteenth and nineteenth centuries served as the balancer, attempting to strengthen any weak state in coalition in order to prevent any major power from dominating the Continent. One could argue that Britain played that role in particular between France and Germany in the late nineteenth century. When Berlin contributed to a Franco-British alliance through its policies, its position was ultimately doomed. At all costs, states in a triangular relationship must avoid emerging as the pariah power with whom no one will associate. The Soviet Union in the early 1980s, after its invasion of Afghanistan, maneuvered itself temporarily into that position *vis-à-vis* the United States and China.

The Israeli–Palestinian–Jordanian Triangle

In the Israeli–Palestinian–Jordanian relationship, each brings advantages and debits to the triangle. Israel is the militarily and economically strongest and has the best political contacts outside the region, but it is the most unpopular of the three in the region, especially in the Arab world and *vis-à-vis* Iran. (Its strong relations with Turkey is an exception.) Jordan has acceptable relations with both the Israelis and Palestinians and has maintained solid communication with both, but it is weak economically and has a small population. Its relations (or designs) *vis-à-vis* the Palestinians have often been suspect in the eyes of other Arab states. The Palestinians have the best link of the three to other Arabs, and indeed, for several decades, they have been the litmus test of Arab unity. But they are only an emerging state, exceptionally weak economically, with part of the supposed Arab affection being only symbolic, and with severe limits on any pretense of sovereignty. Given these parameters, each has a variety of countervailing calculations in terms of its own interests and needs in the triangle.

Jordan is the most natural balancer and pivot. It has maintained close contact with the Palestinians and even controlled the West Bank from 1948 to 1967. Even afterward, until 1988, King Hussein continued to lay claim to the area. Jordan's relations with Israel go back to the Hashemite contacts with the Zionist movement after World War I. Although Jordan was not the first Arab country to sign a peace treaty with Israel, its relationship with the Jewish state has been the warmest. Therefore, the balancing role comes easiest for Jordan, as long as there is not too much conflict forcing the Jordanians toward the Palestinians. Their pivotal role is also jeopardized if a high degree of Palestinian-Israeli cooperation develops; then the logical balancing of their position is destroyed. Thus, it is in Jordanian interest for a degree of tension to remain in Israeli-Palestinian relations, since it forces Amman to the forefront. But if the conflict is too severe, then their maneuverability is destroyed.

The Palestinians, by contrast, need to bring in outsiders to ward off the natural affinity between Jordan and Israel. This is not surprising, in part because they are located geographically in the middle and have often found themselves over the decades squeezed between the other two. For the Palestinians, it is actually hardest to play balancer or pivot. Their natural compensation comes from alliance with such countries as Egypt, Syria, and Russia, as we have seen over the years. The Palestinians logically worry about pariah status between Jordan and Israel. They historically have had poor relations with both sides, fighting a 100-year conflict with the Israelis and suffering through historically tense relations with Jordan, highlighted by King Abdallah's conquering of half of their territory in 1948 and the war between Arafat's Palestinians and Jordan in 1970. It is obviously not in the Palestinians' interest for close relations to develop between Jordan and Israel. It is also not in their interest to avoid both sides, but rather to maintain a degree of contact with each. The Palestinians have only rarely achieved this position, however. In the 1970s, for example, Arafat managed to alienate both Jordan and Israel.

The Israelis benefit from cooperation with both sides. Like the Palestinians, they also seek to avoid becoming the pariah, a position they have often occupied. On the rare occasion when they are in a position of cooperation with both the Jordanians and Palestinians, they have the potential of becoming the pivot, a position that was possible only under Rabin and Peres. More frequently, the Israelis have been alienated from both sides and therefore can only hope for Jordanian–Palestinian alienation to prevent the two from uniting against them, a condition from which they benefited particularly in the 1970s. The Israelis were also strengthened when their peace treaty with Egypt temporarily neutralized Cairo, the Palestinians' classic protector. But that good fortune was dissipated by the assassination of Sadat and the invasion of Lebanon.

History of the Triangle

The history of the last several decades reflects these conflicting interests and interactions. In the 1920s, the Zionists failed to establish a working relationship with the Palestinians. Those opposed to the growth of the Jewish community gained ascendancy within the Palestinian community. This left the Palestinians divided between those such as the Nashishibis, who were moderate *vis-à-vis* the Jews and closer to the Hashemites, and the Husseinis, who were more radical in their views against the Jews and antagonistic to the Hashemites. These divisions became clearer during the Arab Revolt of the late 1930s. With the killing of many moderate Palestinians by their Palestinian opponents and the increased contact between Zionists and Hashemites, the stage was set for later developments. Palestinians and Zionists were at complete loggerheads, leaving the opening for the Hashemites in the pivotal role.

In the 1940s, the flirtation between Jordan and Israel collapsed in the 1948 war when they fought against each other. The Palestinians, however, were the big losers as Jordan and Israel basically divided their territory, leaving only the Egyptian-controlled Gaza Strip as a Palestinian enclave. In the 1950s, the resulting bipolarity between the Jordanians and Israelis exacerbated conflict between the two; the triangle basically did not exist despite *Fedayeen* raids into Israel. By 1964, the PLO had been formed by the Arab League. Functioning largely as a tool of Egyptian policy, the Palestinians did not play a major role until after the war. In 1967, the Israelis and Jordanians again fought each other, but this time with Israel capturing Jerusalem and the West Bank from the Amman government. The Palestinians reemerged under Yasser Arafat and soon threatened to overthrow King Hussein, but he defeated them in 1970 with support from American-Israeli political and military maneuvering.

The Palestinians had once again emerged as pariah, but Israel failed to secure this opening. King Hussein did not believe himself strong enough to move beyond the Arab consensus, and the Israelis were not prepared to return all of the territory captured in the June 1967 war. Nevertheless, Palestinian terrorism and alienation from Jordan left them as the pariah through the 1970s. Jordan did not join with Egypt after its treaty of peace with Israel in 1979, but it remained the balancer. When Israel fought against the Palestinians in Lebanon in the 1980s, Jordan did not back the Palestinians militarily, but maintained sporadic secret contacts with the Israelis and continued implicit cooperation on their border and the West Bank.

Thus, Jordan remained partially aloof from both sides, but its policies were sufficiently delphic that it could, through its maneuvering, change the direction of the triangle if it sided totally with the Israelis or the Palestinians. Encouraged by the 1982 Reagan Plan which envisioned a Jordan-Palestinian Confederation, in the mid-1980s King Hussein and Yasser Arafat explored a possible coalition, but in the end they could not reach an agreement. King Hussein then tried to make a deal with Israel in 1987 when he explored the possibility of an international conference, but that idea also ran asunder of internal Israeli coalition politics.

The pivotal position of the Jordanians was temporarily undermined by the *Intifada,* which began at the end of 1987 and which thrust Jordan to the sidelines as the Israeli-Palestinian communal war escalated. King Hussein withdrew his claim to the West Bank in 1988, and the Israeli-Palestinian confrontation emerged center stage. In this sense, the bipolarity of the 1950s and early 1960s between Jordan and Israel had been transformed into a Palestinian-Israeli clash. Jordan's maneuvering in the 1980s demonstrated its underlying weakness because it could not conclude a successful deal with either side. It was the only party to maintain contacts with both sides, but it was not strong enough to dominate the triangle either. In part, the King could not succeed because his potential partners were too limited internally. Yet, if either the Palestinians or the Israelis had accepted Hussein's overtures in the mid-

1980s, the history of the triangle in later years might have radically diverged. Instead, Arafat was too weak after his defeat in Lebanon to take decisive measures, and by 1987, Israel's "national unity" government was, ironically, too divided. Hussein's failure and the Palestinian *Intifada* which followed threatened to push him to the sidelines, the pivotal position having now become temporarily irrelevant.

In 1990, the action of an outside power – Iraq's invasion of Kuwait – again altered relations within the triangle. Both Jordan and the Palestinians miscalculated in backing Saddam Hussein. The Israelis then used their strong support of the anti-Iraq coalition to recoup part of their lost international prestige at the expense of both Jordan and the Palestinians. After the Gulf War, the Madrid conference in 1991 and the beginning of regional negotiations partially resurrected the Jordanians. But the Oslo agreements and the Declaration of Principles, signed with the famous Arafat-Rabin handshake in September 1993, represented a major Israeli-Palestinian breakthrough. For the first time in 100 years of conflict, the possibility appeared of an Israeli-Palestinian rapprochement within triangle politics, coming at the expense of the Jordanians. Instead, King Hussein in the following year resurrected his central position as pivot in the triangle by signing a peace treaty with Israel. But the Israelis were even in a position to bid for the pivotal role, as their concessions to the Palestinians elevated their place in the region and made them acceptable contacts for both the Palestinians and the Jordanians.

This position was decimated by the internal convulsions which gripped Israel between 1995 and 1996, covering such events as the assassination of Prime Minister Rabin and the series of terrorist bombings in late February and early March 1996. The result was a hard-line victory in the May 1996 elections and a new Likud government under Prime Minister, Benjamin Netanyahu. With this new Israeli government, Jordan again emerged as the undisputed pivot, and Israel and the Palestinians returned to a pattern of intense and ongoing conflict.

The natural ebb and flow among the players in the triangle has seemed to resurrect the pivotal position of Jordan repeatedly. Amman has not been strong enough to singlehandedly determine consequences by throwing its weight to one side or the other, but it has been the only party able to maneuver consistently between both sides. In other words, it has been more effective at pivoting than at balancing. Jordan has been sought after as a potential ally by both and also feared by both, especially the Palestinians. The pivotal role of Jordan has been reasserted over and over again because Israel and the Palestinians fear its joining with the other side, as was clearly suggested by the triangular politics that took place in the months following the May 1996 elections. While Netanyahu and Arafat confronted one another, King Hussein's actions, judgments, and statements often determined which one would be seen by the regional and especially global audiences as stronger diplomatically, and which policy would be viewed as more just and more appropriate to ongoing circumstances.

The Record of the Parties

With this historical perspective, how should we evaluate the performance of the three sides in triangular politics over the decades? Clearly, Jordan has been the most successful and the Palestinians the least. The continual reassertion of its pivotal standing suggests the essential cleverness of Jordanian diplomacy, beginning with weak resources and a difficult diplomatic position. There are only two exceptions to this otherwise exemplary record: Jordanian behavior in the June 1967 war and the Gulf War in 1990/91. Otherwise, the Jordanians have historically presented themselves as the party which both sides thought they had the best chance of attracting.

The Palestinians, by contrast, have been the weakest. They have continually lost opportunities, underestimating the strengths of both the Jordanians and the Israelis by thinking that they could do better through aligning with outside parties. By failing to play triangular politics, they have consistently lost. We can see this recurring pattern in the defeats they suffered during the Mandate, the loss of sovereignty in the 1940s, the failure to take advantage of the Camp David accords, the slow adjustment by the Palestinian leadership based in Tunisia to the potential gains of the *Intifada,* Arafat's slow adaptation to the Declaration of Principles and its full implications for the possibility of Palestinian sovereignty, and his failure to take charge of the terrorist issue quickly enough before March 1996, which might well have prevented the Netanyahu victory. One need not agree with Abba Eban's famous aphorism, "The Palestinians never lose an opportunity to lose an opportunity," to see the weaknesses of Palestinian diplomacy.

Israel's record falls between the successful Jordanians playing a weak hand strongly and the Palestinians making a weak hand much weaker. In all fairness, the Israelis have had to maneuver for most of their existence in a triangle where their best card was to avoid pariah status. Within this context, Palestinian-Jordanian antagonism was essential. Yet, after 1967, the Israelis failed to seize sporadic opportunities which might have opened possibilities for increased maneuverability. After the disastrous October 1973 war, in particular, greater generosity toward the Jordanians might have opened the way to an early quashing of the PLO. Less likely, an opening to the PLO might have stemmed the growth of terrorism within the Palestinian movement at a relatively early stage. By failing to play triangular politics, the Israelis did not unite the Palestinians and Jordanians against them, but they still left themselves as odd-man out with little opportunity for a breakthrough. The stalemate continued after Camp David and further accelerated with the Lebanon war. Prime Minister Shamir's major miscalculation in giving up the opportunity for a Jordanian-Israeli sponsored international conference in the spring of 1987 exacerbated Palestinian frustration, which then led to the *Intifada*. Along the way, Israeli support for the initiation of *Hamas* as a balance against the PLO contributed to the opening of the Pandora's box of fundamentalist extremism within the Palestinian movement.

While most possibilities for Israel to break out of its isolation in the triangle were admittedly problematic, together they add up to a legacy of sorry diplomacy and limited vision. The Israelis were certainly plagued by domestic politics, a growing messianic movement, the ghost of a tragic Jewish past – especially the Holocaust, and decades of suffering inflicted by Arab neighbors. Such a history meant that to gain concessions, the Arabs would have to approach Israel openly and dramatically in order to convince a skeptical public. In the 1970s, only Egypt could afford such a strategy and most Arabs were unwilling to do so.

This Israeli legacy of failed flexibility in an admittedly hostile environment was reversed by the Oslo accords and its Declaration of Principles. From 1993 to 1996, Israeli diplomacy demonstrated unusual ingenuity and alacrity, causing the Israelis to emerge as the dominant figures in the triangle. The painful susceptibility to terrorist attacks and the deep suspicion of the Arab world remaining within part of the Israeli population led to the reversal of Israeli politics. With the assassination of Prime Minister Rabin and the election of a new government, traditional Israeli behavior patterns resumed, leading again to Israeli isolation and candidacy for pariah status within the triangle. Thus, throughout most of the period since World War I which we have reviewed, this has been a triangle distinguished by successful Jordanian maneuvering, abysmal Palestinian moves, and an uneven Israeli record marked by a successful military policy mixed with only partial diplomatic success and often hindered by domestic divisions, ideological blunders, Arab intransigence, and serious diplomatic blunders.

Overcoming the Triangle

The theory of international relations systems analysis leaves little room for overcoming the dynamics of a triangle through peaceful means. In the past, Americans often mentioned a Jordanian-Palestinian confederation as embodied in the Reagan plan of 1982, but the reemergence of a Likud government seemed to diminish interest in such a resolution after 1996. In any case, if a confederation worked to unify the Palestinians and the Jordanians, it would destroy the triangle and replace it with bipolarity. If the two retained their individual identities, then the triangle would remain and the confederation would be mere window-dressing.

The other way to escape the triangle would be some kind of unity among all three, at least in the economic sphere. Politicians and analysts have occasionally discussed a Benelux-type arrangement, where some kind of common market or confederation would exist among the Jordanians, Israelis, and Palestinians. But that possibility has always seemed highly improbable, even during the hopeful signs toward peace of the mid-1990s, because of economic and political incompatibilities between the three parties.

It remains to be seen whether future developments might allow some kind of amelioration of the hell of the triangle as Sartre's play depicted, but judging from the experiences in the twentieth century of the Israelis, Palestinians, and Jordanians, that would be a difficult task indeed to accomplish. The best they might hope for would be to regularize their relations so that the triangular competition between them might be played out by non-violent means based on an underlying consensus regarding the ultimate political disposition of their relations, the territorial demarcations between them, and the accepted patterns of behavior which should rule their relationships. Certainly, this is a triangle that cries out for non-violence and a fundamental consensus on the nature of the members' relationships. Until that goal is achieved, the triangular pattern predicted by the systems theorists keeps reasserting itself to the consternation of all concerned. Consistent with the Realist school of systems theory, it never seems to dawn on leaders that the only way to escape from a triangular trap is to agree among themselves.

Notes

1 The systems theorists referred to in this chapter are mainly realists, those preoccupied with a power structure and who believe that a state must protect its own vital interests, political independence, and territorial sovereignty at any cost in the "dog-eat-dog" world. Described by the realist paradigm, military power is often a necessary ingredient for national survival. In this context, the system is anarchic and all states are unitary, rational actors. Their primary concern is survival. For further information

on different types of realists and other systems theorists, see: Spiegel, Steven L. *World Politics in a New Era* (Port Worth: Harcourt Brace Publishers, 1995), ch. 13.

2 For further discussion, see: Waltz, Kenneth, *Theory of International Relations* (New York: Random House, 1979); Mearsheimer, John, "Back to the Future: Instability in Europe after the Cold War," *International Security* Vol. 15, No. 1 (Summer 1990); Deutsch, Karl and J. David Singer. "Multipolar Power Systems and International Stability," *World Politics* Vol. 16, No. 3 (April 1964); Rosecrance Richard, "Bipolarity, Multipolarity and the Future", *Journal of Conflict Resolution*,Vol. 10, No. 3 (September 1966).

3 Rourke, John T. *International Politics on the World Stage*, 5th edn (Guilford: Dushkin Publishing Group, 1995), pp. 83–4.

5

The Jerusalem Triangle

Moshe Ma'oz

In his address to an international conference in Amman, on 9 September 1995, Crown Prince El Hassan Ibn-Talal said, *inter alia*: "An area which includes Jordan, the Palestinian National Authority (PNA in the West Bank and Gaza Strip) and Israel lies at the heart of all nations of the region. This area forms a natural pivot between the eastern Mediterranean, the Red Sea, the Gulf and the hinterland, which includes the countries north of the Arabian Peninsula. In building the definition of the region and a vision for its future, we may begin with this heartland and work toward expanding the circle of peace."[1]

Indeed, this region constitutes, in many respects, a geographical unit, characterized by strategic, political and economic interdependence among its three entities. The inhabitants of this region – Israelis, Palestinians and Jordanians – have strong historical, religious, nationalist, demographic and emotional ties to various parts of it, notably to Jerusalem. Unfortunately, for many decades these strong ties have contributed to creating intense political disputes and military conflicts, rather than to peaceful coexistence among the three peoples of this region, particularly between Israeli Jews and Palestinian Arabs. One of the major bones of contention among these three peoples has been the Jerusalem issue.

Thus, for example, during the late 1920s, Palestinian Arabs and Zionist Jews were engaged in violent conflicts regarding the "Western Wall" at the Temple Mount / *Haram-Al-Sharif* site. During the 1948 war, Israeli and Jordanian armed forces vehemently fought over the Old City of Jerusalem, which was subsequently captured by Jordan and later fell under Israeli control in the war of June 1967. Shortly afterwards, Israel formally annexed East (Arab) Jerusalem, including the Old City, despite strong protests by all Arab and Islamic nations, as well as most of the international world community. To be sure, this Israeli act particularly deepened the antagonism toward the Jewish state by the Palestinians and, seemingly, also by the Jordanians (although in practice, Israel and Jordan tacitly agreed that the *Haram Al-Sharif* would be autonomously administered by the Jordanian-appointed Muslim Waqf authority).

It would seem that the recently signed agreements between Israel, on the one hand, and the PLO and Jordan, on the other, carry certain prospects for a peaceful solution to their disputes while preparing the ground for regional cooperation among the three entities. Nevertheless, it appears that these prospects apply mostly to the Israeli-Jordanian equation, and less to the Israeli-Palestinian relations. The Israeli-Jordanian peace treaty of October 1994 – being, in many ways, a formalization of the close strategic relations between the two states since 1967 – may indeed serve as a model of peaceful coexistence and cooperation in the region in terms of most, if not all, bilateral issues. Regarding the highly sensitive issue of the future status of Jerusalem, the treaty stipulates that Israel respects the special role of Jordan in the holy Islamic sites in Jerusalem and will grant high priority to this role during the negotiations for the permanent status of the city.[2]

By contrast, the Israeli-PLO agreements of September 1993 and of May and August 1994 were, as we know, of an interim nature,[3] practically dictated by Israel and stipulating that the permanent agreement would be concluded only toward the end of the 1990s. By the end of 1996, Palestinian self-rule was established in the Gaza Strip and in small parts of the West Bank, several institutions were created by the PNA, and democratic elections were carried out of for a new legislative council.

Yet, the prime and ultimate goal of the PLO and most Palestinians is to establish an independent state in the West Bank and the Gaza Strip with its capital in East (Arab) Jerusalem. The prospects of reaching this goal could have been fairly promising had Shimon Peres and his Labor-leftist coalition won the Israeli national elections of late May 1996. According to the Israel-PLO agreement, the issues of the final borders (between the two states?) and the status of Jerusalem were to be determined in the negotiations on the final status issues, which also include the problems of Jewish settlements and Palestinian refugees. Prior to the Israeli elections, there had been certain indications that the Peres government was inclined to settle these issues in ways which might have been acceptable to the PLO. Thus, in early November 1995, Israel's Minister Beilin and PNA Minister Abu-Mazin apparently agreed on a format to settle the final status issues, including the creation of a Palestinian state in the West Bank and the Gaza Strip.[4] Indeed, on the eve of the May 1996 elections, the Labor party erased from its platform its long-standing objection to an independent Palestinian state in the West Bank and the Gaza Strip.

With respect to the Jerusalem issue, the Labor party continued to stress that the undivided city would always remain under Israel's sovereignty. But a few Labor leaders apparently entertained the idea of creating a capital of the Palestinian state in certain suburbs of East Jerusalem (*Al-Quds*) to be linked to other Palestinian sections of the city, which would enjoy municipal autonomy.[5]

However, with the ascendancy of Benyamin Netanyahu and his Likud-rightist coalition in the May 1996 elections, the prospects for establishing an independent Palestinian state in the Gaza Strip and the West Bank, with its capital in *Al-Quds*, seem to be very slim for the next few years. In fact, the guidelines of the new Israeli government stress its strong objections to the creation of an independent Palestinian state west of the Jordan river, while stating that "Holistic Jerusalem, Israel's capital, is one city, holistic and united, that will remain for ever under Israel's sovereignty."[6]

Indeed, the new Israeli government has deliberately delayed the implementation of the Oslo agreements, particularly with regard to the withdrawal from Hebron. Only following diplomatic efforts by US President Clinton and Jordan's King Hussein did Israel carry out its commitment regarding Hebron in early 1997. As for the issue of Jerusalem, the Netanyahu government has insisted that the entire city must continue to be under Israeli sovereignty. It has demonstrated this position by adopting unilateral acts which were severely criticized by the international community, particularly Arab and Muslim countries, and negatively affected Israeli relations with the Palestinians and with Jordan, namely: the opening in September 1996 of a tunnel near the *Haram Al-Sharif* and the initiation of construction for a new Jewish neighborhood on *Har Homa*, on the southern outskirts of Jerusalem.

If such policies are further pursued by Netanyahu's government, then the Israeli-Palestinian peace process may very well come to a halt, if not collapse entirely, and Israeli-Jordanian relations could be impaired, throwing the whole region again into instability and violence. Under such crucial circumstances, can Jordan play a role that would serve the interests of the three parties and settle the Israeli-Palestinian conflict? Against the background of the long-standing strategic cooperation between Israel and Jordan and the disputes of each of them with the PLO, one way would be to form an uneven triple system. For example, both Israel and Jordan would accept a Palestinian state in the Gaza Strip, while the Palestinian-inhabited parts of the West Bank would have merely municipal autonomy, under military and political control of Israel, or joint Israeli-Jordanian control. United Jerusalem would continue to be under Israel's sovereignty, and the Islamic holy sites – the *Haram Al-Sharif* – would continue to be supervised by Jordan.[7]

Yet, such a scheme, which is likely to be designed by the Netanyahu government, would be totally unacceptable to the Palestinians as well as to other Arab nations. It is also highly doubtful as to whether Jordan would be able to support such a design, given the negative position of most Arab states and its own policy on this matter. It would seem, then, that an essential prerequisite for creating a credible Israeli–Jordanian–Palestinian tripartite system would be the establishment of an independent (but demilitarized) Palestinian state in the West Bank and the Gaza Strip, with mutually agreed border amendments (of the pre-1967 lines, possibly along the Alpher plan[8]) in order to satisfy Israel's security needs and include many Jewish settlers within its borders. The remaining settlers would have to choose between evacuating or becoming law-abiding residents of the Palestinian state.

Jerusalem would remain undivided, while two municipalities or several boroughs both – Israeli and Palestinian – would be established under an umbrella city council composed of Israeli and Palestinian representatives in accordance with their demographic strength. A Palestinian capital in *Al-Quds* would be set up in the eastern section of the city around Abu-Dis or Azariyya, to be linked to the Palestinian municipality of the city. The Muslim holy sites would be controlled by a joint Palestinian-Jordanian committee, while the Old City would be administered by the umbrella municipal council, assisted by an interfaith advisory committee – Jewish, Christian, and Muslim.

The Old City would be the site and headquarters of the *Jerusalem Triangle* – an Israeli–Jordanian–Palestinian alliance. This alliance could take the shape of a tripartite confederation – a Jordanian-Palestinian confederation alongside Israel – or might consist of the three separate states. It would serve as a forum of cooperation and coordination in strategic, security, political, economic, and cultural matters relevant to the whole region or to the various partners. For example, it would design and supervise the regional infrastructure projects of water resources, electrical grids, roads and railways, hotels and tourism, trade, agriculture, industrial parks, and the like. More crucially, this tripartite alliance would be charged with tackling and solving the problem of the Palestinian refugees, and with securing international financial help to provide for their settlement in various parts of the region. It should also prepare and carry out a major project for peace education by using the media, designing new textbooks for schools, and arranging exchanges of educators, writers, youth music bands, and sport teams among the three peoples.

Finally, while the Jerusalem Triangle will seek to safeguard the security and the strategic interests of the region and its peoples, it must not negate or threaten the interests of the neighboring Arab countries. This is particularly relevant to the case of Syria and Lebanon, which still have territorial conflicts with Israel and have long harbored some 650,000 Palestinian refugees in several camps. In order to settle these refugees and incorporate Syria and Lebanon in the Arab-Israeli peace process, political solutions must be sought to their conflicts with Israel. This would be accomplished by a formula which was almost reached in 1995 between the Israeli Labor government and Syria,[9] that is, Israeli withdrawal from the Golan and southern Lebanon in return for peace treaties, diplomatic relations, normalization, and mutually agreed-upon security arrangements.

Failure to secure a Syrian-Israeli peace settlement is likely to entice Damascus to sabotage the Israeli–Jordanian–Palestinian triangular relations, particularly if they seem to be advancing toward an acceptable design by the three parties. Alas, at this juncture, in early 1997, the prospects for such an acceptable design or for a Syrian-Israeli settlement seem to be very bleak. One of the main reasons for this state of affairs is the rigidity of the guidelines of the new Israeli government: No to a Palestinian state (in the West Bank and the Gaza Strip); No to a redivision of Jerusalem (namely, to a Palestinian sovereignty in any part of it); and No to an Israeli withdrawal from the Golan.

Notes

1 See text of a speech by the Crown Prince in the International Policy Conference, Amman, Jordan, September 1995.

2 See text of the treaty in: *The Peace Process in the Middle East* (in Hebrew), editor Hayim Ufaz, Ministry of Education, Jerusalem, January 1995, p. 34.

3 Ibid., pp. 12–26.

4 *Haaretz* (Tel Aviv), 22 February 1996.

5 Cf. *Haaretz*, 19 March 1996,

6 *Haaretz*, 17 June 1996.

7 For a possible Netanyahu view regarding the Jerusalem issue, see: Dore Gold, *Jerusalem,* Final Status Issues: Israel-Palestinians, Study No. 7, Tel Aviv University, 1995.

8 See: J. Alpher, *Yishuvim u-gvulut* (Settlements and Borders – in Hebrew). The Jaffee Center, Tel Aviv University (no date), pp. 36 ff.

9 On the Syrian-Israeli peace negotiation see: M. Ma'oz, *Syria and Israel: From War to Peacemaking* (Oxford, 1995), ch. 11.

Part II

The Cultural-Sociopsychological Aspects of Making Peace

6

Building Up Peace

Joseph Ginat

Jordanians, Palestinians, and Israelis together form a unique structure of "triangular" relations. First, there are three separate sets of dyadic relationships:[1] Jordanians–Palestinians, Israelis–Palestinians, and Jordanians–Israelis. However, there is also an important "triad" system: the Jordanians, the Palestinians and the Israelis, which is different from each separate system of dyadic relations.

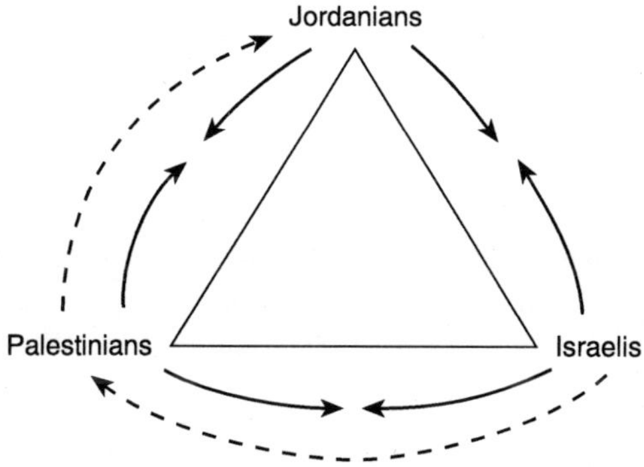

In a discussion I had with Dr Marwan Al-Mu'ashar, who served as Jordan's first ambassador in Israel and who is now Information Minister in the Jordanian government, Dr Muasher mentioned that during the Madrid conference in which he participated, he noticed the differences in the relations between the Israelis and the Palestinians, and those between the Jordanians and the Israelis. The Palestinians and Israelis spoke like old friends, while this was the first time the Jordanians had met Israelis, and they were as yet strangers to each other. After the signing of the peace treaty between Jordan and Israel, a wave of Israeli tourism swept Jordan. It was the Jordanians of Palestinian origin who conversed openly with the Israelis, and a number of them even knew some Hebrew.

For the Jordanians, in contrast with the Palestinians, the encounter with the Israelis was similar to the first encounters between the Egyptians and the Israelis. Both the Egyptians and the Jordanians were very polite, but claimed they did not know where the peace process would lead. In my first visits to Jordan, immediately following the signing of the peace treaty, I asked people on the streets, in shops and even in mosques: "How do you view the peace treaty?" Besides positive answers such as "I am for peace," or "We support the King's decision," there were also those who answered in a negative tone. Some, although not many, said "I am against peace, unless peace is achieved with all the Arab countries," or "I am against peace until you hand back Jerusalem." But there were quite a few people who answered, "I don't know yet – I still have to see what I will gain from this peace." This type of answer is mainly economic and personal: "if peace is good for my business or helps me find employment – then I'm for it." This, then, was the picture during the initial weeks following the signing of the peace agreement. These spontaneous answers teach us how important the personal-familial level is regarding the building up of peace. If citizens feel that peace benefits them personally, they will act to strengthen it.

Before discussing the triadic relationship between the Jordanians, the Palestinians and the Israelis, we must first examine the question "Who in Jordan is the Jordanian and who is the Palestinian?" There is varied information on this subject; both politicians and scientists have noted various statistics of the number of Palestinians in Jordan, in order to state various claims. I do not intend to deal with statistics but with the feelings and definitions of the inhabitants themselves.

The members of the Al Rifai family have held high-ranking positions in the Jordanian government, including the prime ministry – for example, Zeid Al-Rifaí. This family originally comes from Sefat;[2] thus, it is a family of Palestinian origin. The Al Majali family, which also produced prime ministers and ministers, is known to reside in Karak in the south of Jordan, but the family originally came from the Hebron Mountains. The Qalaiyyah (pronounced by the Bedouin Galaiyyah) came at the end of the eighteenth century from the Khan Yunis area to the western Negev as a result of wars between the Tarabin and Tiyaha federations of tribes, and settled among four Negev tribes. During the battles of Israel's War of Independence (1948), parts of the Qalaiyyah family moved to the Madaba area in Jordan and became assimilated into the existing population. They maintain their uniqueness as an independent Bedouin tribe, but define themselves as Jordanian.[3]

Another group are Bedouin of Bani Qais origin, known as the Qaisiyyah. During the wars between different tribes in the Arabian deserts, the Bani Yamman vanquished the Bani Qais, and the latter wandered northward, settling in the southern Hebron Mountains. The Negev Bedouin, as well as the rural inhabitants of the southern Hebron Mountains, considered them inferior to themselves. Neither the Negev Bedouin, nor those of the Judean Desert, nor the villagers of the Hebron Mountains agreed to be married to them. Their inhabitation of the southern Hebron Mountains began at the end of the eighteenth century and continued during the first half of the nineteenth century. During the 1920s and 1930s, some of them moved to the eastern side of the Jordan River, settling in the southern regions surrounding Karak.[4]

There are tribes and federations of tribes, parts of which are found in Jordan and parts in the Negev, unrelated to Israel's War of Independence. Such are the Huitat and 'Azazmah tribes ('Aref Al 'Aref, 1934; Abadi, 1988). There are also tribes and parts of tribes which, due to the 1948 war, crossed over to the "West Bank." As a result, some *khams* (descent group) members live in Israel, particularly in the Negev, while others live in Jordan. All the tribes and groups mentioned are now renewing contacts between them following the peace treaty with Jordan.

Other federations and tribes in Jordan were not separated, and have a long tradition of living in Jordan. These are the Bani Sakhir (Abadi, 1988; Al Fayez, 1995), or the 'Adwan federation in the Jordan Valley area (Abadi, 1988; Layne, 1994). These federations reached the west bank of the Jordan River only during years of drought, when the struggle for survival forced them to raid the fields belonging to the kibbutzim in the Beit She'an and Yizrael valleys.[5]

Many Palestinians emigrated from the "West Bank" to Jordan in various periods since 1948, and not necessarily as refugees.[6] They consider themselves Jordanians. There are those among them who served for many years in Jordanian institutions, including the armed forces, and who feel themselves to be Jordanians and not Palestinians. The author personally knows several people who originate from the "West Bank," and who served or still serve in high-ranking positions in the Jordanian authorities, while their relatives, such as first degree cousins, and in some cases even brothers, serve in top positions in the Palestinian Authority. Thus, the matter of Jordanian citizens of Palestinian origin must be dealt with according to the feelings of the people themselves. Those who are of Palestinian origin must define their identity and affiliation, whether they are Jordanian or Palestinian. We cannot fix some arbitrary date defining someone as one or the other. For this reason, politicians and scientists will find it difficult to determine statistical scales indicating the percentage of Palestinians in Jordan.

Connections between Jordanians, Palestinians, and Israelis

What is peace between countries? Is the signing of a peace treaty the actual "peace"? Is "peace" the ceremony held in honor of the Oslo accords in Cairo and later in Washington, between Palestinian and Israeli representatives? Is it the impressive ceremony held in the Arava, where the peace agreement between Jordan and Israel was signed? Undoubtedly, the signed peace agreement between countries is very important, but the agreement is only the cornerstone. Real, practical peace is the structure built by the people of both nations on the economic and social levels, more than the official or institutional contacts between the two countries. In the relationships between Israel and the Arab countries, the institution's approach to the building of peace is very important. It projects onto the population, and significantly affects the speeding up or slowing down of contacts between economic firms or between individuals. At the academic conference we held in Jordan and Israel, I was told by one of the Jordanian scientists at dinner one evening that "from the moment the peace agreement between Jordan and Israel was signed, the government has not interfered in the matter of the intensity of contacts. There are those who support the peace process, those who oppose it, and many are indifferent. There are those among my friends and relatives who did not approve of my traveling to Israel and participating in the conference. These I told I was going to Lebanon. No representative of any government institution interferes with visits or contacts of Jordanians with Israelis. The decision is in our hands, there is no government pressure or direction."

I met the same scientist two months after the conference, and he told me that upon his return, he discovered that those of his friends whom he told he was going to Lebanon had seen an interview he had given to Israeli television. Some of them accepted this with understanding. The respected Jordanian professor's story suggests the difference between the authorities' role and that of the citizens in building up peace.

Contacts between Jordanian, Israeli, and Palestinian Authority Bedouin

The Bedouin in all three places mentioned, as in other places in the Middle East, try to resolve their conflicts, as far as possible, without involving the state authorities. When there is a conflict, those involved often attempt to resolve it at the local level. If the conflict cannot be resolved at the community level, then it must be resolved at a higher level.

Today, Negev Bedouin who encounter difficulties in resolving their problems by themselves ask for help from mediators and judges from among the Bedouin of Jordan.[7] Sheikhs and dignitaries from among the Bedouin residing in the Judean Desert, some of whose tribesmen live in Jordan, mediated between Israeli and Jordanian Bedouin during the initial period following the peace agreement between Israel and Jordan. They recommended that well-known sheikhs in Jordan help the Israeli Bedouin resolve difficult conflicts.[8] Freilich (1983) stresses that conflicts exist in every society: between the young and the old, the strong and the weak, and between different groups. The Bedouin in Israel try to resolve their conflicts using the local systems. When they face difficulties, they act according to the rule that every mechanism has a wider mechanism – a safety net – surrounding it. Schneider (1965, 1967) notes that whatever is not resolved at the low level must rise up to a higher level. (See also Schneider and Homans, 1966.) Thus, as mentioned above, when the Israeli Bedouin find that they need to act in a broader cultural system and on a higher level, they call upon the sheikhs in the Palestinian Authority areas and on the Jordanian sheikhs.

Abadi (1988) states that despite the abolition of the Bedouin Control Law, including the abolition of the *bish'a* practice[9] in 1976, tribal law is still in practice among the Bedouin tribes, and moreover, it is still operative in civil courts, although unofficially. Linda Layne (1994) discusses this issue in her research: "The Jordanian press regularly published articles in both English and Arabic debating the pros and cons of 'tribalism' under headlines such as 'Jordanian Bedouins Enshrine Arab Virtues,' 'Can We Afford These Archaic Customs?' and 'Detribalisation – Toward the Rule of One Law'. Those in favor of 'tribalism' portrayed it as the embodiment of a value past, whereas those against it saw it as outdated and standing in the way of progress." Layne quotes Marwan Al-Mu'ashar before he was appointed ambassador in Israel and Minister of Information in the Jordanian government, in the period when he was a newspaper columnist. She claims that "Al-Mu'ashar criticized the government for support of tribal practices that 'are followed not only by Bedouins but also by many urbanite, educated Jordanian families' . . . 'this way of life has survived the modern social transformation Jordan has gone through. . . .These are the eighties, not the twenties, not the fifties, not even the seventies'" (Al-Mu'ashar, *Jordan Times*, 19 January 1985; Layne, 1994, p. 97).

Layne gathered various criticisms, including severe criticism against the continued practice of Bedouin laws and customs. She quotes from Ahmad al-Anani's book: "We are unable to extricate ourselves from some outdated nomadic habits, such as the processions and ritual meals held on occasions of marriage, settlement of blood feuds, rituals of consolation and congratulation . . . and a long list of similar habits which were extant in Jordan since pre-Islamic times" (Layne, 1994., p. 98). Layne brings additional excerpts from those opposing the continued tribal jurisdiction, and notes that some emphasize that the primary loyalty is the tribal one, while other loyalties remain secondary. As Layne puts it, "Like the modernization theories, Jordanian critics of tribalism assumed that loyalty to a tribe is 'automatic', whereas loyalties such as those to class, party, or professional organizations are 'pragmatic'" (p. 99). Thus we can see that, although the practice of laws and customs originating from Bedouin tradition was abolished in 1976, reality remains stronger.

When sheikhs from Jordan are invited to function as mediators and judges in conflicts between the Bedouin of the Negev, their honor and prestige is increased. Lately, there occurred a severe incident between two descent groups of the Afinish tribe in the Negev. The members of this tribe live in the town of Rahat. A quarrel between children flared up, and one man from the head of the tribe's *khams* was killed. The event was a serious and complicated one. Dignitaries from among the sheikhs of the Negev tried to deal with it; several Negev mediators understood the difficulties inherent in the resolution of the conflict, and suggested bringing in experienced and famous sheikhs from Jordan.

The delegation of Jordanian sheikhs included over twenty dignitaries. Some of them were the descendants of heads of tribes who lived in the Negev before 1948, and some were of pure Jordanian tribal origin. They met several times with representatives of the two descent groups. The members of the offending *khams* were expelled from the tribe to another area. The Jordanian sheikhs announced that they would not return to Jordan until the conflict was resolved, or until an *'atwa* (cease-fire) was achieved, thereby promising that no blood would be shed.

Meetings between Israeli and Jordanian Bedouin also result in various business deals. The author is familiar with two Israeli Bedouin who purchased land in Jordan in the Madaba area. One of them even married a second, Jordanian wife, who lives next to the plot of land he purchased, thus emphasizing his ownership of the land.[10] In another case, an Israeli Bedouin who owns a heavy machinery company searched for a Jewish Israeli who would be interested in investing capital in the establishment of a hotel, on land belonging to a Jordanian Bedouin in a location with a good view, south of Amman.

Relationships of a different kind began to form between Bedouin in

Israel and Jordan, based on past kinship. The tribe of Hureishat is located in Jordan, and one of its descent groups moved to Lebanon because of a blood feud. The event took place in the nineteenth century. At the beginning of the twentieth century, one lineage moved to the north of Israel, and at the present time they live in 'Usfiyya on Mount Carmel. The tribesmen in Jordan married their daughters to the sons of the Bani Sakhir federation of tribes; such marriage ties created an alliance with this strong tribe.[11]

Members of the Hureishat tribe living in 'Usfiyya are now renewing their contacts with the members of the tribe living in Jordan. These are completely new relationships, since none of the tribesmen in 'Usfiyya actually know the tribesmen in Jordan. The establishment of these relationships is an attempt to replace tradition with actual relations, that is, establishing family ties based on stories passed down during several generations within the lineage now living in 'Usfiyya. Similar relationships are forming between descendants of Arab Turkeman living in the villages in the Wadi 'Ara area in Israel and Bedouin of the Turkeman tribe living in Jordan.[12]

Another example of searching for relatives to form relationships is that of the Al 'Uqbi tribe, or as it was originally called, Bani 'Uqba, which live in the Hura area of the Negev. The Bani 'Uqba live in the Karak area of Jordan, but in the course of time, their name was changed to Bani 'Amr. The tribe is mentioned in writing as far back as the Mamluk period, in the days of Baybars.[13] The tribesmen, presently called Bani Amr, still preserve the tradition of their previous name. Some Bedouin of the Al 'Uqbi tribe visited the tribe members in Jordan, emphasizing the family kinship.

Other relationships formed are those between the two Circassian villages in the Galilee and the Circassians living in Jordan.[14] Mutual visits are made. A Circassian from Kafar Kamma is presently trying to encourage commerce between Israelis and Jordanians.

Contacts on a different level between Israeli Arabs and Palestinians, and Jordanians as well, are conducted through The Islamic Movement and the Democratic Arab Party. During the struggles between the Palestinian Authority and the *Hamas*, parliament member Darawasha and Abdalla Nimmer, and other representatives of the Israeli Islamic Movement, served as mediators between the two groups. In the author's opinion, this activity should not be considered as part of the increased process of Palestinization among the Arabs of Israel, but as a reflection of the Israeli Arabs' desire to be involved in contacts resulting from the peace process (see below). Representatives of the above mentioned Arab movements and parties visit Jordan regularly, and their representatives conduct meetings with various communities in Jordan.

Economic Ties between Jews and Jordanians

An Israeli agricultural company, represented by Zvi Karchi, professor of agriculture and genetics, initiated a business enterprise in Jordan. Karchi was the scientist who developed the Galia melon and other cross-breeds of fruits. I accompanied Professor Karchi and other people from the company during meetings at agricultural farms in various places in Jordan. The first to cooperate with the Israeli company's initiative was a farmer of Palestinian origin, who grows melons in the Azraq area. Professor Karchi and his men acted in a positive and interesting manner. In spite of his academic background and his rich experience in growing various fruits, Professor Karchi did not come as one who teaches, or as one who instructs those who lack knowledge. He formed a good relationship with the work supervisors in the field, and acted as an equal among equals, in a non-patronizing manner. Several Jordanians told me, "This is the only way to succeed. When the Israeli and Jordanian walk in the field together, it is clear that the Israeli has the knowledge. But when he says 'We will work *together*,' he establishes good rapport with us. There were people who said, 'You don't know, we will teach you.' This approach creates resistance. We consider it humiliating."

Another agricultural matter introduced by Israeli scientists was the improvement of sheep raising. Professor Karchi is involved in this field as well. A method was developed causing sheep to give birth to three lambs a year, thus significantly increasing the amount of milk the sheep could produce. There were contacts between representatives of the Israeli and Jordanian Ministries of Agriculture. The Israeli experts surveyed potential farms, whose owners were interested in establishing experimental farms, but the Jordanian farmers prefer that the matter be developed privately and not at governmental level. They want to establish experimental farms which will constitute joint ventures with Israeli, non-governmental companies. I visited three farms, whose owners have heard initial details about the possible "revolution" in sheep raising and improvement in milk production, and they emphasized that they are interested in partnerships with private people or companies, without any mediation on the part of the authorities. The emphasis is on the joint venture. They believe that partnerships on the private level have a greater chance to succeed. They claim that this method will create a strong involvement on the part of both the Israeli experts, and the Jordanian farmers and the teams on the farms. Such a partnership will create a shared system of mutual interests for the Israelis and Jordanians involved in the project.

Following the Casablanca Economic Conference, and once again, later on, following the Amman Conference, voices were heard throughout the Arab world claiming that Israel desired to dominate the economy of the Arab countries. I sensed that people in Jordan were significantly apprehensive of doing business with Israelis. But the approach adopted by Professor Karchi breaks through the walls of suspicion and establishes the foundations for business. As mentioned, Professor Karchi created a trust-building mechanism immediately at the first stages of his contacts. This is not done in air-conditioned offices, but by walking with the Jordanians in the furrows of the fields and between the rows of fruit trees.

Professor Karchi's mechanism is also based on the clauses of the written agreement between the Jordanians and the Israeli company. It was agreed that all the expenses of visits to Jordan and experts' salaries would be paid after the end of the agricultural season, after the melons were sold, whether in the local market or through export. This method also adds an important element to the building of mutual trust between the parties.

The first experience, then, was with a Jordanian of Palestinian origin. Later contacts were formed with Jordanians who became familiar with Karchi and his work methods. We find here a parallel situation to that described by Dr Al-Mu'ashar, the Minister of Information, regarding the Israeli–Palestinian encounter in the Madrid Conference. The Palestinians have been familiar with Israelis for years, ever since 1967, and it was easier for them to make contact with Israelis. Thus, the links are: Israelis–Palestinians–Jordanians. There are also square or diamond-shaped contact systems: commercial contacts between Israeli Jews who know Israeli Arabs who are experienced in commercial contacts. The Israeli Arab knows Palestinians in the "West Bank," and through them, commercial ties are achieved with Jordanian Palestinians or with the Jordanians themselves. I found examples of this type of system in the attempts made to create commercial ties for marketing mineral water, as well as in the field of textiles. The phenomenon of using Israeli Arabs as a bridge is interesting, and it should be considered as a permanent level in the making of peace, and not only a stage. For many years, a common phrase was heard: "The Israeli Arabs will serve as a bridge to peace, when the first attempts are made to reach peace talks with the Arab countries." It is a matter of regret that such mottos remained empty and unfulfilled during the talks between governments on the establishment of peace. Both in the peace talks with the Palestinians and in the talks with the Jordanians, representatives of the Israeli Arabs were not asked to join. After signing the peace agreements, various committees were established. Couldn't representatives of the Israeli Arabs have been members of such committees? Couldn't the Israeli Arabs have participated in the joint Jordanian–Israeli, or Palestinian–Israeli, water committee? Could they not participate in the joint committee for environmental preservation? Or in committees dealing with sewage, agriculture, and other joint committees?

The Israeli Arabs felt frustrated for being ignored in the initial stages of peace-making with the Jordanians and Palestinians.[15] The researcher Ori Stendel writes of their desire for peace and of the weight they carry in Israeli politics: "Meanwhile, the *Intifada* has ebbed, and the image of Saddam Hussein has paled. Simultaneously, the longing for a political settlement has grown, and the Palestinians cleaarly want a peace settlement with all their might, with the exception of marginal extremist elements . . . Since the Knesset elections in May 1992, the relative weight of Israeli Arabs has steadily grown, both politically and diplomatically. For the first time in the history of Israel, it is the Arab vote that tips the scale in the deadlock between two evenly balanced sides. The Arab parties made possible an obstructionist bloc against the right, enabling Yitzhak Rabin to form a government" (Stendel, 1996, pp. 21–2). After the Arabs of Israel helped Yitzhak Rabin to form his government, they became doubly frustrated when they were ignored as a possible "bridge to peace."

Although they were not included as a "bridge to peace" in the initial stage, the Arabs of Israel have an important role in the second "bridge" – the bridge to strengthening peace. They can definitely help with trust-building gestures on the public and private levels.

Cooperation in Tourism

An economic field in which strong ties between Israelis and Jordanians have formed is tourism. The direction of most of the tourism is from Israel to Jordan. Jordanian travel agents visit Israel and establish ties and agreements with Israeli agents. The previous Israeli Minister of Tourism, Uzi Bar'am, emphasized in a conversation with the author that he was working on the planning of joint "marketing packages" for Israel and Jordan in the United States and Europe. I do not intend to discuss activity on the national level in this chapter, but it is impossible to separate completely between the authorities' activities and those carried out on the private level. Cooperation is also developing between Palestinian tourism companies in Jerusalem, and Israeli and Jordanian companies.

A Jordanian travel agent told me that the contacts between Jordanian travel agents and Israeli agents have developed into social relationships. For example: the Jordanian agent held a birthday party jointly with an Israeli agent, whose birthday took place in the same week. One party was held in Tel Aviv, in which the members of both families participated, along with other friends, and a week later, a similar party was held in the home of the Jordanian agent, attended by the family, relatives and friends of the Israeli agent. This event strengthened the ties of friendship between the members of the two families. The two agents are now working on joint tourist programs, such as sailing in the Dead Sea and visiting sites on both its sides, a trip for Israelis to the ridges of the Arnon River, and a parallel trip for Jordanians to the ridges of David's River and the springs of Ein Gedi. They have prepared a joint marketing program for Jordan and Israel, and they travel together to meetings with agents in Europe and the United States. They believe that direct, face-to- face meetings will help them succeed.

Academic Cooperation

Another area of contacts is in the academic field. The joint conference held in Amman and in Haifa, 17–22 December 1995, was the first to be attended by Jordanian, Palestinian and Israeli scientists, in addition to European and American scientists. It was the first conference to be held first in an Arab country and then to continue at a university in Israel – the same conference which engendered the chapters comprising this book. As one of the architects of the conference, I admit there were quite a few difficulties throughout the various stages of the planning, and it is important to mention that, when various institutional functionaries, academics and media people in both countries heard of the planned conference, most of them claimed the time had not yet come for conducting such an affair, which would take place in the two countries in one continuous sequence. This approach accompanied the preparations for the conference all along the way. The success of the conference proved that reality is sometimes different from theory and reflection. Ever since the conference was held, academic activity continues, both on the private level and in the form of mutual participation in other conferences.

An interesting and important experience is the joint academic activity including Jordanians, Palestinians and Israelis in the field of applied research. Three institutes presently cooperate between them: Data, Bethlehem; Horizon, Amman; and The Economic Cooperation Foundation, Tel Aviv. Their first publication is "Total Cumulating of Rules of Origin in Exporting to the EU from Israel, Jordan, Egypt and the PNA" (June 1996). Two other publications are "Cooperation in the Field of Insurance" (October 1996) and "Implications on Economic Activity" (also October 1996).

The authors begin their first publication thus:

> Description of the Data-Horizon-ECF tri-lateral industrial and financial projects. Data (Bethlehem – the PNA), Horizon (Amman – Jordan) and the Economic Cooperation Foundation (Tel Aviv – Israel), under the auspices of the Friedrich Naumann Foundation, decided to join forces in investigating in a practical solution-oriented way issues confronting the three respective partners. The general aim of the group is to create innovative ideas and concepts, to be formalized in the form of policy papers, that will incorporate specific proposals for cooperation and suggested policy guidelines that will guide decision makers in forming future relations between the three economies (Israeli–Palestinian–Jordanian Industrial Cooperation, June 1996, Introduction page).

The "triad's" objective is to identify methods of action for the governments, but the establishment of this body and its activity are not under a governmental umbrella. It will constitute an immense contribution if the Jordanian, Israeli, and Palestinian authorities adopt the recommendations of this tripartite academic body.

The researchers emphasize that there are problems on the Palestinian side:

> The Palestinian economy, being a small economy at a crisis situation, is in urgent need of any trade concession that will improve its trade condition. These concessions are of even greater importance when taking into account the existing plans for a border industrial park and other joint projects in the region. Such a park, to be located on the Palestinian side of the border, may encounter problems in attracting Israeli investors . . . (Ibid., p. 6)

The group, consisting of academics from all three research centers, consider their role to raise suggestions for cooperation between the three states. They study the various agreements signed between Israel and the Palestinians and between the Kingdom of Jordan and Israel, and try to suggest solutions for various problems, such as the one mentioned above. Shimon Peres, when serving as prime minister and foreign minister, put a great deal of thought, not only in the formulation of peace contracts, but also into the long-term view, the vision. For several years he has been speaking of an industrial park, to be built in the area between Israel and the Palestinians and between Israel and Jordan, in the Beit She'an Valley. There is also a plan to build an industrial park at the Karni passage, on the border of the Gaza Strip. If a single academic representative of one of the three countries should point at the difficulties and attempt to suggest solutions, he would draw only partial attention; but when a joint research, carried out by academics from all three entities, is presented, the political level cannot overlook it.

In another publication (October 1996), the researchers address the issue of "Cooperation in the Field of Insurance":

> Border zone parks are a special model of economic and business cooperation which provide employment in the PA and meet Israeli security concerns. The unique features of this project, with regard to the need to create adequate insurance and risk-treatment packages, pose a challenge that is of importance to the success of the industrial parks. (Cooperation in the Field of Insurance, p. 9)

The third publication, "Impediments on Economic Activity" (October 1996) discusses the following issues:

> Data, Horizon and the ECF have committed themselves to promoting economic cooperation in the region. In doing so, they recently engaged in two projects under the auspices of the Friedrich Naumann Foundation and the Government of Germany: the "Guidelines for Promoting Industrial Cooperation" project . . . and the "Coordinating Guidelines Regarding Financial Investment and Banking" project . . . Both projects aim to identify the economic and day-to-day issues, which confront small and medium size business activity in the region, and to present policy-guidelines to relevant decision-makers and economic players in the Triad. (p. 4)

Addressing the matter of "small- and medium-size business activity in the region" is very important. Contacts between small business owners from Jordan, the Palestinian Authority, and Israel will contribute to the building up of peace. The wider the network of ties becomes, to include more and more circles, the greater the chances for peace. The more meetings there are between Israelis, Palestinians and Jordanians, the lower the walls of past hatred. If joint Israeli–Palestinian and Israeli–Jordanian projects materialize in the mutual industrial parks – those planned for Beit She'an and the Karni passage – such industries will add not only a layer in the process of establishing peace, but an entire story in the building of peace.

Concluding Remarks

"Peace" between nations that for a very long time were enemies cannot become manifest at the moment in which a peace agreement is signed. The agreement between the states is only the beginning. In the resolution of conflicts between different groups in Arab society, one says: "*Neftah safhah jadidah*" – we will open a new page. This is more than mere *sulha;* it means forgetting the past or repressing its sediments and making a fresh start. "Opening a new page" has great significance. The first meeting between King Hussein and the head of the Palestinian Authority, Yasser Arafat, after a long period of hostility between them due to the "Black September" crisis (September 1970), represented an "opening of a new page." When signing peace contracts between nations, opening a new page is not enough: an entire new book must be opened. Signing the peace treaty is only the first page in that book, as in laying the cornerstone. It is not to be expected that once the ink is dried, peace will take over. After signing the peace agreement, a strong cognitive dissonance may appear because of the contradiction between the hostile positions of the past and the present need for changed behavior toward the new partner. Bar-Siman-Tov addresses this issue, emphasizing that "the dissonance is thus a motivational process which results from the need to change the conflict on the one hand, and from the need to avoid loss of self-identity and to overcome uncomfortable feelings resulting from doing something contradictory to norms and values, on the other" (1996, pp. 11–12). On the national level, this situation must be provided for by the establishment of committees that will deal with arms control and regional security.[16] Meetings held in the framework of these important committees remove past suspicions and help create a more solid sense of security. Such discussions will reduce the negative sediment of the past without damaging the self-identity of any of the parties, which are no longer in conflict but are in the process of building up peace.

Peace must be built consistently by forming and strengthening relationships on the economic and social levels. There is no doubt that the political level has a strong influence on this process. The political level serves as a kind of compass and thermometer at the same time. A political declaration made by some leader might reflect onto the relationship between the nations. Terrorist activity originating from areas under Palestinian authority caused the closure of the territories, preventing laborers from going to work. Contacts between Israeli and Palestinian merchants came to a standstill. Delaying the signing of agreements creates a negative atmosphere, which in turn causes the cooling of economic relations between Jordanians and Israelis, reducing the number of visitors on both sides of the border. Advances or delays in the implementation of the Oslo accords affects not only the relations between Israel and the Palestinians, but between them and all the Arab countries, including those of North Africa, and especially the relations between Israel and Jordan.

My discussion has focused on the Jordanian–Palestinian–Israeli triangle, and on the interpersonal level of relations in the economic and social fields. I have described the development of contacts in the relationships between the various populations, and the beginnings of economic ties and cooperation in the areas of tourism and academic relations.

We are only at the beginning. We have laid only several rows of bricks above the foundations. We have not yet reached the windows, so it is still difficult to look out through such windows to assess our achievements. One thing is clear – the paper upon which the peace accords have been signed cannot be abolished, and peace is irreversible. The more we broaden the economic and social relationships, in which the Israeli Arabs are given a central role, the more chapters will be written in the book of peace.

Notes

1 For a discussion of dyadic relations, see Altman and Ginat (1996).

2 The El Rifa'i family has strong ties with the Sufi Tariqa Rifa'iyya which was active in Sefat. In recent years, a stone was discovered with the name Rifai'yya written on it. See Yossie Stepansky's publication about the stone in his article, "Archaeological News in the Eastern Galilee Caves," *Niqrot Zurim*, No. 17 (Dec. 1990): 21–34. Reference to the stone is on pp. 26–8.

3 The source of the name Qalaiyya is the fortress in Khan Yunis, which in Arabic is called Qalah. About their origin and dispersion in the Negev, see 'Aref al 'Aref (1934): Tarikh Bir Al-Sab'a Wa Qabailiha. Emanuel Marx, in his book *Bedouin of the Negev* (1967), refers to this group. See also Ginat, *Blood Disputes Among Bedouin and Rural Arabs in Israel* (1987), and *Blood Revenge: Family Honor, Mediation, and Outcasting* (1997).

4 On the settlement of Bani Qais on the Negev borders and in the southern Hebron Mountains, see Marx (1967). For a discussion of the blood conflicts among the Qaisiyyah inhabitants of the southern Hebron Mountains, see Ginat (1987, 1997).

5 The historian Malamat, in his discussion of the Midianites and his analysis of their penetration and retreat in Gideon's period, notes the raid of the Bedouin from the eastern bank of the Jordan River to the "West Bank" in the year 1947, which was a drought year. Reference to the raid of the Bani Sakhir Bedouin is made on page 118. See A. Malamat, "The War of Gideon and Midian," in J. Liver (ed.), *The Military History of the Land of Israel in Biblical Times* (Tel Aviv: "Maarachot," Israeli Defense Forces), pp. 110–23 (in Hebrew).

6 In discussions the author has had with refugees in various camps in Jordan,

there were those who mentioned being the second or third generation born in Jordan, and who were unwilling to leave their place of residence to return to the family's place of origin in Israeli territory. See Ginat's discussions on the refugees, "A proposal for a permanent settlement plan for the Palestinian Refugees."

7 For mediation and handling of conflicts on the local or regional level, see Victor Ayoub, "Conflict resolution and social reorganization in a Lebanese village," *Human Organization,* 24 (1965), pp. 11–77; Victor Ayoub, "Resolution of conflict in a Lebanese village," in L. Binder (ed.), *Politics in Lebanon* (New York: John Wiley and Sons, 1966); Ginat (1987, 1997); P. Gulliver, *Disputes and Negotiations: A cross-cultural perspective* (New York: Academic Press, 1979); Amina Farrag, The Wastah among Jordanian villages," in *Patrons and Clients in Mediterranean Societies,* edited by Ernest Gellner and John Waterbury (London: Duckworth, 1977), pp. 225–38; Fredrick Charles Huxley, *Wasita in a Lebanese Context: Social Exchange Among Villagers and Outsiders* (Ann Arbor: Museum of Anthropology, University of Michigan Press, 1978).

8 The sheikhs and dignitaries from among the Jahalin, the Ta'amrah and the Ka'abna, live in the Judean Desert and in Jordan. Those living in the "West Bank" area have had interactions with the Negev Bedouin ever since 1967, and they were the first to renew the ties between the Negev Bedouin and tribes in Jordan.

9 On the bish'a, see 'Aref al 'Aref, *Bedouin Justice* (Jerusalem: Beit al Maqdas, 1933) (in Arabic); A. al Qusus, *Bedouin Justice* (Amman: Al Matbaah al Urduniyya, 1972) (in Arabic); Omari Affendi El-Barghuthi, "Judicial Courts Among the Bedouin of Palestine," in Studies in Palestinian Customs and Folklore, *Journal of the Palestine Oriental Society,* Vol. II (1922), pp. 34–54; Robert Bartlett, *Trial by Fire and Water, The Medieval Judicial Ordeal* (Oxford: Clarendon Press, 1986).

10 During the signing of the cease-fire agreements between Israel and Jordan on the Isle of Rhodes in 1949 (see United Nations. The Rhodes Agreement: Armistice Agreements Between Israel and the Hashemite Kingdom of Jordan. Security Council. Official Records: Fourth Year, Special Supplement No. 1, 1949, New York, 1949), inhabitants living in villages which were transferred to Israel according to the agreement continued to own lands east of the borderline. Some of them left a relative on the land in order to exemplify their ownership. A family from Kafar Qassem left a three-year-old boy with relatives in Meshah, the parent village of Kafar Qassem, to exemplify their ownership of the land. After the Six Day War, the family asked to be reunited with the child who had been left behind in April 1949.

11 Granqvist, in her book *Marriage Conditions in a Palestinian Village,* describes the marriage ties between the inhabitants of the village of Irtas, who were located on the fringe of the Swan Desert border, and the Bedouin of the Judean Desert tribes. The villagers, who feared Bedouin raids in times of drought, married their daughters to the Bedouin's sons, thus creating a safety net for their village. Musil (1928), and Lancaster (1981) say the Rwala

did not give their daughters to the sons of other tribes, being the strongest tribe.

12 In the past the Arab Al-Turkeman lived at the edge of the Jesrael Valley, called in Arabic Marj Ibn 'Amir. During the 1948 battles, they dismantled their tents and moved to the Dothan Valley and the Jennin area, repitching their tents there. Some even live today in the Jennin refugee camp. Most of the Arab Al-Turkeman tribesmen have moved to Jordan. For more information about Arab Al-Turkeman, see 'Alia Al Khatib's book, *Arab Al Turkeman Sons of Marj Ibn Amir* (Amman: Dar El Jaleel for Publishing and Palestinian Research and Studies, 1987) (in Arabic). See also Eugene Rogan, "Turkeman of al-Ruman: An Ottoman Settlement in South Eastern Syria," *Arab Historical Review for Ottoman Studies*, 1–2 (1990), pp. 91–106.

13 For information on Bani 'Uqba in the Karak area during the Mamluk period, and on changing the name to Bani 'Amr, see Jeremy Johns' article, "The Longue Durée: State and Settlement Strategies in Southern Transjordan Across the Islamic Centuries," in E. L. Rogan and T. Tell (eds), *Village, Steppe and State: The Social Origins of Modern Jordan* (London and New York: British Academic Press, 1994), pp. 1–31. According to Johns, "Karak province was dominated by the Bani Uqba (later Bani Amr of Judham)" (pp. 22–3). The Bani Sakhir federation is also mentioned in the Karak area, "long before they became a leading force in the region" (p. 23).

14 For information on the Circassians, see G. H. Weightman, "The Circassians," in A. M. Lutfiyya and C. W. Churchill (eds), *Readings in Arab Middle Eastern Societies and Cultures* (The Hague: Mouton, 1970), pp. 91–98. See also, Ori Stendel, *The Circassians* (Tel Aviv: Am Hasefer, 1973) (in Hebrew).

Upon their arrival in Jordan in the 1870s, the Circassians were settled on "miri" (state) lands. See: M. R. Fishbach, "British Land Policy in Transjordan." In E. L. Rogan and T. Tell (eds), *Village, Steppe and State: The Social Origins of Modern Jordan* (London and New York: British Academic Press, 1994), pp. 80–107.

In Jordan, the Circassians were the first to build modern Amman, and they live in independent villages and in mixed Circassian–Arab villages. See N. Lewis, *Nomads and Settlers in Syria and Jordan, 1800–1980* (Cambridge: Cambridge University Press, 1987), pp. 107–17.

The Circassians hold seats in the Lower House. "Seats in the Lower House are allotted in each administrative government on a sectarian basis, with a certain proportion of seats reserved for Muslims, Christians, Bedouin and Circassians, and are filled by vote by the entire plebiscite within each government" (Layne, 1994, p. 111). They have a representative in Parliament, and this time it is a woman, who is very active in Parliament discussions.

15 In surveys conducted on the extremist positions of Arabs, it was discovered that Jews tend to attribute to the Israeli Arabs much more extreme views against the state and the Jews than the Arabs attribute to themselves. The surveys show that most of the Arabs accept the existence of the State of Israel, while only a small minority of the Jews in Israel trust the Arab

population. See John F. Hoffman's book, *Arab-Jewish Relations in Israel* (Wyndham Hall Press, 1984). See also J. F. Hoffman's article, "Social Identity and Readiness for Social Relations between Jews and Arabs in Israel," *Human Relations*, Vol. 35, No. 9 (1982), pp. 727–41. Thus, there is no doubt that the perceptions of Jews regarding the Arab minority in Israel affect their inclusion or exclusion from various roles.

16 For more information on arms control and regional security, see the two volumes on this subject edited by Steven L. Spiegel and David J. Pervin (eds), *Practical Peace making in the Middle East*, Vol. I, *Arms Control and Regional Security*, and Vol. II, *The Environment, Water, Refugees, and Economic Cooperation and Development* (New York and London: Garland Publishing Inc., 1995). While the various chapters of the first volume deal with issues which can only be discussed on the national level, the second volume deals with problems of water and refugees, which also belong to the institutional level; but the chapters dealing with the environment and economic cooperation and development belong to the overlapping area between the state and the academia and private initiative (as mentioned above, regarding the activity of Data, Horizon and the ECF).

References

Alfayez Mefleh, *Bani Sakhir Tribe*. 'Amman: Aljamiah al Urduniyyah markaz al lughat, 1995 (in Arabic).

Abadi al, Ahmad Aweidi, *The Jordanian Tribes*. 'Amman: Al-Dar al 'Arabiyya Liltawazi'a Wansher, 1988 (in Arabic).

Altman, I., and Ginat, J., *Polygamous Families in Contemporary Society*. New York: Cambridge University Press, 1996.

'Aref al 'Aref, *Bedouin Justice*. Jerusalem: Beit al Maqdas, 1933 (in Arabic)

——, *The History of Beer-Sheva and its Tribes*. Jerusalem: Beit al Maqdas, 1934 (in Arabic)

Ayoub, V., "Conflict resolution and social reorganization in a Lebanese village." *Human Organization*, 24: 11–77, 1965.

——, "Resolution of conflict in a Lebanese village." In L. Binder (ed.), *Politics in Lebanon*. New York: John Wiley and Sons, 1966.

Barghuthi, El, Omari Affendi, "Judicial courts among the Bedouin of Palestine." In Studies in Palestinian Customs and Folklore, *Journal of the Palestine Oriental Society*, Vol. II, pp. 34–54, 1922.

Bar-Siman-Tov, Y., *The Transition from War to Peace: The Complexity of Decision-Making – The Israeli Case*. Tel Aviv: Tami Steinmetz Center for Peace Studies, Tel Aviv University, 1996.

Bartlett, R., *Trial by Fire and Water, Medieval Judicial Ordeal*. Oxford: Clarendon Press, 1986.

Data, Bethlehem; Horizon, Amman; and The Economic Cooperation Foundation, Tel Aviv. Total Cumulating Rules of Origin in Exporting to the EU from Israel, Jordan, Egypt and the PNA. Tel Aviv: Prepared and published within the project for Israeli–Palestinian–Jordanian Industrial Cooperation.

Sponsored by the Friedrich Naumann Foundation, June 1996.
——, Impediments on Economic Activity, October 1996.
——, Cooperation in the Field of Insurance, October 1996.
Farrag, A. "The Wastah among Jordanian Villagers." In E. Gellner and J. Waterbury (eds), *Patrons and Clients in Mediterranean Societies*. London: Duckworth and Co., 1977, pp. 225–38.
Fishcbach, M. R., "British Land Policy in TransJordan." In E. L. Rogan and T. Tell (eds), *Village, Steppe and State: The Social Origins of Modern Jordan*. London and New York: British Academic Press, 1994, pp. 80–107.
Freilich, M., "The two worlds of homo-sapiens: Yet another explanation for war." In M. Freilich (ed.), *The Pleasures of Anthropology*. New York: A Menton Book, New American Library, 1983, pp. 432–45.
Ginat, J., *Blood Disputes among Bedouin and Rural Arabs in Israel, Revenge Mediation, Outcasting and Family Honor*. Pittsburgh: University of Pittsburgh Press, 1987.
——, *Blood Revenge: Family Honor, Mediation and Outcasting*. Brighton: Sussex Academic Press, 1997.
——, "A proposal for a permanent settlement plan for the Palestinian Refugees." To be published in a forthcoming publication of the Institute on Conflict Cooperation, University of California, San Diego.
Granqvist, Hilma. *Marriage Conditions in a Palestinian Village*. Societas Scientiarum Fennica, Commentationes Humanarum Litterarum, Vol. 3, No. 8 and Vol. 6, No. 8. Helsinki: Akademische Buchhandlung, 1931–5.
Gulliver, P., *Disputes and Negotiations: A Cross-Cultural Perspective*. New York: Academic Press, 1979.
Hoffman, J. F. et al., *Arab-Jewish Relations in Israel*. Bristol, IN: Wyndham Hall Press, 1988.
——, "Social Identity and the Readiness for Social Relations Between Jews and Arabs in Israel." *Human Relations*, Vol. 35, No. 9, 1982, pp. 727–41.
Huxley, F. C. *Wasitah in a Lebanese Context: Social Exchange Among Villagers and Outsiders*. Ann Arbor: Museum of Anthropology, University of Michigan.
Johns, J., "The Longue Durée: State and Settlement Strategies in Southern Trans Jordan Across the Islamic Centuries." In E. Rogan and T. Tell (eds), *Village, Steppe and State, the Social Origins of Modern Jordan*. London and New York: British Academic Press, 1994.
Khatib, Al-Alia, Arab Al Turkeman, Sons of Marj Ibn Amir. Amman: Dar El-Jaleel for Publishing and Palestinian Research and Studies, 1987 (in Arabic).
Lancaster, W., *The Rwala Bedouin Today*. Cambridge: Cambridge University Press, 1981.
Layne, L. L., *Home and Homeland: The Dialogics of Tribal and National Identities in Jordan*. Princeton: Princeton University Press, 1994.
Lewis, N., *Nomads and Settlers in Syria and Jordan, 1800–1980*. Cambridge: Cambridge University Press, 1987.
Malamat, A., "The War of Gideon and Midian." In J. Liver (ed.), *The Military History of the Land of Israel in Biblical Times*. Tel Aviv: "Ma'arachot" Israeli Defence Forces, 1965, pp. 110–23 (in Hebrew).
Marx, E., *Bedouin of the Negev*. Manchester: Manchester University Press, 1967.

Musil, A., *The Manners and Customs of the Rwala Bedouins. Oriental Exploration and Studies,* No. 6. New York: American Geographic Society, 1928.

Qussus, el A., *Bedouin Justice.* 'Amman: Al Matba'ah al Urduniyya. 1972 (in Arabic).

Rogan, E. L., "Turkeman of al-Ruman: An Ottoman Settlement in South Eastern Syria." *Arab Historical Review for Ottoman Studies,* 1–2, 1990, pp. 91–106.

Schneider, D. M., "American Kin Terms for Kinsmen." In E. A. Hammel (ed.), Introduction to Formal Semantic Analysis. *American Anthropologist,* Vol. 67, No. 5 (part 2), 1965, pp. 288–308, .

——, *American Kinship: A Cultural Account.* Englewood Cliffs, NJ: Prentice-Hall, 1967.

Schneider, D. M. and Homans, G. C., "Kinship Terminology and the American Kinship System." *American Anthropologist,* Vol. 57, 1966.

Spiegel, S. L. and Pervin, D. J. (eds), *Practical Peacemaking in the Middle East, Vol. I, Arms Control and Regional Security.* New York and London: Garland Publishing Inc., 1995.

——, *Vol. II. The Environment, Water, Refugees, and Economic Cooperation and Development,* 1995.

Stepansky, J., "Archaeological news in the Eastern Galilee Caves." *Niqrot Zurim,* No. 17, Dec. 1990, pp. 21–34 (in Hebrew).

Stendel, O., *The Arabs in Israel.* Brighton: Sussex Academic Press, 1996.

——, *The Circassians.* Tel Aviv: Am Hasefer, 1973 (in Hebrew).

United Nations. The Rhodes Agreement: Armistice Agreements Between Israel and the Hashemite Kingdom of Jordan. Security Council. Official Records: Fourth Year, Special Supplement no. 1, 1949, New York, 1949.

Weightman, G. H., "The Circassians." In A. M. Lutfiyya and C. W. Churchill (eds), *Readings in Arab Middle Eastern Societies and Cultures.* The Hague: Mouton, 1970, pp. 91–8.

7

The Emotional Aspects of the Path to Peace

Aaron Ben-Ze'ev

The path to peace has to overcome many difficulties; one of them, which is often neglected, is the emotional obstacle. A successful peace process requires a substantial change in the emotional attitudes of all parties concerned. Such a change is not easy to achieve, as emotional attitudes express our most profound values and implicit knowledge.

Emotions among Enemies

A considerable psychological change which is implied in the path to peace is the change from a distant relationship typical of enemies to a close interaction associated with friendly relationships. Each kind of relationship is related to different emotions. In distant relationships between enemies, hate, contempt, and fear are dominant; friendly relationships involve positive emotions, such as happy-for, hope, and gratitude, as well as different types of negative emotions, such as anger, resentment, and envy. I focus my discussion on hate and anger, which are, respectively, the major negative emotions in relationships among enemies and those among former enemies (see also Ben-Ze'ev, 1992).

Hate may be characterized as involving a global negative attitude toward someone considered to possess fundamentally evil traits. Anger is similar to hate in involving a negative evaluation, but it is the evaluation of a specific action. Love is similar to hate in involving a global evaluation, but in this case it is a positive one. The negative evaluation in hate is global not in the sense that every aspect of the hated person is considered to be negative, but in the sense that the negative aspects are so fundamental that other traits become insignificant. The positive evaluation in love is global in a similar manner: the beloved is believed to be an essentially positive person rather than a perfect being without flaws.

Like other emotions, hate is typically directed at a particular person. However, hate does not usually stem from a specific act by this person which is more likely to evoke anger, but from what are believed to be general traits that are not limited to specific circumstances. The negative characteristics of those we hate are perceived to be "in their blood." Hate is a long-term attitude whose generation is frequently not triggered by a personal offense. The hated person may not have harmed us at all, or at least not in the present or the recent past, but the supposed negative character of this person is thought to be capable of such harm. The particular details of the hated person are often unknown to us.

To a certain extent, hate involves depersonalization. As in prejudice, hate often feeds on partial or distorted information, which ignores the object's real personality. The general nature of hate is also reflected by the fact that hate is often directed at groups and not at individuals, regardless of the individual differences among group members. Although the object of hate is more general than that of anger, it has to have some degree of specificity and closeness in order to maintain a high level of emotional intensity. Thus, terrorist groups begin their activity by adopting a unifying general ideal. However, very soon this general ideal turns into more proximate and specific matters, such as revenge for a comrade's death or fighting against the oppression of parents and past generations.

Hate does not contain abstract fear about the other's continued power, but fear that this power will harm us or those related to us. Those we hate do not have to be actively responsible for their negative traits. Since these traits are considered to be more or less permanent, they probably do not bear actual responsibility for their generation. In hate we usually believe that changing the other's basic faults is beyond our power, since their source is not transient; consequently, hate is often associated with perceived self-impotence.

In light of the fundamental nature of the conflict in hate, the hater believes that the situation can be changed only if the other person is avoided or even eliminated, and that this is what the other person deserves. While hate is not always expressed by non-standard forms of behavior, in extreme cases physical elimination may be the only way that we believe to be effective in fighting the dangers associated with the hated other. Typical hate involves an extreme type of intolerance and opposition to diversity.

While hate does not have to seek physical elimination or even the wish to hurt the other physically, it must involve the creation of some psychological distance. In marital relationships, for instance, hate is usually expressed by evading the situation and acting coldly, as if the partner were no longer within the close relationship which is supposed to prevail in marriage.

Describing the intensity of hate is a complex issue. On the one hand, because of its more general and less personal nature, the feeling dimension of hate is sometimes of a lesser intensity than that of anger; it is as if a given intensity is spread over a longer period of time. Hence, killing can be done in "cold blood" without having intense feelings. This kind of hatred was manifested in the behavior of the Nazi Germans. On the other hand, hate can sometimes be quite intense. Since there is no hope for changing the object, the situation is viewed in extremely negative terms, thereby increasing emotional intensity. In extreme cases of hate, when physical elimination is not possible, emotional tension is created and various substitutes are sought. A major substitution is verbal aggression, which enables us to express our negative attitudes within the limits of acceptable standard behavior.

Due to the profoundly negative evaluation of the object in hate, we attempt to detach ourselves from the object, namely, to increase the subject–object distance as much as possible by avoiding or eliminating the object. If total detachment were possible, our attitude toward the object would be indifference, which is the typical attitude toward strangers. The problem typical of hate is that such detachment and indifference are impossible.

The wish to avoid or eliminate the object, together with the realization that this is impossible or at least very difficult, generate the emotional intensity typical of hate. Hate is directed at people whom we perceive to be too close to us, and from whom we wish to further distance ourselves. When this wish is not fulfilled, we are compelled to cope and even communicate with this object. The wish to avoid or eliminate is contrary to the wish to understand; the latter is what underlies genuine communication. The need for communication is then in conflict with a basic desire of hate, and therefore communication is ambivalent and often negative. Anger is typical when positive, normal communication is possible and when modifying the object's negative deeds does not require a radical change in the object's identity.

Like hate, contempt is also a long-term attitude, although usually less intense than hate. The difference between hate and contempt is that in contempt, the emphasis is on the inferiority of the object, whereas hate stresses the object's dangerous nature. In contrast with hate, contempt allows for competitive coexistence.

Both hate and prejudice involve a global negative evaluation of the object and can become epidemic. One who hates or has some prejudice against a given group will hate friends of this group, and then those defending the friends, and so forth. The struggle against hate is similar to the fight against prejudice. A major means of fighting both is to know the other person better. Such knowledge will force us to exchange the negative global evaluation for a more specific evaluation having both positive and negative elements.

Emotions among Former Enemies

The path to peace is first of all the path to being closer and knowing each other better. Such a path may considerably reduce the negative emotions typical of enemies, mainly hate and contempt, and give rise to some positive emotions. When people are getting together and peaceful solutions are in evidence, the likelihood that hate will be the prevailing emotional attitude decreases. However, other negative attitudes, such as anger, resentment, and envy, are more likely to prevail. I will focus on anger which replaces hate as the main negative emotion in the transition from relationships among enemies to those among former enemies. Awareness of the differences between the two types of negative emotions is of great importance for a successful peace process.

Anger is typical of close relationships. We are usually angry at those who are closest to us, such as partners, children, and colleagues. Those are the people whom we care most about and whose actions are most likely to upset us. Anger is an immediate response to what we consider as unjustified harm that someone has inflicted upon us or those related to us. In anger, the harm is often a kind of personal insult, and thus the wish for revenge is personal. Unlike hate, which implies fear for our own existence, anger arises from a less profound worry: it is related to a specific demeaning offense against us. Issues of social status and honor are far more relevant in anger, in that the other's action is not merely perceived as unjust, but also in some sense as depreciating our position.

A schoolteacher who is angry with pupils who talk while she is speaking, for instance, believes that their behavior is unjust and depreciates her position in the sense that she is not the only one to whom everyone is paying attention. Similar considerations probably explain why people typically do not appreciate when their guests are playing with the remote control of their TV, or when someone on the telephone is busy with something other than the conversation. These seemingly minor issues are interpreted as demeaning offenses and acquire great emotional significance in close relationships.

People are unlikely to respond with anger if they judge the other person to be justified, non-arbitrary, or not in control. The issues of justification and controllability constitute the main discrepancy between the description of anger by those who experience it and those at whom anger is directed.

People provoking anger are most often viewed as doing something voluntarily that they had no right to do, or as doing something that they could have avoided had they been more careful, whereas people who are the target of anger consider that they were justified in their actions or that the incident was beyond their control.

The personal harm to the angry person is assumed to be inflicted by a blameworthy person. Improper treatment by a blameworthy person is deemed to be hurtful not only because of the damage it inflicts, but also because the wrongdoer is perceived as sending the message that we are inferior and that our needs are insignificant. We do not become angry with inanimate objects that damage us, unless we construe these objects as agents rather than as inanimate objects. Since inanimate objects cannot treat us improperly, we cannot be angry with them.

Anger has a higher functional value than hate. The major functions of emotions, namely, mobilization of our resources and means of social communication, are quite evident in anger. Hate may be functional in the first sense of mobilizing resources, but it can hardly have any social role insofar as it attempts to disconnect all ties. Anger is quite important as an energizer and organizer of our behavior. Anger serves an important social function in that it is often perceived as a means for strengthening or readjusting a relationship. As such, both parties usually regard it as beneficial to the relationship in the long run, despite its short-term unpleasant circumstances. Like other emotions, anger is functional when it is in the right proportion and is expressed in a socially constructive way without becoming highly aroused. On the other hand, a high level of chronic anger and aggressive behavior can be harmful and are related to higher mortality and in particular to coronary heart disease.

In addition to anger, other negative emotions, such as envy and resentment, are typical of close relationships. Resentment is similar to anger in many respects. Like anger, it is a negative attitude toward a particular action of a blameworthy person rather than toward the person himself. Resentment is usually directed at an action which repeats itself or at a general pattern of actions, whereas anger is typically directed at actions which never before occurred. Like anger, and unlike hate, fear is not a significant factor in resentment, yet resentment lacks the urge to attack that is so typical of anger. Resentment may be characterized as an emotional protest against injustice. Unlike anger, which refers to immediate personal harm, resentment is mainly directed at moral injustice whose consequences are more remote.

Like anger and resentment, envy is directed at those who are relatively close to us; we envy those who are like us or equal to us. In envy, our attention is focused on those perceived to be immediately above us, since these people occupy the first rungs on fortune's ladder which we will have to climb. These are the people with whom we are most likely to be compared and whose accomplishments are most likely to demean us. Where no closeness exists, comparison is less likely to arise and we are less prone to feel inferior. Those who are close to us, but still above us, emphasize our own inferiority more than do those who are distant from us.

I have suggested that the transition from hostile to peaceful relationships involves a change in emotional attitudes. The most significant change in this regard is the change from global negative emotions, such as hate and contempt, to more specific negative emotions, such as anger, resentment, and envy. The next section discusses the ways to cope with such a change.

Coping with the Change

The negative emotions associated with relationships among enemies are more fundamental than are those typical of former enemies. Thus, whereas hate requires an evaluation of the object as possessing inherent dangerous traits, the object of anger is guilty of merely instrumental negative actions. Accordingly, the object of anger seems to be "less negative" than that of hate. Nevertheless, the risks involved in having these seemingly less negative emotions are quite profound because of their greater frequency and sometimes even greater intensity.

Since anger entails a belief in the effectiveness of our acts, the motivational domain is strong and is often expressed in non-standard aggressive behavior. The urge to attack is essential to anger even if it is expressed in more acceptable, non-aggressive behavior. In anger, we want to personally punish the other party who is seen as deserving of punishment. That is, objects of anger are to be blamed and punished, not avoided or eliminated, since they are assumed to have some responsibility for their actions. The willingness to become personally involved is much stronger in anger than in hate, due to our belief that it is easier to change the undesired circumstances. This may be one reason that despite the more negative nature of the object of hate, we are often more aggressive toward the object of anger.

Negative emotions, such as anger and resentment can be expected to occur more frequently when the interaction between the two parties is greater, as there are far more events which can generate these emotions. This is true not only for individuals, but for political entities as well. Consider, for example, the relationship between Israel and Syria, which is currently one of enemies, and the relationship between Israel and Egypt, which is one of former enemies. There are hardly any negative incidents taking place between Israel and Syria, as there is no actual relationship that exists. However, Israel's relationship with Egypt is full of such incidents, and the negative emotions of anger, resentment, and envy are quite frequent and intense.

The value of the peace process from an emotional point of view is that the proportion of positive emotions increases, making the negative emotions less destructive. Nevertheless, negative emotions do exist and, as indicated, can be more frequent and even more intense with increased interaction. Ignoring this fact may endanger the whole peace process. The initial stages of the peace process are especially vulnerable, since at these stages expectations are high, while fulfilling them remains difficult. Such difficulties stem from two major sources: (a) there are still many objective obstacles to overcome, and (b) the emotional attitudes have not yet been completely changed. The second factor, which is a psychological one, is more relevant to our discussion.

Making peace may solve the most profound existential issues related to the two parties, thus considerably decreasing the likelihood of hate. Nevertheless, it raises a host of psychological problems concerning the situation of living close together. These problems do not have a quick one-step solution, but should be dealt with in a painstaking, long-term process; in this sense, they are harder to address. Emotional attitudes express our most profound values and beliefs, and changing them therefore requires time and maturity.

In light of the high expectations associated with suddenly becoming closer together, people are usually not ready for the long and rocky process of adjusting to the new situation. People would like to immediately enjoy the benefits of becoming closer, even as they often lack the psychological tools needed to cope with the problems inherent in the new relationship. When we have high expectations, small negative incidents loom larger, and small positive steps are perceived as insignificant. Accordingly, suspicion and frustration are likely to prevail.

From a psychological point of view, we can compare the peace process to a love affair. In the same way that it is easier to fall in love than to stay in love, it is easier to make peace than to maintain peace. Staying in love is an extremely difficult task, since it requires continuous effort and compromise. Being close together in marriage, for example, can be a wonderful and happy experience – indeed, research indicates that married people are usually happier than single ones. However, marriage is also a difficult and demanding experience whose chances of breaking down are quite high. This is particularly true of the first years of marriage when expectations for positive outcomes are very high, and negative outcomes are not considered as natural and are likely to cause suspicion and frustration.

One way to cope with clashes between expectations and reality in both love and the peace process may be to lower expectations. This approach has the disadvantage of being less convincing about the positive outcomes of a future relationship and hence less conducive to investment of effort and other resources. Like love and other positive emotions, a peace process has the nature of a self-fulfilling prophesy, whereby optimism often increases the chances of success, which in turn enhances optimism.

A better way of coping with the difficulties involved in love and peace is to allow more time for the fulfillment of our expectations and to be ready for the anticipated obstacles. The greatest remedy for anger is delay, namely, taking a broader perspective not limited to the current, specific situation. Awareness of the presence of other perspectives, as well as awareness of the likelihood of clashes between expectations and reality, are crucial for coping with the difficulties typical of an initial friendly relationship between former enemies. Such an awareness would increase the probability that the newly found close relationship declared by the leaders of Israel and several Arab countries will not collapse into a failed, brief encounter.

Reference

Ben-Ze'ev, A. (1992). "Anger and hate," *Journal of Social Philosophy*, Vol. 23,pp. 85–110.

8

The Cultural and Social Context of the Triangle

Asher Susser

With respect to the cultural and social context of the Israeli–Jordanian–Palestinian triangle, it is especially relevant to address two main issues:

1 The corporate identity of the peoples concerned.
2 The building of peace on normal interaction and mutual political, cultural and social acceptance.

The Historical Evolution of Corporate Identity

The British Mandate in Palestine and the Arab-Jewish conflict over the fate of Palestine led to the emergence of three distinct political entities: Israel, Jordan, and the Palestinian community and national movement. Though distinct, all three have developed, in no small measure, as functions of the conflictual interaction between them, defining their respective corporate identities largely in reference to their adversaries.

Since these corporate identities have evolved with the Arab-Israeli conflict, historical watersheds in the conflict have been of formative importance. These are, in the main, the war of 1948 and the war of 1967 and their respective consequences.

The war of 1948, for the Jews of Israel their war of national liberation, was for the Palestinians their traumatic defeat and dispersal. This, more than any other single event, was the formative crucible of the Palestinian national identity, powerfully derived from their national setback and tragedy.

Jordan, initially carved out of the original British mandate over Palestine, and thus linked from its very inception to the Palestinian question, now became the home for most of the Palestinian people. The West Bank was unified in 1950 with the Hashemite Kingdom of Jordan, and all Palestinians in the Kingdom, refugees and non-refugees alike, became citizens of Jordan. However, from the late 1950s onward, there has been a steady revival of the Palestinian entity and identity, symbolized by the establishment of the Palestinian Liberation Organization (PLO) in 1964 and further accelerated by the consequences of the June 1967 war.

Jordan's loss of the West Bank to Israel in the June 1967 war arrested the process of "Jordanization" of the Palestinians and "re-Palestinized" the Arab-Israeli conflict. The deployment of the PLO in Jordan and the tension this aroused with the government there eventually led to the outbreak of the 1970–71 civil war (know as the "Black September"). This was yet another traumatizing event which sharpened the distinctive corporate identities of both Jordanians and Palestinians. The armed conflict between Jordanians and Palestinians reinforced a separate sense of Jordanianism, fueled by a powerful desire of the original East Bank Jordanians to preserve their own political patrimony. King Husayn's old slogan of "Jordan is Palestine and Palestine is Jordan" was gradually replaced by a new concept of "Jordan is Jordan and Palestine is Palestine." Rather than assuming the historical role of inheritor of Palestine, Jordan now sought a partnership with the Palestinians.

Jordanian policy and aspirations since the early 1970s, have evolved from an attempt to restore total unity with the West Bank to the current acceptance of a separate Palestinian identity and to satisfaction with some form of federative or confederative relationship with the Hashemite Kingdom. Israel has reluctantly come to terms with Palestinian nationalism as well. The logical dynamics of the Oslo accords of September 1993 are paving the way toward the establishment of a Palestinian state or entity of one form or another, if and when the final status negotiations are concluded.

The internal balance within the triangle of Israel, Jordan, and the Palestinians is changing as Israel begins the arduous process of disengagement from the West Bank and Gaza. How this process will culminate is difficult to foresee, but it is worth noting at this juncture some observations on the political and ideological priorities of the Israeli public. Polls conducted since the late 1980s have shown that a clear majority of Jewish Israelis value the preservation of their state as the state of the Jewish people (i.e., a state with a stable Jewish majority) more than they value the concept of Greater *Eretz Yisrael*. The cultural and national identity of the state and the preservation of this facet of the

Zionist *raison d'être* is of greater importance to most Jewish Israelis than the eternal control of the West Bank and the Gaza Strip.

If, as a result of this proclivity, Israel chooses to disengage from much of the West Bank, whether by providing for limited Palestinian self-rule or for the establishment of an independent Palestinian state, this could have potentially far-reaching consequences for Jordanian-Palestinian relations. The West Bank is landlocked and geopolitically "sandwiched" between Israel and Jordan. The more Israel detaches itself from the West Bank, the more dependent that territory will become on Jordan. The less integrated the Palestinian territories are with Israel, both economically and politically, the more they are likely to develop political and economic links with Jordan, especially considering Jordan's massive Palestinian population and the fact that Jordan will always be the natural major outlet for the West Bank to the hinterland of the Arab East *(Mashriq)*. Indeed, it is not unlikely that, in the future, Jordan and the Palestinians will come to an agreement on closer economic and possibly confederative or federative political ties. One may safely assume that both parties would do their utmost to preserve their respective separate identities in such an association. At the same time, however, there is an obvious cultural and social affinity between these two Arab and predominantly Muslim peoples.

The Israeli–Jordanian–Palestinian triangle is not symmetrical. Though all three parties are products of the struggle for Palestine, Israel, as the state of the Jewish people, does not share in the cultural, linguistic, and religious affinity that links Jordanians and Palestinians. It is therefore most unlikely that future bonds with Israel would ever be as close as those that may link Jordanians and Palestinians.

Arab Views of Israel's Place

Precisely because of these differences, the conflict with Israel has been so protracted and its solution so problematic. Indeed, the peace process with Israel is much more of a "pragmatic peace" than it is the product of an ideological transformation within the Arab world. The Arab world is coming to terms with Israel far more out of acquiescence in the regional balance of power than as the result of a substantive change in the pervasive delegitimizing ideological perceptions about Zionism.

In the effort to build on this pragmatic peace, the parties involved have to contend with conflicting self-images and a profound perceptual divide. Israelis tend to see themselves and their history as essentially defensive, viewing the Zionist endeavor as a heroic feat of self-defense and collective preservation against all odds and in defiance of the Jewish fate. Having endured the struggle, the Israelis therefore seek reassurance and ideological acceptance of their community and their collective identity in the family of Middle East nations.

The Israeli need for such ideological acceptance is also a function of perceptions about time. On whose side is time perceived to be? Israelis are far more confident about the short-term regional balance of power than they are about the long-term balance. If peace is but a function of the existing balance of power, and not the consequence of profound ideological change, then how would this peace be affected by a shift in the regional balance of power in the longer term? This is more or less a mirror image of the radical Arab perception of time. It is the radicals in the Arab world, such as *Hamas*, who argue against the peace process, contending that in the long run Israel is doomed to ultimate defeat ("the disappearance of Israel is pre-determined by the forces of history" – *zawal Isra'il hatmiyya ta'rikhiyya*). Why, therefore, hinder this process by concessions and peace treaties at a time of relative Arab weakness, which is bound to change in the future?

Israelis are consequently perturbed by Arab reservations about "normalization" since these reflect a reluctance about ideological acceptance, as opposed to the mere pragmatic, and possibly even transient, acquiescence in an historical aberration. For Israelis, diplomatic, economic and cultural ties with the Arab states are of crucial importance as a reflection of Israel's long-term acceptance as a normal and natural member of the region, far more than any strictly economic or other benefit.

The Arab view of these matters, however, is markedly different. Even in countries that have made their peace with Israel, like Egypt and Jordan, there is a widely held view amongst intellectuals that peace with Israel is essentially an admission of historical defeat. Moreover, this is not simply a setback within the narrow confines of a territorial dispute, but yet another and even more resounding defeat in the cultural and civilizational conflict in which the Muslim Arab Middle East has been engaged for the last two centuries with the West.

From this point of view, Israel is not a defensive enterprise of formerly oppressed Jews, but an aggressive, intrusive, domineering outpost of the West that has imposed itself on the region through the use of force in alliance with the Western powers. Israel, therefore, is not a "natural" or "normal" member state of the region, but a monument to Arab and Muslim failure to contend effectively with the challenge of Western-style modernity. Israel's quest for normalization, when addressed within this frame of mind, is seen as no more than the thin wedge of further cultural, economic and political "invasion" (*ghazw*), designed to ensure its own hegemonistic domination.

Prospects for Change

For such deep-seated attitudes to evolve and to "smooth the path to peace" it is essential for both sides to pursue an intensive social and intellectual interaction. A mutual learning process should be set in motion in order to break down conceptual barriers and pave the way for a political and cultural acceptance that goes beyond the purely pragmatic acquiescence in the collective existence of the "other." The role of the media and the educational systems are obviously crucial in the creation of mutual images. Yet perhaps even more important is the role of intellectuals in the promotion of empathy for the respective perceptions of history, communal identity, and cultural preference.

This, however, is easier said than done. Precisely those who should play the key role in this mutual learning process and in the transmission to their respective societies of a more empathetic perception of the former enemy, the intellectuals – the writers, academics and professionals – are, in the Arab world, the most reluctant to do so. The intellectuals, as pillars of the educated elite, have been for decades the standard bearers, guardians and articulators of Arabism or Islamism, as an essential component of the political and cultural confrontation with the West. It is they more than others who for generations have internalized and disseminated the vision of the conflict with Israel as a clash of cultures and civilizations and who have consequently presented the notion of normalization with Israel as a symbol of defeat. It is these images of struggle that rest in the minds of Arab intellectuals who make the historical reconciliation with Israel such a difficult undertaking for the societies in which they set the agenda of public discourse.

Israelis would do well to bear these realities in mind when pressing for normalization. Such pressure is often misunderstood as encroachment on the Arab collective identity. Equally, Arabs would do well to bear in mind that what motivates Israelis more than anything else is their need for the preservation and the acceptance of their own collective identity rather than regional domination.

One can only hope that an extended period of political and pragmatic coexistence will itself, with time, erode the mutual fears of domination and loss of identity and pave the way for the development of empathy essential to conflict resolution and peace.

9

The Role of People in Building Peace

Fredrik Barth and Unni Wikan

The overwhelming emphasis and attention in the Israeli-Palestinian peace process so far has been on the channels and strategies of negotiation between empowered political representatives among the surrounding states and, to some extent, among other established factions and interest groups in the affected societies. No doubt, the establishment of high-level direct negotiations between Israelis and Palestinians has been most crucial during the first stages of opening any form of intelligent communication at all between the two sides. But as the process moves on, the connection between progress on the higher levels of negotiation and the changing understandings and support of the broader populations that form the constituencies of the negotiators, becomes increasingly important.

Smoothing the way toward peace, then, can no longer focus narrowly on facilitating negotiations at the highest levels only and relying on a top-down vision of the political process whereby the negotiated agreements, or the negotiators themselves, are presented to the public through an electoral process. An active promotion of peace must also aim at the broadest popular level: laying the foundations for greater support for peaceful forms of coexistence and promoting the attitudes, communication links, social relations, and organizational tools among ordinary people so as to create the conditions for peace and give impetus and broad support to the achievements of peace negotiators.

In order to explore these popular bases for peace, we must adopt the more humble approach of anthropology, by which we look not to states, or economies, or international negotiations, but to ordinary people and the way things seem to them. On the basis of the understanding that this view can give us, we can then try to design, and put into effect, situations in which people's active engagement in the peace process is facilitated: either by changing their understandings and attitudes, or especially by enticing them to develop a personal stake in the peace process – both the securing and expansion of peace – through particular activities and engagements that they themselves desire and are able to pursue.

On the first item of changing people's attitudes, this sets a far larger agenda than simply looking to distribute information and propaganda to voters. Much more creatively, it can be promoted by creating arenas – occasions, meetings, and interactions – where people *experience* something new and positive that will affect their subsequent views. With regard to their developing a personal stake, it is of course true that the public is already looking to the peace process and trying to see and judge how it may affect them – mainly in terms of security, but also in terms of what it may imply for economic improvements or hardships. The additional contribution of the anthropological approach would be to ask how people can be encouraged to increase their commitment to the goal of peace: by *investing individually* in various activities, enterprises, or relationships that give them a greater stake in continued and expanded peace. In other words, these would be processes whereby people's material and social interests in the peace process are enhanced by investments that they themselves choose to make and that depend on continued peace for their value and success.

The political gains of such processes would be that they effect a certain decentralization and *devolution* of the peace process itself. The initiatives do not all remain with the political negotiators, who are constrained in their moves by the need to mobilize organized political parties and public opinion and, in the last instance, voters. If a greater degree of decentralization could be achieved, then some of the initiative would pass down directly to ordinary people, who through their own acts and choices could build new, individual stakes in peace and thus, by small increments, build the foundations for peace by shifting the options and the political support for these options in public opinion.

Changing People's Attitudes

The critical issues here are how to humanize the enemy, counteract gross stereotypes, and create space and tolerance for a greater diversity of social relationships, and thereby also for an enhanced diversity of opinions and practices in one's social environment. This will be promoted by all forms of social contact that increase mutual communication and familiarity, particularly in settings where an expanded range of topics are addressed, and specific conflicting or tabooed subjects are aired. Most directly relevant to peace between peoples are the conversations that bridge the division between those peoples. We understand that there is already an instituted pattern in Israel whereby dialogue groups are created among circles of Jews and Arabs, who meet once a month or so and telephone each other as they see fit. The social processes that are accordingly set into motion must be of fundamental importance. It should be a high priority to find ways in which to increase the number of such groups, and to ensure that they criss-cross the current separation between Israeli and Palestinian territory.

Somewhat similar devices can also be of great importance for bridging factional and ideological differences within one's own group. Quaker congregations in US, for example, use institutionalized "question groups" when a member is facing difficult life decisions, in which a small group of sympathetic equals visits the person, asks questions, and listens to his or her reflections, but without offering advice or drawing conclusions. The effect is often to give the person a broader and deeper grasp of his/her situation and options. Recently, in response to the deep public divisions over attitudes toward homosexuality, this device has been developed into a "listening project" by liberal-minded couples who visit more conservative or fundamentalist opinion leaders and elicit their reflections, without entering into debate with them. The result seems to be the expression and subsequent adoption of considerably more nuanced and complex positions than those that had previously been expressed – both on the part of the conservatively entrenched person, and his/her liberal-minded interlocutors. As a method of combating fundamentalism in one's own group and improving the subtlety of internal discussions, devices like this may have a considerable potential.

However, it is clearly also important that people of good will are heard within their own group in *public* debate, engaging spokesmen of other factions in serious analytical discussions rather than simplistic confrontation or dismissal, acrimony or avoidance. Academics and intellectuals among both Israelis and Palestinians have a special role and responsibility in this respect: to speak out against the fanatical rhetoric that otherwise may easily dominate public discourse. The broader public is in need of articulated counter-arguments to such simplicities and confrontation, and these are far more effective when spoken by someone within one's own group than by spokesmen from the other side.

There is much rhetoric spewing forth from the various extremist wings, and recognized scholars and intellectuals can claim a certain authority and stature that gives them public influence in such matters of conflict. We need to consider ways by which to increase the sense of moral obligation among intellectuals in both groups to make their voice be heard in public, and we need to consider the various possible arenas for this kind of public speaking, like the teach-ins of American universities in the 1960s.

There are, of course, real costs in taking a public stand on these issues: the risks of social ostracism and of sudden violence at any time, and the risk of total disaster if the political situation changes. What might constitute counterbalancing benefits to the individuals who come out in public and thereby take these risks? How can such benefits be enhanced so as to make public acts of rapprochement more attractive in terms of the trade-offs that are involved? There are already brave people who choose to make their views public, despite the risks. But the number of persons who might be willing to do it, and who might thereby create a snowballing effect that changes the entire public climate, would be enhanced if factors could be introduced that would positively change the balance of these trade-offs.

Developing a Personal Stake

The other way to change attitudes and to involve people in action that promotes peace is to create situations in which people make growing material and social investments that give them a stake in the condition of peace. The fields for such investment may be purely economic, or they may be organizational, social, and symbolic.

Every form of economic entrepreneurship that crosses the national borders creates links that will increase the interests in maintaining the peace among those involved in the enterprise. Professor Gilbar notes a very good example of such entrepreneurship: the potential for Palestinian-Israeli cooperation in the field of international tourism. Here a growing market for joint services could be created, and the profits and livelihoods derived from such activity would represent, for those involved, a heavy stake in maintaining a situation that would allow the flow of tourism to continue, namely peace and order with regard to border crossings. Such activity also has a ripple effect within a wider circle involving local deliveries and services, thereby also giving these subsidiary participants a greater stake in the maintenance of peace and cooperation.

Other forms of enterprise that link Israeli and Palestinian territories should all have a similar effect: businesses that deliver goods or services across the borders and wage laborers that depend on crossing the borders for work. So long as such interdependencies are not primarily experienced as exploitative or frustrating, they give those involved a positive stake in peace. We must look for ways of smoothing the conditions for such interdependence and securing them in order to counteract tendencies – driven by the pressures of danger and insecurity – toward an increasing disengagement between the two populations. The personal material benefits of lowered barriers in the search for better wages, lower costs, enlarged markets, and more secure benefits can all contribute to creating investments and positive commitments to peace.

In the organizational field, we must search for the optimal forms of cooperation, adjustable to the changing security situation. Labor unions and professional associations should be encouraged to develop active links to strengthen them for their own purposes; and some of these links could be expanded into the whole triangle or the whole region.

In the field of education, many forms of cooperation would be constructive and must be explored. The work presently being done to revise the constructions of history taught in Israeli and Palestinian schools is of the greatest importance. But purely social initiatives would also be valuable. Classes and schools can pair off in "friendship" links, with intervisiting and joint outings, if the security situation allows. Between advanced training schools and universities, the possibility of transfer of credits and equating of exams and licenses to practice should be established and maintained. Cooperation in scientific research, scientific meetings, visiting lectureships (from abroad and between the two units), seminars, and traineeships can be supported, possibly by bonuses or other benefits.

We have not investigated what arrangements have been made for judicial and legal functions, but one should look into such arrangements and see that they are not so cumbersome as to create excessive barriers. The possibility of free legal services for some inter-territory purposes should be explored. The field of sports is an important but ambiguous topic: on the one hand it involves large audiences and great public interest, and on the other hand, its competitive format can generate confrontation and hooliganism, rather than friendship. The possibility of joint facilities and training meets, rather than public competitions, may be explored. One should also consider the potential for other forms of cultural cooperation: performances, recitals, lectures, and exhibits. Access to religious sites and celebrations will, of course, be highly charged matters. Innovative formats for secular celebrations on historical sites might possibly serve to contain and defuse such conflicts.

A further point about all these organizational matters is that they inevitably engage some particular persons as entrepreneurs in their creation and pursuit, in ways that activate them and require an investment of prestige and work, thereby giving those persons a real stake in their success. Their organizers will have engaged themselves in the links that are created, and will have come out in public for the value of the peace that they presume. The work invested in building such organizations thus not only creates organizations that are more capable of functioning across the barriers – it also creates a cadre of organizational leaders who are committed to cooperation and to peace.

Reducing Violence

An important facet of the task of securing peace is to find ways to reduce the incidence of public violence by identifying its main social and cultural wellsprings. We may note at the outset that these activities are overwhelmingly performed by males between adolescence and early middle age, so we should direct our attention toward the particulars of the situation of such person.

Comparative global scenarios (especially Cambodia, Bosnia, Central America, Argentina, Nazi Europe) suggest two factors of importance for the practice of violence: the social and conceptual separation of perpetrator and victim, whereby the victim is depersonalized, excluded, and ideally unknown as a particular individual, and the presence of an ideology that fervently demonizes the victim population. These factors are exacerbated where there is an idle population of frustrated young men, marginalized and unemployed, who can obtain material benefits or a sense of importance and belonging by joining secret, violent organizations. Prevention should thus take three main directions:

1 Improving conditions of employment and perceptions of an achievable future for young men, particularly by giving them a realistic (but preferably reasonably resource- and energy- consuming!) path toward marriage and establishing a family. By means of comparison, our data leave little doubt that among the poorer classes in Cairo, the necessity for young men to accumulate a dowry so as to be able to marry, serves both to channel much of their activity toward a constructive purpose and also deflects them from seeking peer arenas for competitive display and gang formation.
2 Embedding male youth in the widest possible social networks of kinsfolk of all ages and both sexes tends to reduce macho displays and violence; and drawing young men into arenas where they must also mix socially with those who would be their potential victims counteracts tendencies to anonymization and demonization.
3 There is, finally, the need to be vigilant and effective against nascent centres and social circles of ideology production that justify violence. These must be counteracted, not just dismissed or

condemned as confused ramblings, since they can give shape and direction to the frustrations, energies, and need for belonging among marginal young men.

While working to establish these three conditions should be the conscious policy of all parties, their effectuation will of necessity mainly depend on persons within the group. One needs to explore their many implications and work conceptually to design practical actions suited for the particular conditions of various age and class groups of Palestinian and Israeli young men.

Reflections on Current Ideas of Ethnicity and Peace

The current conception of conflict resolution among the vast majority of Israelis and Palestinians seems to favor separation and disengagement. It would not be politically feasible to come out strongly against this current at the present moment; but, we can have justified doubts both about how persistent this mood will be as circumstances change, and about how compatible it is with the long-term goal of prosperity and peace. Although it agrees with current political moods in much of the industrialized world, in terms of public attitudes toward immigrants and minorities, it is opposed to the actual current global trend toward multicultural communities. It is also directly contrary to the deeper social traditions of multi-ethnic social formations in the Middle East. While conflict, bloodshed, and massacres have always accompanied the traditionally mixed settlements and districts of the great civilizations of Asia, it is undeniable that the whole political and social fabric, particularly of the Ottoman realm, was fundamentally based on ethnic pluralism – though much of this has been recently dismantled throughout the whole region. It is not clear, however, whether this dismantling has promoted peace or, on the contrary, war and violence in the twentieth century. Many, perhaps most, of the suggestions in these brief notes seem to plead for a curbing of the current processes of segregation and separation between Israeli and Palestinian populations, and for diverse compensatory actions to create new kinds of links and alliances. It is worth repeating that one needs to think carefully about how far such recommendations are politically feasible and practicable at this moment, and whether other means to strengthen people-to-people peace must be sought. But one cannot only think of the shorter term: one also needs to consider the question of how best to secure the long-term feasibility and security of peace between the populations and in the Middle East region as a whole.

10

Some Social and Cultural Implications of the Triangle

Uri M. Kupferschmidt

While the triangular relationship between Jordanians, Palestinians, and Israelis is the focus of this book, there is another triangle that must be discussed: the relationship between political steps, economic projects, and the building of peace in social and cultural respects. This is perhaps a rather more difficult side of the triangle to discuss.

First, the topics involved are, at least in part, more extensive, more diffuse, and more difficult to pin down. The notions of society and culture embrace a wide range of human activities and attitudes. Moreover, they involve moods, sentiments, and emotions. Second, it is more difficult to get "things from the conference table to the ground," that is, down to the people. It has been remarked that peace so far has been pragmatic rather than ideological, and more on the level of leaders than of the people. Leaders can create a modus of mutual understanding among themselves, decide on certain strategic and political steps, and even carry them out, as well as initiate economic projects. However, in the long run, the peace process cannot be sustained if there is no broader support from among the lower strata of public opinion. Hesitations, doubts, second thoughts, and in general a lack of confidence or understanding may seriously hamper any further progress toward a normalization of relations between once antagonistic populations. Several commentators have dwelt on the urgent need to distribute the dividends of the peace process to "the people," but here, it would seem, is an area where massive investments are still needed before the first dividends can be reaped.

The question of how to go about this must be preceded by a careful scrutinization of our expectations, and of the objective possibilities and limitations. Although by now I have lived most of my life in Israel, I cannot ignore the historical and political record of Western Europe where I grew up. Indeed, several colleagues, particularly our German friends at the conference, have alluded to the European experience. One participant has sought comparisons with peacemaking processes in Ireland (and, indeed, South Africa). As I see it, that continent, which has gone through so many wars, even in the immediate past, is still searching for the right formulas to subdue former animosities. Workable forms of equilibrium may be found in a less rigid, more pluralist type of nation state. There is hardly a state in Europe today with one monolithic culture, one social ideology, and one exclusive national language; divisions flow over from one state to another. Regionally, the desired solutions involve smaller cultural, linguistic and ethnic units, but larger frameworks of economic cooperation, integration, and unification. Even within the much heralded peaceful Benelux, which is nowadays cited as a model of peaceful coexistence, there was a war going on still in 1830, and not all mutual prejudices have been eliminated. The behavior of the spectators at international soccer matches – not only between the Netherlands and Belgium, but even more so between the Netherlands and erstwhile enemy Germany – shows how high latent nationalist feelings can still rise.

It is important to realize in this respect that even in a peaceful regional system of international relations, certain old feelings may persist. This is a social and cultural limitation which we also have to bear in mind for our future in the Middle East. But, of course, even such a state of affairs, yet to be achieved in this region, is much better than that of the past, and its drawbacks can be reasonably coped with, controlled, and stabilized.

It is particularly with regard to the social and cultural topics that the importance of devolution has been emphasized. It has even been suggested that states, as such, have been, or still are, obstacles, rather than helpful instruments, in furthering what has been called a people-to-people peace. What is meant is that leaders and (all) state-systems have often constrained – and in some cases even strangled – the legal and practical options of private initiative on the peace scene. Indeed, it would appear to me that we must distinguish between the differential roles which governments and peoples can play.

King Hussein, and before him Egyptian President Sadat, have masterfully played on Israeli public opinion; so far, Syrian President Asad's coolness has achieved exactly the opposite. The impact of their direct addresses to an Israeli audience may have been limited and short-lived, but at critical moments they could forge a change in public opinion. No doubt, academics, educators, writers, artists, or professionals in general, can contribute a lot by further developing relations with their counterparts across the borders. Of course, possibilities are not limited to "intellectuals" alone. However, two preconditions have to be met: The reality of our area is, for better or for worse, that in most cases governments either have to give an initial signal or have to emphatically endorse and encourage the process.

In addition, a healthy measure of interest must evolve in the other's culture and society, which cannot exist as long as the other is dehumanized, or even despised. Such understanding and appreciation cannot develop without free and open contacts. Political circumstances, moreover, may temporarily widen or narrow the scope of interest. Following the assassination of the Israeli Prime Minister Rabin, one could discern in some Arab quarters a genuine, deeper interest in the motives behind it, and therefore in Israeli society at large. The explanation possibly lies in the fact that the dramatic event affected joint hopes and aspirations. The subsequent change of elected government in Israel- and a *de facto* change in peace policies – has since then led to a decline in real curiosity again.

The triangles discussed are not symmetrical in their political and economic aspects, and even less so in their cultural respects. This is a major problem to overcome. Considering the three peoples – Jordanians, Palestinians and Israelis – there appears to be, at least at first glance, a diadic rather than a triadic relationship. Distinctions between Jordanian and Palestinian cultures, whatever degree of crystallization we assume to exist, remain "strange" for many Israelis in that both belong to the larger orbit of Arab-Muslim civilization. Certain political and ideological Arab emphases, more so in the past than in the present, have blurred delicate local and regional cultural particularities. In the modern era, no culture is a closed, "pure," untouched world unto itself.

Similarly, language and religion form a divide with Israeli culture, the Western character of which is often exaggerated. But here too, the existence of a distinct Israeli culture has, over the years, domestically been the object of much debate and controversy. Interpretations have ranged from an overemphasis on "Ashkenazi" attitudes and tastes to a more "Mediterranean" mixture (or "Levantine" in its pejorative form). Deeper investigation into the latter may yield only few genuine, concrete expressions which can be pinned down, and many of these are of a global nature. There may be something to commending this interpretation as an ideal conceptual framework.

Moreover, we have to pay attention to two important subgroups that could play a role in creating broader common ground: first, those who used to be called Israeli Arabs, or who are nowadays more appropriately called Palestinian Israelis, and who have always been seen as a potential bridge to peace with the Arab world; and second, the large segment of Israeli Jews with roots in Oriental-Muslim communities and cultures.

Music may be a good medium. Israeli singer Ofra Haza is popular with Palestinian audiences, and her colleague Zehava Benn has been invited to perform Umm Kulthum's songs in Gaza. Even if an invitation to the former to perform in Yemen has not yet materialized, just the raising of the possibility itself is a significant development.

Indeed, I would argue that, in general, sheer cultural curiosity in the other's culture is an important new departure. In this respect, the live television appearances of the Jordanian comic duo Hisham & Nabil in Israel deserve some mention. One may wonder about the meaning of this interest inside Israel – it may be the fact that their technique of satire moves a familiar string; it may also be the fact that personalities on both sides of the line are equally lampooned. A Jordanian pop group has also performed in Israel; here too it seems that the starting point of success lies in a sort of globalized culture.

The Oriental-Jewish population is all the more interesting because it has shifted its position, in the course of the "conflict," away from its Islamicate heritage toward what is problematically defined as the Israeli-Jewish standard culture. But there are also some signs of an opposite swing of the pendulum, which makes this discussion even more complex. Given the large segment of the Israeli population that is of Moroccan origin, it would sometimes seem that many of them are not politically in support of the peace process as it was conceived by the Rabin–Peres government. Paradoxically, however, they feel closer to Islamicate than to European culture and tastes.

Obviously, and inevitably from a territorial point of view, there have been manifold mutual Arab-Jewish influences in the past. Some decades ago, anthropologists spoke about acculturation processes in our region, but we have come to understand that these have often been reflections of political or economic power. In fact, we are aware of the strong fears which continue to exist today in the Arab and Muslim worlds of cultural (and economic) domination by Israel.

This should not divert our attention from certain healthy aspects of cultural emulation that have occurred in the past, and which in themselves may recur in a positive sense in the future. We should remind ourselves that the early Zionist settlers at the beginning of the twentieth century, in a sort of romanticist phase, consciously borrowed from the larger Arab environment: Some adopted items of Arab dress or emulated Arab styles of architecture and furniture, while others composed songs in Arab metre. Even today, it is difficult to convince many an Israeli that humus and falafel are not their own authentic, national dishes. With open borders, tourism, and other direct contacts, we may see another phase of Arab impact on the Israeli cultural scene, simply because emulation will become legitimate again.

We can also think of influences coming from the Israeli side, as indeed already abundantly exist on the Palestinian scene. Modes of dress, housing, leisure activities, not to speak of certain aspects of political culture – whether seen as "Zionist" or Western – are cases in point. Here too we have to distinguish between spontaneous and state-directed activities, between what can be done from below and what must be done from above. It is especially in the educational field that room has to be consciously created for the other, that is, respect and appreciation for Arab culture has to be instilled, and vice versa.

The need for a very thorough revision of the contents of school books came up, time and again, during the conference. New textbooks for such fields as history, geography, literature, and folklore have to be devised, and erstwhile prejudices have to be eliminated. This is a typical task for academics, educators, and writers, as well as a welcome field of cooperation. Some encouraging projects are indeed already underway on both sides of the cultural divide. None of us – Jordanians, Palestinians, or Israelis – can claim to be exempt from the need for thorough self-scrutiny. Israel, on its part, will have to make more room than thus far for the learning of Arabic, the dominant language of the region, as well as for the proper teaching and understanding of Arab and Islamic culture in the widest sense of the term.

One often tends to forget that there have been not a few places and periods in which Jews and Muslims have lived peacefully side by side, in fruitful economic, if not social, interaction. True, there are instances of tension and antagonism too, but the positive episodes deserve renewed study and emphasis. The Golden Age of Andalus is only one example of many more. Even Hebron may serve as a case in point: It is relatively simple for Israelis and Palestinians alike to relate massacres of the past, but it may be more helpful to retrieve and better understand the record of centuries of coexistence. More can be done to identify common denominators and to actively look for like-minded points of interest or cultural similarities. There are, indeed, ample similarities in the realms of Judaism and Islam as civilizations.

In Israel, school curricula devote a fairly large share of time to the meaning of its own religious and national festivals. Festivals figure high on social agendas in general. But, in fact, there is at present not one single religious or secular festival celebrated by Jordanians or Palestinians which can be adapted to serve as a joint, synchronous festival with the Israelis. Maybe such an option should be created from above. It could be found in May Day, which is an official holiday in most

Arab countries, but which has recently been discarded as a proletarian anachronism in Israel. Possibly, it could be given new meaning as a day to celebrate the achievements of the peace process in the Middle East. An alternative suggestion, put forward at the conference, was to lend such a meaning to *Arbor Day* in Jordan, which has a parallel in the *Tu biShevat* festival in Israel. The latter, however, is defined by the *Mishna* in religious terms as the New Year of the Trees, which could make a change of meaning more controversial. In theory, also, the Egyptian festival of Shamm Al-Nasim, or the Moroccan-Jewish *Mimuna,* could be mobilized for this purpose. As popular spring festivals with outings for the entire family, they have their parallels under various names in the entire region. It really does not matter which day can be made free for this purpose. What is important is that educators, as well as intellectuals and politicians throughout the region, create an opportunity to simultaneously address all issues of peace and mutual understanding.

Participants at the conference were careful not to bring up the most controversial issues of religion, although all sensed that they would not and should not be totally ignored. It is the hope of all that liberal education will contribute its share toward the smoothing of the most virulent forms of fundamentalism. It is necessary to show that all religions in the region know a wide variety of shades of experience and interpretation, ranging from ultra-orthodoxy to mysticism and to libertarianism. All possess radical and militant manifestations, but equally all share tolerant and non-bigoted attitudes toward society at large.

Here too, it is easy to forget that for centuries there have been holy tombs and holy men, especially in this very area, who have been the object of popular religious worship. Often the same places were revered by adherents of different religions, and common people of one denomination sought relief for their personal predicaments with holy men of the other's system of worship. I am not saying that we should engineer a wholesale revival of such phenomena, or enhance a renewed type of popular religion, or even that as a policy this would be feasible at all. In any case, such phenomena continue to (co-)exist abundantly in the region. There would be some benefit in it if Israeli spiritual leaders would indicate their awareness that the Patriarch's Tombs in Hebron, Joseph's Tomb near Nablus, or Rachel's Tomb near Bethlehem, have a strong meaning for Muslims as well. Something similar could also be advised to the other side. This is an important didactic aspect to bear in mind – one which may be of avail in emphasizing the idea that religions are not necessarily as divisive as orthodox leaders and politicians have sometimes manipulated them to be. Even the undertaking and publicizing of more studies on such cross-religious phenomena in the past and the present can serve a useful purpose.

This brings me to the issue of developing deference for the other's culture, or "humanizing" the other, which was brought up frequently at the conference. In addition to our educational systems, mention must be made of the actual and potential role of the mass media. The mass media have in the past often played a destructive role and have, under different degrees of guidance by states and leaders, demonized rather than humanized erstwhile enemies. Stereotypes, prejudices, and unsavory caricatures – deviating from a certain standard of legitimate and healthy satire and ridicule – can only flourish in a climate of ignorance and alienation.

But mass media, and in particular television, more than any other means, are also capable of translating the peace process into visible realities. Potentially at least, television can also relay the day-to-day difficulties encountered and make them discussible and understandable. Television may be a window to the other's society, as well as a mirror for understanding one's own.

Many people in Israel watch programs on Jordanian television, ranging from movies to the news. Jordanians and Palestinians may likewise tune into Israeli channels. There is, in my view, an urgent need to bring the day-to-day realities of the Palestinians onto the screen of a wider Israeli population of spectators. I remember an interview with a Palestinian waiter, once employed in Tel Aviv and since working at a beach cafe in Gaza, enthusiastically inviting his former customers to come to Gaza, in fluent Hebrew. While perhaps unrealistic at the present time, this sort of attitude is just what is required for a people-to-people peace.

In this respect, the expansion of a Palestinian television broadcasting system is an urgent domestic requirement. Subscribers to the Israeli cable networks should have the option to receive Palestinian television programs, as they can currently do with Egyptian, Moroccan, and Turkish stations. News or talk shows may bore some and interest others. But the transmission of standard fare soap operas, cartoons, and even commercials will nevertheless be a positive humanizing gain.

A more ambitious proposal would be the initiation of a regional television peace channel. After all, currently in Israel one can watch a cultural channel as well as a Lebanese station with missionary overtones. Resources would be a major problem, of course. However, the idea should not be dismissed out of hand, for the production of a joint Israeli-Palestinian version of the popular children's programs Sesame Street is already underway.

But present-day technology offers even more options, such as working with three or more regional interlocking studio facilities (including Egypt). In terms of programming, any peace-related issue, both in terms of the achievements and the problems of peace, could be raised, with a clear preference for dialogue and comparison. Even the possibility of involving the various academic schools and departments of journalism deserves consideration. This would make peace relations an educational experience for the younger generation, as well as one in real time. At least one such distant learning project, focusing on the benefits of tourism and cultural exchanges in the Mediterranean, is already operative, jointly managed by universities in Marseille, Bethlehem, and Beer-Sheva. The possibilities of the Internet era with regard to the peace process has still to be explored

Finally, I would also like to say something on the point of fraternization which has been raised at the conference. For the time being, we should try not to reach too high. A conference such as this has been a wonderful and very rewarding experience, but one held under particularly artificial and sterile conditions. No doubt, many personal friendships and forms of academic cooperation are in full swing. Some of these friendships may be fairly recent, as a result of the breakthrough since Oslo; others date back longer. However, the experience of the last few years has shown that the will to meet, to socialize, and to exchange opinions is often stronger than the reality on the ground. This is to be regretted, but it is a fact nevertheless. On the purely political level, deceptions and setbacks may hinder academic establishments; potential physical dangers may prevent people from traveling across borders; and temporary closures and other security rulings may make face-to-face meetings impossible altogether. Thus, while scholarly conferences, mutual visits by school classes, exhibitions and other exchanges have already taken place on a limited scale, these will become a critical mass only when the general political climate allows.

With an eye to the future, some word is in place on the *mahasim* (the Arabic plural of the Hebrew word *mahsom* for barrier – an interesting linguistic neologism in itself) which have been mentioned frequently by our Palestinian friends. Indeed, only government orders can remove bureaucratic obstacles and facilitate easier access. But this divide also works the other way around. May I remind readers that in the 1970s we Israelis moved about freely – true, often in a too euphoric mood – in the West Bank and the Gaza Strip. In fact, I then lived in Jerusalem, and few weeks passed without some visit to the West Bank. Many hours were spent sightseeing, talking and shopping at *bazaars*, or enjoying meals. All guests from abroad could be taken on a relaxing excursion to Bethlehem or Jericho or elsewhere. The *Intifada*, however, put an end to all that. One should hope for a restoration of the pre-*Intifada* period as far as this aspect is concerned and as far as immediate, spontaneous personal contacts are concerned.

We all realize that popular tourism, if correctly and respectfully conducted, has an eminently educative role to play. Many Israelis who have already visited Jordan have been pleasantly surprised and have even revised their previous stereotypes, and this may translate into a more positive attitude toward the peace process.

April 1997 I took a renewed look at a pamphlet dating back to my student days, called *The Middle East in the Year 2000*, published by an otherwise unknown Association for Peace in Tel Aviv in 1968. Subtitled *Beyond the Frontiers of Time*, it carries chapters on free and rapid communication, educational networks superseding defence, cooperation in health, agriculture, desert reclamation, and tourism – in short, a completely utopian, if not surrealistic, publication at the time. The Israeli side in the Casablanca and Amman Economic Summit conferences of 1995 and 1996 published a bulky brochure (entitled *Development for Cooperation: The Middle East/East Mediterranean Region*), which comprises numerous economic projects, but also some social and cultural targets. Comparing the above two publications today, many of the objectives mentioned still appear to be remote, but they are definitely not as unrealistic as in the past.

11

The Cultural and Social Situation and the Peace Process

Musallam Abu-Helu

Despite the fact that the Israeli-Arab conflict has been marked by primarily military and political aspects, and although the economic side has also manifested such conflict, the most important aspect which requires evaluation of its contents and dimensions is that of cultural and social peace. Since 1948, the Arab-Israeli conflict has resulted in a new social and cultural situation which has affected and will continue to affect the overall situation. This has a strong and immediate influence on the overall peace process. The conflict also involves economic aspects, represented in competition over resources and changes in investment strategies and methods.

Therefore, it is vital to concentrate upon the following related aspects and how they can be seen as a unit:

1 The social and cultural issues that should be addressed.
2 What do such issues include in terms of the triangular dimensions?
3 What relations exist between the present social context and the economic and political context?
4 What steps could be followed with regard to the possibility of implementing and forecasting their effects?

It is not possible here to present a comprehensive view about past results of the social factor on the above-mentioned dimensions. Therefore, I will concentrate on the key issues which have had a clear effect on the peace process and may still exert a negative impact in the future:

1 The educational dimension and its social results.
2 General freedom rights and the *de facto* policy.
3 A comprehensive view of the social and cultural context.
4 Social equality.

The Educational Dimension and its Social Results

Here the focus is on the present educational system, both formal and informal, in addition to its content, philosophy, curriculum, methods, and effects. It is critical to evaluate how close such systems are in terms of forming individual attitudes and behaviors. The problem is not only how to present a unified strategy, but also how to achieve such a strategy. It is worthwhile to mention the importance of education during the previous decades. Just as an individual will not easily forget what he has learned, it is likewise vital to prepare an atmosphere which strengthens credibility in mutual dealings. Considering the differences in the educational systems, it is difficult to achieve our goals.

This can be considered as one of the most complicated issues requiring analysis. For instance, despite the similarities between the philosophies of education in Jordan and Egypt, there are discrepancies in the effects of the implementation of both philosophies in the West Bank (Jordanian education) and the Gaza Strip (Egyptian education). The process involves more than that. How can we control the educational content presented in the minds of the public?

General Freedom Rights and the *De Facto* Policy

All peoples and societies aspire to reach a certain level of democracy. This may be reflected in the selection of their representatives and the capacity of these representatives in proposing laws. Many factions within Palestinian society, if not all of them, reject what the Israeli or even the international laws – at least those related to their citizenship – state in regard to general freedoms. This is due to the fact that such laws are not clear enough, thereby allowing for the possibility of being interpreted against the Palestinians and being implemented unjustly. Denial of these freedoms will cause the individual to be deprived of many rights, such as: self-determination, repatriation, ownership, citizenship, and democracy (free expression of speech). The individual finds himself obliged to accept the *de facto* situation or to justify the fact of being told that he would misuse these rights if they were given to him. But, is the solution to deprive him of such rights and until when?

A Comprehensive View of the Social and Cultural Context

The policy of arranging issues according to priority does not conflict with solving the problems of social and cultural context. However, what is being done, prepared for, or declared about the delay in starting or planning for it on the cultural or social level is one of the most important issues. I mean by this the issues of refugee and forced deportees, which have been and are still key issues of conflict. I believe that no active atmosphere for cooperation among peoples in the area or between Israel and its neighbors (especially those who are hosts of refugees) will be achieved without the solution of such issues.

So, how can an atmosphere of interaction be created between more than half of the Palestinian people and the Israelis while the Palestinians find themselves obliged to accept the *de facto* situation and those who deal with them are depriving them of their rights? This is not acceptable to the supporters of peace.

Even locally, such a situation will not be helpful for interaction in a society in which one party has been wronged (i.e. refugees). The refugees in the West Bank and the Gaza Strip have similar views as those outside the country; and this is clear from their refusal of relocating in any way.

Social Equality

Providing conditions and facilities to secure interaction is one of the factors affecting social interaction. Likewise, that of providing complementary levels in living standards, income, education, and culture (which is basic and described as the first issue). Here, we find distinctive differences between Israeli society and other societies. The Palestinians prefer and aspire to be treated similarly, for they are a people with land, culture, rights, and a representative. That is to say, most of them look forward to the day when Israelis change their view toward them (such as describing them as terrorists, killers, and undeveloped). This can be seen and heard throughout the media, as well as read in books and literature about Palestinians. This is also true for Israelis who are described as occupiers, criminals, etc. In view of the above, educational, social and cultural establishments should be encouraged and supported. Furthermore, the citizens should be helped to develop their lives and achieve some sort of comfort and security. The bridges of trust and cooperation should be built toward joint institutions and establishments. In such a situation and environment, peace will be not only real but true.

What Can Be Done?

Although our talk will generally deal with the social and cultural content of the triangle in order to see the cultural and social obstacles facing the peace process, the major aim of the conference, in this regard, was to propose strategies that will contribute to overcoming such obstacles and ensure that making and practising peace is the responsibility of those concerned. Discussion of the problems facing the peace process and hindering its execution is no more than an approach to determining the importance and priority of such obstacles by first acknowledging their content and dimensions.

The next step can be summed up in unifying the different views concerning these obstacles in terms of defining, studying, analyzing and evaluating their effects by proposing practical solutions. Despite the importance of the general talk at this stage, it will not be enough, and more precise and deeper steps must be taken so as to get the peace process off the ground from the conference table. It is not easy to handle all social, economic and political aspects at the same time; it is necessary to separate them and deal with them separately. Thus there is much to be done, not only with respect to the cultural and social sides, but also to the political and economic ones.

In order to understand more about the obstacles facing the peace process, and to determine them precisely and take practical steps based on such insights, two approaches can be taken. First, by organizing workshops and preparing studies regularly on the most important issues proposed, with the contribution of specialists from all parties, in order to arrive at a joint understanding and solutions of these obstacles. Here, I present some of the important issues that require further study. Second, workshops, studies, and seminars should be formal (i.e. all concerned parties should be informed about decisions being made so that they will be committed to the results).

The peace-making process, especially a comprehensive peace, is difficult and requires much effort, expense, and time. As for effort, it exceeds the personal efforts of the society, the state, and the whole international community. With respect to time, we should be cautious. It is not important just to sign an agreement or treaty, but to see that what was signed becomes real, not only for those involved in making it but for everyone concerned and represented. In other words, to see that decisions and agreements have become agreements between peoples and not between rulers. Before we judge any agreement with respect to content, success or failure, we should be sure of its contribution to all the groups in the society as well as their interest in its success. As for expenses (whether material or not), despite the fact that it is not difficult to calculate the material expenses these studies require, compared with the difficulties encountered when calculating immaterial expenses, we still need some creditable criteria to determine costs because of the large differences held by the parties regarding their relative importance.

Thus, when we see that the way to peace is long, difficult and expensive, and that the peace process is an accumulated product of successive efforts in various spheres of life (namely, social, economic, and political), and that the peace desired is a function of the interaction and cooperation among individuals and groups, not only between governments and leaders, we recognize that putting forward issues affecting peace for discussion among the various sectors of society will be of great value for achieving a more accurate understanding of such issues, provided that this takes place in a complementary way under the auspices of specialized establishments whose ultimate aim is to support the peace process more than to emphasize the propaganda aspect.

Finally, there are many issues which need to be studied in order to create a base that might be used for moving to practical and executive stages in the working for peace. Besides what has been mentioned earlier concerning the social situation, it would be beneficial to investigate the following topics:

1 The role individuals might play in designing the suitable way to peace, and how it could be achieved.
2 The effect of the culture, habits, and social form of people as important factors in determining the way to peace, rather than just the reaction of a people or group with respect to the decisions arrived at by decision makers.
3 Not only must success factors be studied, but also failures must be studied, especially where the future involves entrenched, hostile attitudes.

Economically, there are important issues to be considered when talking about the present situation and the economic future of the area in a situation of peace. And this despite the great optimism indicated through the mass media and political circles. It is true that peace creates cooperation and vice versa. However, matters of independence, authority, and equality remain important issues which can determine the level and steps of this cooperation. This is because such matters are looked at differently by the various parties as a result of difficult economic systems and their strategies, demand and product means, as well as other influences. It is not sufficient, according to experience, to propose outlines for cooperation in a certain field before tackling in depth the possible obstacles. If this is not done, any particular proposal might generate an adverse situation, with more negative effects than what was originally the case.

Economic affluence and what it brings about, such as a substantial increase in per capita income and more flexibility of capital and product transfer, will surely have a great effect on paving the way to peace provided that it will not devalue the other aspects mentioned above (i.e. independence, supremacy, and equality). For example, Jordan has experienced various stages of economic growth, followed by other stages which were not as successful. The political factors, and possibly the social ones, were major reasons affecting the economic direction, and thus led to instability in the investment sphere. In contrast to the economic content of the parties involved are the social, demographic and cultural spheres, which are based on compete and well-revised criteria. Thus, analytical studies on a micro level are essential. This will help us to understand the real situation accurately and draw credit where deserved, and is thus a practical step toward peaceful cooperation.

Planning and constructing joint projects will contribute to preparing an atmosphere of cooperation and peace between parties. However, such projects will remain partial and gradual if political, social, and cultural aspects are not taken into consideration. Over the last 30 years, more than 40 percent of the labor force in the West Bank and the Gaza Strip have worked in Israel. That has now changed through a political decision based on a social, political and cultural situation; the percentage of workers has been drastically curtailed. As a result, this impinges on policies in other areas.

Therefore, let us rethink many times in order to specify the problems and obstacles that we might face. Cooperation in every field should lead to equality and remove imposed attitudes. We should choose areas of economic cooperation which strengthen social and political ties. Above all, we must stay optimistic: pointing out the dangers does not necessarily indicate pessimism.

Part III

The Economic Factor of the Peace Process

12

Regional Economic Cooperation in the Middle East: Prospects and Problems

Mary E. Morris

The peace process that began in Madrid in 1991 and that was given impetus by the Oslo agreements of 1993 and 1995 presents the Middle East with opportunities for unparalleled change in political, economic, and social arenas. Yet the strategic visions that are currently being constructed cannot be divorced from historical experience. The lessons of the past, if learned, can provide the means for developing a bright future. If unheeded, they can provide a stumbling block to solution of both immediate problems and long-term challenges.

This chapter surveys past approaches to Middle East economic issues and discusses current challenges and opportunities in light of the ongoing peace process. It looks at both barriers and incentives to economic development and examines the relationship between politics and economic progress, with particular focus on the triangle.

A Look at the Past

For decades the economic development of the Middle East has been held hostage to political considerations. Political energy and economic resources were spent on regional conflicts and rivalries at the expense of economic development. Oil wealth was channeled into activities with high payoffs for elites, but with low social returns. Labor distortions designed to help the disadvantaged resulted in underuse of investments in human capital, while the region's natural resources fueled the process. The peace process, however, has reduced the region's political risks and created the opportunity for establishing economic stability by rationalizing economic decisions and encouraging basic economic reforms. Countries in the Middle East, pressured by domestic demands for reform and attention to elemental human needs, are in the process of economic liberalization and gaining access to global markets through cross-regional associations.[1]

Beginning in the early 1960s, Arab countries embarked on a series of ambitious economic development projects, mobilizing resources and injecting large amounts of capital into their programs. However, they were unable to develop economies that could compete with the economies of newly-emerging industrialized states. The collapse in oil prices of the mid-1980s, combined with deteriorating productivity, also made it difficult to sustain a reasonable economic growth rate – and, in fact, produced an economic crisis. Real per capita incomes have fallen by an average of 2 percent annually since 1986, while both investment and productivity took sharp dives.

Although the Middle East is primarily agriculture-based, economic policies of past decades stressed the development of industrial and service sectors. Negligence of the agricultural sector led to a continuous wave of rural–urban migration, which industrial and service sectors were unable to absorb and which overstretched national budgets with the burden of coping with problems of over-urbanization. Firms adopted capital-intensive technologies, despite the need to create a large number of work opportunities for a growing population.

During the 1960s, many Arab countries began to nationalize private companies and impose rigid state controls. This was done in the belief that the public sector was the appropriate mechanism for mobilizing resources and distributing them to the public. Profitability is not the overriding concern of public social institutions; thus, motivation and initiative were frustrated by public companies' conduct of business as essentially governmental organs. Despite their inefficiency, these companies continued in business, since their clients were either local markets or East European markets, where business was conducted under barter or "contra-deal" arrangements.[2]

State-owned enterprises were effective, however, at generating growth in an era of mass production and relatively little competition, while large oil and other rents meant that non-oil exports and international competitiveness were not a priority. Indigenous private sectors were small and did not constitute a major growth engine.[3] Both foreign investments and intra-Arab capital flows were discouraged by the predominance of the public sector in economic activities. Arab capital, instead, flowed to industrialized countries where there was a certainty of profit. Ibrahim Oweiss has identified three distinct economic groupings of states in the Middle East:[4]

(1) *Low income states*, such as Yemen, Sudan, Mauritania, Djibouti, and Somalia, where life expectancy at birth is less than 52 years and adult illiteracy rates range between 60 and 81 percent. Per capita income in these countries averages $500.[5] In addition, these countries suffer from low labor force productivity, malnourishment, widespread poverty, famine, diseases and epidemics, poor health conditions, scarce financial and natural resources, crude technology, lack of training and research facilities, and the prevalence of internal upheaval.[6]

(2) *Middle income states*, such as Syria, Tunisia, Jordan, Iraq (pre-1991), Lebanon, Algeria, Egypt, and Morocco, where life expectancy is 67 years. Adult illiteracy is between 20 and 50 percent, and per capita income between $640 and $1750.[7] During the 1990s, many of these states adopted structural economic reforms and a policy of privatization and economic liberalization; however, their economies continue to face serious challenges. These include 20–25 percent unemployment, budget and balance of payments deficits, declining national revenues, severe shortages in housing, a drop in workers' remittances, and crushing foreign debt amounting to $200 billion – about one and one-half times their combined GNP (Gross National Product).

(3) *Upper income countries*, such as Kuwait, Qatar, Bahrain, the United Arab Emirates, Saudi Arabia, Oman and Libya, rely upon oil export as the primary revenue. The main challenge for these rich states is how to adjust their budgets to correspond with the fluctuations in the price of oil.

In the view of many analysts, the prospects for Arab economies in the 1990s are not promising unless and until old patterns are broken. The low-income group will have no way to escape the "vicious circle of poverty" and famine if internal factional disputes and wars continue; countries in the middle-income group are riddled by economic problems that are difficult to solve in the short run; and the upper-income group faces economic uncertainties in view of oil price fluctuations.[8]

The vast majority of Middle Eastern countries are poor. In the past, this poverty made them dependent upon outside assistance from the two superpowers and from the oil-producing Arab states. The flow of this foreign aid was governed by the presence of mutuality of interests between donors and recipients, and the latter's rendering of services to the former. Thus, in a crisis situation, the aid-receiving states were obliged to side with the donor or risk the termination of foreign aid.

Foreign assistance has also been a function of the health of the economy of the donor states. During the "oil boom," from 1973 to 1987, the wealthy Arab states extended $100 billion in "Official Development

Assistance" to poorer Arab countries.[9] State-to-state aid preserved the economic health of the recipient states, while Arab financial aid and workers' remittances were greater than all investment for Jordan and Yemen. American and Gulf aid to Egypt led to the stabilization of the Egyptian pound and the drop in inflation from 30 percent to 10 percent by the early 1990s.

Between 1973 and 1987, however, the flow of Gulf financial aid dropped from 7 percent to 0.95 percent, largely as a result of falling oil prices. The deterioration in interstate political relations also had a negative effect on the flow of foreign assistance: Gulf financial assistance to Jordan, Yemen, Tunis, Sudan, and the PLO ended as a consequence of their perceived sympathy for Iraq during the 1991 Gulf War. Furthermore, the end of the Cold War and the demise of the Soviet Union compounded the economic misfortunes of these states.

Jordan's case is instructive in gauging the extent of change in the past five years and in appreciating the nature of the regional economic challenge. For over two decades, Saudi Arabia, Kuwait, and Iraq (until the Iran–Iraq War) were major aid donors to Jordan through state development fund loans or through contributions to the Kingdom mandated by Arab League summits in 1967, 1974, and 1978. Saudi Arabia and Kuwait also imported large numbers of Jordanian workers to build and staff both state bureaucracies and private sectors. These countries became employment safety valves as well as suppliers of hard currency through workers' remittances.[10]

They were also major trading partners: oil from Saudi Arabia and Iraq, fruits, vegetables, and labor to Saudi Arabia, Kuwait, and Iraq. Iraq also imported Jordanian light manufactures and pharmaceuticals, while transit trade from Iraq, Syria, and Saudi Arabia became an important source of revenue and labor.[11] Almost all of these relationships were severely curtailed, if not ended completely, as a result of the 1991 Gulf War, provoking a serious economic crisis in the Kingdom, but also precipitating a determination on the part of the government to undertake dramatic reforms, both economically and politically.

Unemployment and Rapid Population Growth

Productivity in the Middle East fell dramatically between 1960 and 1990, with unemployment rates in the region ranking as the highest in the world and real wages falling more than in any other region – even as massive investments in human capital continued:

> "[Middle East] countries devote a greater share of their national income

> to education than any other region. But these investments in human capital appear to have generated poor returns, as evidenced by low completion rates, high unemployment among graduates, and low labor productivity. Extensive distortions create incentives for the wrong kinds of education and training services, reduce the social returns to investments in human capital, and lower the external benefits associated with the accumulation of skills. Quality also has deteriorated especially where student numbers have increased rapidly under publicly dominated systems.[12]

Unemployment ranks as one of the region's most serious problems, with rates as high as 20 percent or more in some Arab countries.[13] Causes include an average 3 percent annual increase in the size of the labor force and the mass return of workers from the Gulf countries as a result of the Gulf War in 1991. Average population growth annually in the Middle East is 2.7 percent, while the labor force is growing at 3.3 percent. During the period 1973–93, the Middle East's population growth rate was the highest in the world; at current trends, the region's population will reach 400 million before 2010, with half the population already under the age of 15.[14]

Poor economic planning and the slow economic growth of many Middle Eastern countries has slowed the demand for new workers as well, while the decline in oil prices and the termination of the Iran–Iraq War shrank the Gulf countries' demand for foreign labor. The problem promises to grow worse, not better, with a projected doubling of the labor force between 1990 and 2010. A larger labor force can bring increased production and economic growth if there is sufficient investment to employ people productively. Investment in the Middle East in recent years has been low, however, and formal sector employment has lagged behind growth of the labor force.[15] As a consequence, poverty has increased throughout the region, particularly in rural areas and among the unskilled or self-employed in the major urban areas.

Rapid population growth in relation to resources also means that the greater part of investment is absorbed by population increase and is not available for raising per capita GNP and income. Merely keeping up with growing numbers in the provision of education, health, and housing is a major challenge for most of the region's governments. Additionally, the age pyramid results in a high dependency ratio, that is, the number of persons under the age of 15 or over 65 who are supported by the population between those ages. Reducing educational access and quality is not an option if the Middle East is to compete in the skilled job markets necessary for overall economic improvement.

The results of escalating population growth for the Middle East as a whole have been unmanageable and chronic debt, poor performance, low per capita incomes, corruption, and extreme poverty for the many, juxtaposed against extreme wealth for the few. Further results are a low quality of life and widespread misery, as well as a sense of powerlessness and frustration that brings about a vulnerability and receptivity to radical ideologies, especially among the younger generation. Political instability has been an inevitable consequence. Paradoxically, while more young Middle Easterners are becoming educated and progressing through college and university, there are fewer jobs, especially in the traditional bureaucratic and governmental areas where the educated elites formerly found employment. Many of these jobs are held by professionals who entered the work force twenty years ago and who will not reach retirement age for another 10–15 years.

The Growth of the Cities

Since the end of the Second World II, urban growth in the Middle East has been explosive. Indeed, the potential problems of political and social instability caused by unregulated urbanization in almost all developing countries are cause for serious concern. In 1950, 29 percent of the global population was located in urban areas; by the year 2000, almost half the world's population is expected to be urban, with 40 percent in developed countries and 78 percent in less developed countries (LDCs).[16] These increasing population concentrations provide the potential for violent upheaval, as deteriorating urban infrastructures struggle to cope with demands for housing, health care, sanitation, employment, and other services that are already overextended. Additionally, environmental pollution, high crime rates, and the insidious attraction of radical fundamentalist and terrorist groups to disenchanted urban populations are likely to undermine the coping mechanisms of local and national governments. As governments continue to fail the test of providing for their people, alternatives have emerged – most in the form of organized and politically sophisticated radical groups.

In the Middle East, urbanization is proceeding at an unregulated rate – from 4 to 6 percent per year. Estimates are that most cities in the region will triple or quadruple in size by the year 2000.[17] Within the next two decades, the urban population in the Middle East may be as high as 73 percent. Unmanaged population growth across the region is responsible for much of the increase in urbanization, as agricultural and rural growth are less able to keep up. People are drawn to the cities because of declining agricultural opportunities and the lure of urban employment. But as urban populations increase, governments are less able to provide for their services and needs.

Government policies have traditionally favored industrial and urban growth over agricultural progress in order to address the most immediate problems of concentrated populations and to protect regimes from unrest and instability resulting from dissatisfied populations. The result, however, is to further diminish or degrade the resource and agricultural base upon which most populations depend, and to make many countries net food importers. At the same time, efforts made to favor urban areas are insufficient to cope with the ever-expanding number of urban dwellers. Governments tend to keep prices low in an effort to make services affordable, for example, but in the long run they cannot cover the costs of maintenance or expansion, and thus large segments of the population – mostly the poor – remain unserved.[18] A "vicious circle" has thus been created. Overall, regional governments have not been able to deliver the goods, either to rural or to urban populations. The basic social contract between governments and their people has been broken, and regime threats have been the result.

Cities can represent venues for employment, socialization, and intellectual enrichment on both individual and national levels, providing that workable national infrastructures guarantee that growth is proportionate to available resources. In dysfunctional states and urban systems, however, urban areas can become toxic environments, both literally and figuratively. Cities are ideal places for either spontaneous or planned riots and demonstrations insofar as they are the showcases of a country and a regime, and contain concentrations of transport, communications, production, and administration that support established wealth and power. Attacks on urban targets, many with symbolic importance, cannot be met with indifference from regimes; they provide the publicity and attention required by terrorist and insurgent groups. They can become arenas for conflict and seedbeds for terrorism and ideological intimidation, as was demonstrated in Turkey (1976–80) and in Lebanon (1975–90), where the concentration of disaffected populations offered opportunities for dissident groups to consolidate, communicate, disseminate information, and inflict grievous damage to the existing order. Turkey was able to gain control of its terrorists; Lebanon was not so fortunate.

The rate of urban growth in the Middle East presents cause for alarm not so much because of dense urban concentrations, but because most cities in the region cannot cope with the influx. Cities such as Tehran, Cairo, Algiers, Damascus, Istanbul, Amman, and Sana'a have all grown at dangerous paces, condemning millions to perpetual squalor as they pose intolerable strains to overstretched infrastructures. From 1965 to 1990, the urban population of Iran increased from 37 percent to 57 percent; Algeria's increased from 38 percent to 52 percent, and Iraq's from 51 percent to 71 percent.[19] By the year 2012, the number of Iranian cities with populations over one million will reach thirteen. These tremendous increases have led to growth in traffic congestion and pollution, as well as breakdowns in water supplies and sewage treatment plants. Enormous strains have been placed on housing, education, health services, labor and agriculture, as well as on vital natural resources such as water. Development needs consistently outrun the capacity to satisfy these needs. The struggle merely to keep pace with expanding populations forecloses the ability to move ahead of it. Infrastructural problems are also magnified. In Cairo, for example, the demand for waterlines, electricity, and sewage treatment facilities has skyrocketed. Cairo generates 4,000 tons of garbage daily, with 600 tons of it remaining uncollected and untreated.[20]

The Costs of War

The region's numerous conflicts over the past fifty years, including the Arab-Israeli wars, the Iran–Iraq War, and the 1991 Gulf War, have also depleted the financial resources of the region, slowed economic growth, and precluded investment in sound social structures, both within states and within the region. These wars have diverted scarce available capital from developmental projects to the procurement of massive military arsenals. Between 1975 and 1990, Middle Eastern states spent $300 billion on weapons purchases alone. In the years between 1972 and 1991, the Middle East, as a whole, spent an average of 15 percent of GNP and 35 percent of central government expenditures annually on military expenditures.[21]

Beginning with the April 1948 Soviet delivery of Czechoslovakian rifles and light machine guns to the Israeli independence fighters, the numbers of both weapons and weapons suppliers to the Middle East have increased steadily. Conflicts between Middle Eastern states have been the major elements spurring the regional arms race. Attempts at territorial dominance by the Shah of Iran, the conflict between Iraq and post-revolutionary Iran, Syria's quest for "strategic balance" with Israel, the pervasive mistrust between Iraq and Syria, Turkey's strategic importance to NATO, Iraq's invasion of Kuwait and the resulting sense of vulnerability of the Gulf states, and the series of Arab-Israeli conflicts have provided the impetus for the enormous arms build-up in the Middle East.

By the 1980s, the Middle East accounted for between 30 and 40 percent of the world's total arms imports – and more than 80 percent of the weapons now present in the Middle East originated with one of the permanent members of the Security Council.[22] In the aftermath of the 1991 Gulf War, the arms bazaar reopened, with Russia, the US, North Korea, Czechoslovakia, China, France, and Great Britain providing arms and assistance to various states in the region while providing themselves with markets as well as limited leverage within the region.[23]

There is hope – if not expectation – that the Arab-Israeli peace process will significantly reduce regional military spending, allowing resources to be reallocated to economic growth and prosperity. The reality is that, for most states, such a reduction will only happen over time. The reasons for this are rooted in the diverse purposes that military forces and weapons serve. In many countries in the Middle East, the armed forces are used to support regimes in addition to their function of defending against foreign aggressors. Saudi Arabia, for example, has increased its military spending since the 1991 Gulf War, not out of fear of an Israeli attack, but to protect against internal unrest and the possibility of aggression from Iraq or Iran.

Likewise, it is difficult to imagine significant reductions in Syrian militarization in the short term. The rationale for Syria's authoritarian state has been the Israeli threat. The reality is that Assad's regime is a small Alawite minority, so regime protection must continue to be a concern even if peace with Israel is achieved and the large – and expensive – Syrian contingent in Lebanon is withdrawn. Additionally, Syria still has to factor in its fear of Iraq, as well as its ongoing dispute with Turkey and Iraq over Euphrates water.

A military drawdown also poses economic and social problems, for instance, how to employ demobilized soldiers in economies already suffering from dangerous levels of unemployment. The growth of extremist groups, especially in countries such as Egypt and Algeria, has rationalized the need for continuing military spending.

The Necessity for Regional Cooperation

In the words of Khalid Abdallah, Chief Representative of the Arab League to the United States, "Dangers to the security of any country do not arise from military threats only, but also spring from other threats. No society can be secure when it is poor, illiterate, indebted, and unhealthy."[24] What is required is a new concept of security followed by a new concept of alliances. The fact of the matter is that, despite the continuing potential for aggressive behavior by states such as Iran or Iraq, the Middle East today is a region facing not so much external threat as internal crisis. The tentacles of this crisis reach into the area's economics, its environment, its social and political life. Many, if not most, states face problems of political legitimacy, as increasingly aware and aroused populations question the efficiency of regimes and decry their lack of response to political, social, economic, and humanitarian concerns.

While these problems have specific manifestations in individual states, they also, by nature of their similarity, possess a transnational character. Water, for example, is a major regional problem as well as an individual resource issue for most Middle East states. While managing this problem requires individual actions by states, its eventual resolution will depend upon regional cooperation – alliances – that can treat the area's three major river systems as ecological and hydrological entities. Such alliances are dependent upon a minimum level of political stability and a willingness to establish regional rules of conduct and implementation.

Alliance systems that will strengthen the health of the Middle East, as an economic, social, and ecological organism that is the sum of its parts, are an indispensable requirement. Conversely, systems that continue to isolate pieces of the whole, that direct attention away from critical internal problems, that continue the practice of diverting massive amounts of GNP toward military expenditures rather than toward economic development and restructuring, will exacerbate existing tendencies toward factionalism, fractionation, and state failures. Most states in the Middle East, as in the rest of the world, are dependent upon others: for labor, for jobs, for resources. The denial of this mutual dependency, and the perpetuation of mutual mistrust, the continuation of exclusionary politics both within and among states, is a recipe for disaster. It is a disaster that will affect not only the Middle East, but those states in the international community which have critical ties with the region. The question, then, is how cooperative efforts can be encouraged and implemented in the Middle East. One lesson to be learned from the region's past efforts at cooperation is that there are prerequisites: a comprehensive and durable peace between Israel and Arab states leading to political and social stability, sound economic policies that equalize the region's unequal endowment of human and natural resources through complementarity, and development of a scientific and technological base in Arab countries to enable the Middle East to compete in global markets.

Barriers to Economic Development

Peace and political stability are a necessary condition to attracting private investment, particularly foreign. They are not sufficient, however, without the potential for investors to obtain maximum return consistent with minimum risk for capital. These are conditions that remain more readily available in advanced industrialized countries which have succeeded in achieving and maintaining high rates of economic growth. For example, there has been little foreign private investment in Saudi Arabia, other than in oil refineries and petrochemicals, since foreign investors have found few profitable areas for investment in Saudi industry. Similarly, the formal peace between Egypt and Israel has resulted in little foreign investment, particularly in Egyptian manufacturing. In fact, Egypt's economy has been stagnant, on a per capita GNP and income basis, since the end of the oil boom in the mid-1980s.[25] Egypt's economic problems, like those of most Arab countries, are primarily internal. Without deep structural reforms, attracting foreign investors will continue to be difficult.

As Roger Owen has noted,[26] it is difficult to imagine a regional scheme for economic cooperation not preceded by political cooperation, including peace treaties between Israel and all its Arab neighbors, and the end of both Arab and Israeli trade boycotts. The validity of this position is borne out by a look at the history of attempts at economic cooperation in the Middle East. Two notable examples are that of the League of Arab States and the Gulf Cooperation Council – the first, an attempt at pan-Arab cooperation and the second, a sub-regional group comprising the Gulf states.

Both the Arab League and the GCC have fallen short of their objectives. In the case of the League, economic integration was planned through development of an Arab Common Market, modeled on the European Common Market. There were formidable economic impediments from the outset. Egypt was considerably more advanced industrially, and other Arab states feared impeding development of their own industries by giving Egypt free access to their own markets. The League's economic plans were further hampered by emphasis on guarding the sovereignty and independence of individual states, as well as by the lack of an overarching strategy to guide the League and its member states in an integrated manner. The GCC, for its part, lost much of its momentum as a consequence of the 1991 Gulf War, following which many states turned not to each other but to the West for bilateral agreements.

The objectives of both the League and the GCC were primarily frustrated by the political and military disputes of the last decades, which closed boundaries, stopped trade, and froze economic deals and agreements. Since the end of the 1991 Gulf War and the beginning of the Arab-Israeli peace process, however, there is considerable hope that new forms of alliances will be developed, based on both internal and trans-regional economic and structural reforms that can be more productive and better grounded in regional realities than the old political/military alliances that set state against state, group against group, and brother against brother. Indeed, in the past four years, several Arab countries, such as Jordan, Syria, and Lebanon, have liberalized internal rates, promoted capital markets, and launched privatization as well as reform programs to improve the management of public enterprise. These reforms are having the effect of widening the scope of the private sector and improving the efficiency of economies.

The Jordanian–Israeli–Palestinian Triangle

One of the most promising of the potential economic alliances is the development of dialogue and joint ventures among Jordan, Israel, and the Palestinians. Jordan, in particular, has taken great strides to liberalize its economy and integrate it with global markets. The country, which experienced a 25 percent increase in exports in the past year, has entered a three-year International Monetary Fund (IMF) program that will help integrate its stock market into global capital markets and will include the formation of mutual funds with foreign participation. The plan will also cut restrictions on foreign investment, amend the companies law, and simplify land acquisition for companies.[27] Corporate income tax will fall to 15 percent from 40 percent in major areas of economic priority, including mining, industry, and hotels, while tax on banks and financial, insurance, and brokerage firms will fall from 50 percent to 30 percent.[28] Moves such as this should enable Jordan to compete with other countries in the region, and may help to allay pervasive fears that Israel, as the region's strongest economy, will dominate any regional alliance.

Israel, for its part, appears concerned to avoid arousing fears of Israeli "economic imperialism." It sharply curtailed the number of its attendees at the October Amman Economic Summit, for example, cutting its representatives to 100 from the 300 who came to the 1994 Casablanca Summit. In fact, cooperative efforts between Israel and Jordan have moved forward considerably since the signing of the Jordan–Israel peace treaty in October 1994. The bilateral trade agreement, signed 25 October 1995, for example, signalled the opening of trade between the two countries and expressed the desire for acting jointly to create commercial ties and economic cooperation. Specifically, both countries pledged to work toward removing trade barriers, economic discrimination, and the boycott of goods. The treaty also established procedures for conducting inquiries, increasing trade, and exchanging information. Future negotiations are to be held to complete the process of opening markets, with a commitment to a future free trade zone.[29] Cooperative agreements between Israel and Jordan also imply Palestinian involvement. For example, plans are under discussion for a "riviera" running the length of the Dead Sea and connecting Israel and Jordan with Aqaba, building a joint Israeli-Jordanian airport in Aqaba, and a Palestinian airport in the Gaza Strip.

The question mark in contemplation of a Jordanian-Israeli-Palestinian triangle, however, is the current and projected economy of the West Bank and the Gaza Strip. Over the past decade, income levels have stagnated, unemployment and underemployment have risen rapidly, public infrastructure and social services are grossly overstretched, and the fragile natural resource base is threatened with irreversible damage.[30] There is an urgent need for stimulating economic development and for reducing the high vulnerability of the Gaza Strip and the West Bank to external forces. This is a difficult task, as the area undergoes a painful transition from occupation to a still ambiguous future, with many of the key issues, such as allocation of land and water resources, the future status of expatriate Palestinians, the territorial issues surrounding Jerusalem, and the final self-governing arrangements, still in flux. Thus, optimal solutions for the Gaza Strip and the West Bank may be at variance with ultimate political arrangements.

Nonetheless, there is hope that the inclusion of major West Bank towns, such as Ramallah and Nablus, in the Palestinian self-governing agreement will boost the prospects for the Palestinian economy. These towns, within easy reach of Jordan, have the potential to become commercial centers. With mature businesses and industries, and better infrastructure than either the Gaza Strip or Jericho, they offer the promise of a more attractive quality of life to potential Palestinian returnees. The Gaza Strip may be the biggest problem in terms of Palestinian economic (and political) integration. It is physically isolated from the rest of Palestinian territory, and continuing Israeli security fears mean that the free movement of people and goods between the Gaza Strip and the West Bank is likely to remain highly restricted. Also, the Gaza labor force is likely to remain dependent on work inside Israel. At present, the unemployment rate in the Gaza Strip is 40 percent, with 10,000 people entering the work force each year. Job creation is thus an urgent priority for policy makers.[31]

Much has been made of the proposal for creation of industrial zones on the border between Israel and the self-rule areas. These zones would enable Israeli firms to use Palestinian laborers without them entering Israel. However, on their own, these zones will not solve Gaza's unemployment problem. There is also fear that goods from the industrial zones will destroy the little local manufacturing that currently exists in the Gaza Strip.

While many of the structural problems and strategic choices affecting the West Bank and the Gaza Strip are similar, there are notable differences that may present problems for the Palestinians – and by extension, for Israel and Jordan – in both the near- and long-term. These include:

1 Population density in the Gaza Strip, which is almost 10 times that of the West Bank at 1,870 persons per square kilometer.
2 Per capita income, which is approximately $1,230 (US$) in the Gaza Strip, as compared with $2000 in the West Bank.
3 Investment per capita, which in the Gaza Strip is less than half that of the West Bank.
4 Water supply and demand, which is far more precarious in the Gaza Strip than in the West Bank.
5 Composition of the populations: Refugees make up over two-thirds of Gaza's population, as compared with approximately 40 percent in the West Bank.
6 Dependence on the Israeli market for employment in Gaza: About 40 percent of the Gaza labor force depends upon Israeli employment, as compared with approximately 30 percent in the West Bank.[32]

Also problematic have been the absence of sizable development schemes to encourage donor money in addition to the economic policies of the Palestinian Authority. Funds intended for development have been diverted to cover recurrent rather than capital expenditures, as in support of the Palestinian police force. Many of these problems may be resolved as Israel withdraws from the West Bank and as Palestinian elections begin the process of democratization of Palestinian institutions.

The recent Amman Economic Summit may also result in real forward movement. Among the Summit's achievements were establishment of a $5 billion Middle East Development Bank along with regional tourism and business councils. The US has been the main backer of the bank, which will be based in Cairo and which will operate like a merchant bank to promote regional projects. Although the concept of the bank has been controversial, with European countries such as Germany and France contending that it will duplicate the efforts of current institutions, it is significant that the idea originated with and enjoys the support of Israel, Jordan, Egypt, and the Palestinians.[33]

Steps to Economic Health

What steps must be taken to promote economic health and stability, not just in the Jordanian–Israeli–Palestinian triangle, but throughout the Middle East? First, greater regional political security to facilitate mechanisms for promoting prosperity through economic cooperation and development. This goes beyond the present Palestinian–Jordanian–Israeli reconciliation to comprehensive regional peace between Israel and all Arab countries, among Arab countries, and between them and Iran. Second, the creation and implementation of effective national economic development plans and programs such as:

1. Promoting consistent trade liberalization.
2. Developing flexible investment environments, including securities markets, payment and trading systems, and regulatory capacities.
3. Upgrading infrastructure services, preferably with private sector funding.
4. Promoting the privatization process in the region.
5. Encouraging foreign investment through simplified, transparent rules and publication of economic data.
6. Integrating education and economies by making vocational training demand-driven and by focusing on basic skills as well as technological capabilities.
7. Reforming policies on natural resources to rationalize their use and preserve their value.
8. Increasing the availability of employment.
9. Encouraging creative political leadership to dispel the "zero-sum" concept that one party's gain is the other's loss.
10. Targeting critical regional problems as priorities, including water resources and river basin development, environmental hazards and control, land degradation, and the use and care of human resources.
11. Promoting regional cooperation among scientific and technological institutions for planning and dealing with critical issues.
12. Focusing on economic development strategies within states that promote open markets, economic empowerment, and regional prosperity.

Conclusion

> "No country is destined to be poor because of a bad endowment of natural resources, an isolated location, or a concentration on certain products."[34]

At present, there is great potential for economic regeneration, underwritten by political stability, in the Middle East. Major advances have been made by individual countries toward lowering the barriers erected by political differences and sustained by rigid state systems. Peace agreements between Israel, Jordan, and the Palestinians have been the major factor in this process. But many difficulties remain, including the uneven distribution of resources throughout the region, as well as the remnants of state-controlled economies and barriers to intra-regional trade. Most important, however, are the remaining political differences, not only between Israelis and Arabs, but within and among Arab states. Internal instabilities in many Middle Eastern countries, fostered by stagnant or deteriorating economic conditions, can undermine political achievements. There is a legacy of mistrust in the region, resulting in a quest for self-sufficiency that is the antithesis of integration and that must be transcended if the Middle East is to compete in the global marketplace.

There have been significant improvements across the region in the last five years. Debt problems, for example, have been significantly reduced, relieving serious external payment problems. Morocco, Tunisia, and Jordan are making great strides toward privatization, and even Algeria, in the midst of internal turmoil, has carried out effective exchange rate reforms, liberalized its trade system by removing layers of bureaucracy, and begun to sell government assets. A primary problem, however, remains employment and the concern that Middle Eastern states have not achieved the levels of growth necessary to have a sufficient impact on employment in order to alleviate poverty.[35]

Economic cooperation and growth depend on political stability across the region to provide an attractive investment climate. In turn, political stability must rest on stable economies. The two elements are intertwined; the health of each country in the region guarantees the health of every other country. It is a great adventure and a great experiment, and to the minds of many it is against all odds. But to a region that has come so far on a long and difficult road, political stability and economic cooperation arising out of a comprehensive peace in the Middle East represent the best hope that generations to come will not repeat the lessons of the past and suffer the pain of the present.

Notes

1 World Bank, *Claiming the Future: Choosing Prosperity in the Middle East and North Africa* (Washington, D.C., October 1995), p. 64.
2 Khaled Abdallah, "Today's Arab World Presents New Business Opportunities," in *al-Hewar* (September/October 1995), p. 15.
3 World Bank, *Claiming the Future*, p. 38.
4 Ibrahim Oweiss, "Economic Development of the Arab Countries in the 1990s," unpublished paper presented at RAND Conference on the Middle East, August 1994.
5 United Nations Development Programme (UNDP), *Human Development Report 1994* (Oxford and New York: Oxford University Press), 1994, pp. 102–3.
6 Ibid., p. 155.
7 Ibid., p. 102.
8 Oweiss, "Economic Development."
9 Shafik Nemat, "Has Labor Migration Promoted Economic Integration in the Middle East?" Paper presented at the 17th Annual Symposium of the Center for Contemporary Arab Studies, Georgetown University, Washington, D.C., April 1992.
10 See Laurie A. Brand, *Jordan's Inter-Arab Relations: The Political Economy of Alliance Making* (New York: Columbia University Press), 1994.
11 Ibid., pp. 6–7.
12 World Bank, *Claiming the Future*, p. 28.
13 Abdallah, "Today's Arab World," p. 16.
14 World Bank, "A Population Perspective on Development: The Middle East and North Africa," Middle East and North Africa Region, Washington, D.C., 1994.
15 Ibid., p. 11.
16 Gregory D. Foster, "Global Demographic Trends to the Year 2010," *The Washington Quarterly* (Spring 1989), p. 8; see also: H. Jeffrey Leonard et al., *Environment and the Poor: Development Strategies for a Common Agenda* (New Brunswick, Washington, D.C.: Transaction Books for Overseas Development Council, 1989), pp. 167–8.
17 Foster, "Global Demographic Trends."
18 World Bank, "A Population Perspective," p. 9.
19 "Nightmare of the Teeming Millions," *The Middle East* (August 1992), p. 6.
20 Yahya Sadowski, *Political Vegetables? Businessman and Bureaucrat in the Development of Egyptian Agriculture* (Washington, D.C.: Brookings Institution, 1991), p. 22.
21 Compiled from World Military Expenditures and Arms Transfers, Arms Control and Disarmament Agency, various years.
22 Richard Dalton, *Winning Peace in the Gulf: A Long-Term Perspective* (London: The Royal Institute of International Affairs, 1992), p. 12,
23 See: Mary E. Morris, *The Persistence of External Interest in the Middle East* (Santa Monica, CA, RAND, 1993), ch. 6.
24 Khalid Abdallah, remarks to U.S.-Arab Chamber of Commerce (Pacific),

San Francisco, 9 June 1995.

25 Eliyahu Kanovsky, "The Economic Aspects of Arab-Israeli Peace Agreements: Myths and Realities," BESA Institute, Bar-Ilan University, Ramat Gan, Israel, January 1994.

26 Roger Owen, "Middle East Economic Security: 21st Century Options," unpublished paper presented at conference on *New Frontiers of Middle East Security*, Middle East Technical University, Ankara, June 12–15, 1995.

27 Suleiman al-Khalidi, "Jordan Says Will Adopt Wider IMF Reform Plan," Reuters report, 28 October 1995.

28 Peter Feuilherade, "Jordan: Facing the Challenges of Change," *The Middle East* (October 1995), p. 22.

29 "Israeli and Jordanian Trade Ministers to Sign Trade Agreement," provided by Israel Information Service, Industry and Trade Ministry, Jerusalem, 25 October 1995.

30 World Bank, *Developing the Occupied Territories: An Investment in Peace*, Vol. 1, 1993, p. 1.

31 *MEED* (18 August 1995), p. 6.

32 World Bank, *Developing the Occupied Territories*, p. 7.

33 Marjorie Miller, "Israelis, Arabs Get Down To Business at Conference," *Los Angeles Times*,1 November 1994, p. D1.

34 The World Bank, *Claiming the Future: Choosing Prosperity in the Middle East and North Africa*, (Washington, D.C., October 1995), p. 63.

35 *MEED* (22 September 1995), p. 5.

References

Abdallah, Khaled, "Today's Arab World Presents New Business Opportunities, *al-Hewar*, September/October 1995.

Al-Khalidi, Suleiman, "Jordan Says Will Adopt Wider IMF Reform Plan," Reuters report, 28 October 1995.

Ash, Toby, "Palestine: Progress is Taken Hostage by Politics," *MEED*, 18 August 1995.

Brand, Laurie A., *Jordan's Inter-Arab Relations: The Political Economy of Alliance Making*, New York: Columbia University Press, 1994.

Butter, David, "IMF Makes Job Creation a Priority," in *MEED*, 22 September 1995.

Dalton, Richard, *Winning Peace in the Gulf: A Long-Term Perspective*, London: The Royal Institute of International Affairs, 1992.

Foster, Gregory D., "Global Demographic Trends to the Year 2010," *The Washington Quarterly*, Spring 1989.

"Israeli and Jordanian Trade Ministers to Sign Trade Agreement," provided by Israel Information Service, Industry and Trade Ministry, Jerusalem, 25 October 1995.

Kanovsky, Eliyahu, "The Economic Aspects of Arab-Israeli Peace Agreements: Myths and Realities," BESA Institute, Bar-Ilan University, Ramat Gan, Israel, January 1994.

Leonard, H. Jeffrey, et al., *Environment and the Poor: Development Strategies for a*

Common Agenda, New Brunswick: Transaction Books for Overseas Development Council, Washington, D.C., 1989.

Miller, Marjorie, "Israelis, Arabs Get Down to Business at Conference," *Los Angeles Times*, 1 November 1994.

Morris, Mary E. , *The Persistence of External Interest in the Middle East,* Santa Monica, CA: RAND, 1993.

Nemat, Shafik, "Has Labor Migration Promoted Economic Integration in the Middle East?" Paper presented at the 17th Annual Symposium of the Center for Contemporary Arab Studies, Georgetown University, Washington, D.C., April 1992.

"Nightmare of the Teeming Millions," in *The Middle East*, August 1992.

Oweiss, Ibrahim, "Economic Development of the Arab Countries in the 1990s," in Emile Sahliyeh and Mary E. Morris (eds), *Challenges to the State System in the Middle East*, State University of New York (forthcoming).

Owen, Roger, "Middle East Economic Security: 21st Century Options," unpublished paper presented at conference on *New Frontiers of Middle East Security,* Middle East Technical University, Ankara, Turkey, 12–15 June 1995.

Sadowski, Yahya, *Political Vegetables? Businessman and Bureaucrat in the Development of Egyptian Agriculture,* Washington, D.C.: Brookings Institution, 1991.

United Nations Development Programme (UNDP), *Human Development Report 1994,* Oxford University Press, 1994.

World Bank, "A Population Perspective on Development: The Middle East and North Africa," Middle East and North Africa Region, Washington, D.C., 1994.

World Bank, *Claiming the Future: Choosing Prosperity in the Middle East and North Africa,* October 1995.

World Bank, *Developing the Occupied Territories: An Investment in Peace, Vol. 1,* 1993.

World Bank, *World Development Report 1994: Infrastructure for Development,* New York: Oxford University Press, 1994

13

The Economic Factor of the Middle East Peace Process: The Jordanian Case

Onn Winckler

In addition to its considerable human costs, the longstanding Arab-Israeli conflict has caused significant economic damage to many Middle Eastern countries, especially Egypt, Syria, Jordan, and Lebanon. Most evident is the need to allocate scarce resources to military expenditures, which has limited their potential to devote such resources to economic and social development plans. By any measure, the amount of resources allocated by the Middle Eastern countries to military expenditures is substantial. In fact, the Middle East region as a whole allocates higher rates of resources for military expenditures than all other developing-country regions. For the years 1972–88, military expenditures (excluding expenditures funded by foreign assistance, mainly by the US and the Soviet Union) accounted for 10.1 percent of the GDP, almost twice the average of 5.3 percent for developing countries as a group.[1] In Jordan, military expenditures constituted 25.3 percent of total government expenditures in 1980, decreasing to 22.1 percent in 1993.[2]

However, the high rate of military expenditures has not been the only economic cost of the Middle East conflict. Until the June 1967 war, the economic implications of the Middle East conflict were not severe for the countries which were directly involved in the conflict, namely, Egypt, Jordan, Syria, and Lebanon. However, the June 1967 war constituted a turning point in terms of the economic implications of the Middle East conflict. As a result of the war, Egypt lost the oil fields of Sinai. In addition, due to the instability along the Suez Canal, Egypt could not use the oil fields on the West Bank of the Canal. This alone damaged the Egyptian public revenues by billions of dollars annually until the end of the Egyptian-Israeli conflict.

Furthermore, between June 1967 and 1975, the Suez Canal was closed, meaning that during this period of seven years Egypt lost one of its most important sources for hard currency. To this direct damage should be added the indirect damage to the Egyptian economy caused by the small number of tourists and the small scale of foreign investments relative to the huge potential in these areas.

As a result of the peace process with Israel, the Suez Canal was reopened in 1975. In addition, Egypt now enjoys an annual grant of $2.3 billion from the US (for both military and civilian purposes); sizable foreign investments, which have created a large number of work opportunities in various economic fields; and revenues of more than $3 billion on average annually from the tourism industry. All in all, it seems that the economic benefits of the peace treaty with Israel to the Egyptian economy have amounted to more than $10 billion on average annually.

The Syrian economy has also suffered substantially from the military conflict with Israel. During the 1980s, Syria fell into the "population trap," namely, a syndrome in which the growth rate of the population was substantially higher than the growth rate of the GDP. In parallel, during the first half of the 1980s, the policy of economic development was subordinated to the policy of "strategic balance" with Israel, which absorbed a large share of the Syrian financial resources.

These two developments caused a severe drop in the level of the population's welfare. The Syrian authorities were forced to recognize that they could not continue with the policy of "strategic balance" because of its social and political costs. As a result, during the latter years of the 1980s, the Syrian government began to limit its military expenditures, a process that continued into the first half of the 1990s. At the same time, investments in economic and social development plans were substantially increased.[3]

The country which seems to have been the most adversely affected by the June 1967 war is Jordan. First and foremost, Jordan lost the West Bank with almost 40 percent of the Kingdom's population, valuable agricultural land, and more than 80 percent of the country's tourism sites which were concentrated in the West Bank, particularly in Jerusalem, Bethlehem, and Ramallah.[4] In addition, as a result of the occupying of the West Bank and Gaza Strip by Israel, Jordan was forced to absorb about 310,000 Palestinian refugees from these areas (see below).

On 26 October 1994, Jordan and Israel signed a Treaty of Peace, ending nearly 50 years of hostilities and severe hardships in all aspects of Jordanian life, especially economic and social affairs. However, there are Jordanians who remain afraid of Israel's power and are suspicious of its motives in making peace with Jordan. They fear that Israeli military dominance will be replaced in the future by economic control. There are also those who reject the peace process altogether, with the most outspoken being the Islamist and leftist political parties. Others feel that the terms of the peace treaty are weighted too much in Israel's favor.[5]

The purpose of this chapter is first, to trace the main economic problems which encouraged Jordan to end the longstanding military conflict with Israel, and second, to analyze the contribution of the peace process to the development of the Jordanian economy.

The Main Economic Problems Facing the Jordanian Economy

1 *Rapid Population Growth*

Jordan's population increased from 433,700 in 1946[6] to 4.3 million in 1995 (see table 13.1). These data show that during the course of the last 50 years, Jordan's population has grown tenfold, representing an unprecedented growth for the entire Middle East region. According to the State of the World Population Report published by the UNFPA, Jordan's population will reach 5.7 million by the end of the year 2000.[7]

Table 13.1 Population of Jordan (East Bank), 1950–1995 (in thousands)

Year	Males	Females	Total
1950	323	277	600
1955	331	311	642
1961	410	431	841
1970	867	801	1,668
1975	993	959	1,952
1979	1,115	1,017	2,132
1985	1,409	1,285	2,694
1990	1,777	1,676	3,453
1994	2,161	1,979	4,140
1995	2,240	2,051	4,291

Sources:
1950–75: The Hashemite Kingdom of Jordan, Economics Department, *Numerical Index for Population and Vital Statistics*, by Issa Jum'a Ibrahim (Amman, March 1979), pp. 1–3, Table 1.
1979–85: ESCWA, *Statistical Abstract of the Region of the Economic and Social Commission for Western Asia, 1977–1986* (Baghdad, 1987), p. 152, Table I–2.
1990: Jordan, *Statistical Yearbook – 1991*, p. 19, Table 2/1.
1994–95: Jordan, *Statistical Yearbook – 1995*, p. 10, Table 2/1.

The first reason for such dramatic population growth is the emigration of Palestinians from the borders of Mandatory Palestine to the East Bank. As a result of the 1948 war in Palestine, about 70,000–80,000 Palestinian refugees emigrated to the East Bank. After the June 1967 war, with the Israeli occupation of the West Bank and Gaza Strip, the East Bank of Jordan received another 310,000 Palestinian refugees (265,000 from the West Bank and 45,000 from the Gaza Strip). In addition, even in peace periods between the wars there has been a general population shifting from the West to the East Bank of Jordan.[8] To those Palestinian emigrants and refugees, one should add about 200,000–250,000 Palestinians who were expelled from Kuwait and emigrated to Jordan as a result of the support given by Arafat and King Hussein to the Iraqi side during the Gulf crisis. Altogether, more than a million Palestinians immigrated to the East Bank of Jordan during the years 1948–91.

Table 13.2 Jordan: natural increase rates, 1960–1994

Year	Crude birth rate	Crude death rate	Natural increase (%)	Total fertility rate
1960	47.4	19.9	2.8	7.2
1970	47.5	15.7	3.2	7.1
1978	48.0	14.0	3.4	6.5
1988	38.7	5.0	3.4	6.4
1994	33.0	5.2	2.8	4.7

Sources:

1960: The World Bank, *World Tables*, The Third Edition, Social Data from the Data Files of the World Bank (Baltimore and London, 1984), p. 49 [hereafter: World Bank, *World Tables*].

1970: United Nations Economic Commission for Western Asia (ECWA), *Demographic and Related Socio–Economic Data Sheets for Countries of the Economic Commission for Western Asia*, No. 2 (1978), country page [hereafter: ECWA/ESCWA, *Demographic Data Sheets*].

1978: ECWA and the League of Arab States, *Statistical Indicators of the Arab World for the Period, 1970–1979* (Beirut, 1981), p. 5, Table I–2.

1988: ESCWA, *Population Situation – 1990*, pp. 94–95, Tables 5.4 and 5.5.

1994: ESCWA, *Demographic Data Sheets*, No. 8 (1995), pp. 50–51, Tables 3 and 4.

The high rates of natural increase in Jordan over the last four decades have created a wide base of the age-pyramid. By 1994, the percentage of the population below the age of 15 within the total population was 42.2.[9] The direct result of the high percentage of the young population in Jordan has been a very low crude economic active rate. By 1988, this rate was only 22.8 percent,[10] with the ratio between breadwinners and those being supported reaching 1:5. Among developed countries, the crude economic active rates are much higher than in the Middle East, due to the differences in the age-pyramid of the populations. In 1993, this rate was 51.3 percent in Japan, 49.4 percent in France, and 50.3 percent in the United Kingdom.[11]

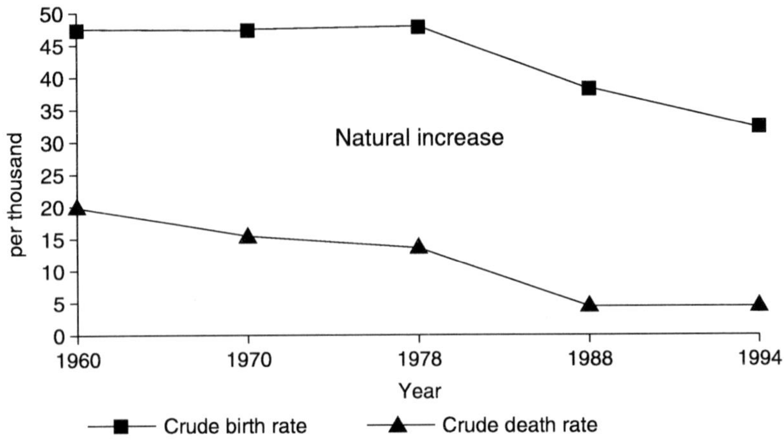

Figure 13.1 Jordan: natural increase rates, 1960–1994
Data taken from table 13.2

In a country such as Jordan, where public services are heavily subsidized, the high percentage of the young population has far-reaching consequences and a substantial negative impact on the rate of economic growth. Children and teenagers are large consumers of public services, such as health and education, as well as subsidised food, while their productive contribution is marginal, if any.

An additional negative result of the rapid population growth has been the creation of a food supply problem. The local agriculture can no longer supply the growing food demand. In 1992, Jordan's net food imports cost the country $483.6 million.[12] Salem Boutros, an economic advisor, claims that:

> To meet the increasing demand, the Kingdom is already importing 82 percent of the national need of wheat, and by the year 2000, it will have to import at least 88 percent of the internal demand.[13]

Furthermore, the rapid population growth in the rural areas has created substantial shortages of work opportunities in agriculture. Those who are no longer needed, due to the lack of arable land, have been forced to look for employment in the big cities, where there is a wider choice of job opportunities. The gradual result of this process has been a reduction in the share of agriculture within the total GDP, dropping from 16 percent in 1960[14] to only 8 percent in 1993.[15] Consequently, the share of the urban population within the total population of Jordan increased from 43.1 percent in 1961[16] to 78.2 percent in 1995.[17] The population of Amman increased from 108,304 in 1952[18] to 1,352,355 in 1995.[19] The rapid urbanization process, in parallel to the concentration of Palestinian refugees in refugee camps located in the big cities, has brought about an imbalance in the distribution of the population between the various districts of the country. By 1995, more than 31 percent of the Jordanian population lived in the city of Amman.

The jump in the size of the major cities (especially Amman) within a very short time has led to severe difficulties in the systems of public services, transportation, housing, water supply, and health services. In this respect, Jordan is no different from any other country in the Middle East where the same process has occurred. According to the 1979 population census, 41 percent of the population of Amman lived four persons per room, and in the poorest areas of the city, the average number per room was higher than six.[20]

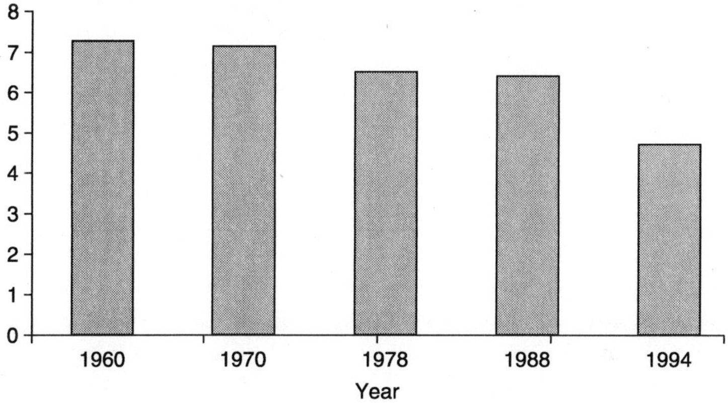

Figure 13.2 Jordan: total fertility rates, 1960–1994
Data taken from table 13.2.

Another critical problem caused by the rapid population growth is the shortage of water. Today, the demand for water already far exceeds the supply, and the gap is widening steadily. In 1990, according to the Water Authority of Jordan (WAJ), the total supply of water was 550 million cubic metres (mcm), while the demand was 900 mcm.[21] Several recent studies predict that by the year 2000, the Kingdom will need 1,554 mcm of water, while the available quantities will total only 980 mcm, representing just 63.1 percent of the demand.

The studies conclude that the shortage in water will hamper the

Kingdom's development process, especially in the industrial and agricultural sectors.[22]

2 Presence of Large Numbers of Foreign Workers

Since the beginning of the 1950s, the Jordanian authorities have shown a liberal attitude toward labor migration. Without extensive labor migration, the Jordanian economy could not have accommodated the influx of Palestinian refugees after the wars of 1948 and June 1967. Despite the loss of skilled and professional workers, the Jordanian government was unlikely to revise its policies encouraging labor migration because of the large role played by workers' remittances in the domestic economy.[23]

In 1984, official estimates of Jordanian workers' remittances reached more than $1.2 billion.[24] By mid-1989, the number of Jordanian citizens working outside the Kingdom was 338,000,[25] of whom 277,000 were located in the rich Arab oil-exporting countries.[26]

The growth of labor outflows during the 1970s and the 1980s created a substantial manpower shortage in the Jordanian labor market, which was additionally fuelled by the investment of workers' remittances, particularly in the construction and housing sectors.[27] As a result, the Jordanian authorities adopted an "open door" policy toward workers from Arab countries, whereby they were exempted from labor permits, while Asian and other workers were not.[28]

In 1975, the number of foreign workers in Jordan was estimated to be 32,000 with an additional 17,250 family members.[29] Data published by the Ministry of Labor at the beginning of 1990 revealed that by the end of 1989, the total foreign work force in the Kingdom numbered 195,995.[30] However, the decrease in the demand for labor in the rich Arab oil-exporting countries and the return of tens of thousands of Jordanian workers from these countries was followed by a substantial escalation in unemployment. Thus, unemployment rate in Jordan increased from 1.6 percent in 1976[31] to about 10 percent by mid-1989.[32]

Despite the unemployment situation, employers continued to prefer hiring foreign workers at lower wages than those demanded by local workers. According to the results of a 1982 sample survey conducted on immigrant workers in Jordan, the average monthly wage for Jordanian workers was JD (Jordanian Dinar) 193, as compared with JD 133 for foreign workers – a difference of more than 45 percent. In some occupations, the gap was almost as high as 100 percent.[33]

As a result of this problematic situation, the Jordanian authorities decided by the mid-1980s to reduce the number of foreign workers. However, the efforts of the authorities, particularly in reducing the number of illegal foreign workers, did not succeed to a great extent.

During the early 1990s, about 65 percent of the foreign workers in Jordan were still working illegally, that is, without the proper labor permits.[34]

3 Economic Recession of the Late 1980s

From the mid-1970s until the mid-1980s, Jordan enjoyed rapid economic growth and a sharp rise in the standard of living, in parallel to political stability. This economic expansion was due to two main factors. The first was the large-scale transfer of workers' remittances, which by the early 1980s reached more than $1.2 billion annually.[35] The second factor was extensive foreign grants, which provided one of the major sources of income for the governmental budget, reaching a peak of $1.3 billion in 1980.[36] Jordan received grants from the United Kingdom during the 1940s and 1950s, from the US during the 1960s, and from the rich Arab oil-exporting countries beginning in the 1970s and ending with the Iraqi invasion of Kuwait.[37] The rapid economic expansion in the late 1970s and early 1980s was demonstrated by the sharp increase in per capita GNP: from less than $400 at the beginning of the 1970s to $2,200 on average by the mid-1980s.[38] As a result, the percentage of the population below the poverty line declined from 24 percent in 1980 to less than 3 percent in 1986/7.[39]

However, since the beginning of 1987, economic development slowed markedly and even took a negative downturn in late 1988, culminating in 1989 in Jordan's worse economic recession in the last two decades. There were two major reasons for the Jordanian economic recession. The first was the substantial reduction in foreign aid from the rich Arab oil-exporting countries as a result of the sharp decrease in oil prices. By 1987, total grants received were only $600 million, less than half the amount received at the beginning of the 1980s.[40] The second major factor was a significant reduction in workers' remittances, also caused by the decline in oil prices, which led the authorities of the oil-producing countries to scale down new projects and reduce the salaries of foreign workers. By 1989, workers' remittances had dropped to a total of $623 million, down from $1.2 billion in 1984.[41]

The economic recession was aggravated by the government's announcement in April 1989 of cuts in subsidies for certain basic items. This led to serious rioting in the southern part of the Kingdom, a region that was traditionally regarded as the backbone of East Bank support for the regime. Jordan's economic recession hit the hardest in the southern part of the Kingdom, fuelled as it was by the end of the Iran–Iraq war a few months earlier, in late 1988. During the war, the level of activity in the Aqaba port, which functioned as a main source of goods and supplies for Iraq, increased considerably. Other related fields, such as transportation, also flourished, and the region as a whole enjoyed economic prosperity. However, with the end of the war, the level of activity in the Aqaba port decreased sharply. Hence, the end of the Iran–Iraq war, combined with the overall economic recession in the country, caused a substantial decline in the per capita income and standard of living in the southern region of the Kingdom.

Nevertheless, the authorities had no intention of lifting the austerity reforms, attempting instead to strengthen their legitimacy among the population through a measure of public participation in decisions relating to resource allocation. As a result, in late April 1989, the King dismissed the Prime Minister Rifai, and the new government announced that general elections would be held in November of that year.[42]

4 The Gulf Crisis (1990/1)

The economic recession of the late 1980s was exacerbated even further as a result of the Gulf crisis. Following the Iraqi invasion of Kuwait, about 350,000 Jordanians and Palestinians returned from the Gulf countries, most of them from Kuwait.[43] This changed the Jordanian labor market dramatically. Within a few months, the population of Jordan increased by 10 percent. Jordan, like other major labor-exporting countries in the Middle East, was not prepared to absorb hundreds of thousands of returnees in the space of only a few months. After a very short time, the unemployment rate in Jordan increased to unprecedented levels. According to official Jordanian figures, by October 1991 unemployment rose to 22.9 percent of the total work force. However, economists and analysts believed that the actual figure, including those not registered with the authorities, was about 35 percent.[44] This placed Jordan among the countries with the highest unemployment rates all over the Middle East region.

Such a high unemployment rate is not only a socioeconomic problem, but even more importantly, a severe political problem. It seems that there is no government, in Jordan or in any other Middle Eastern country, that can survive, at least in the long run, with such a high rate of unemployment. Hence, it seems that the large capital streaming into Jordan (through workers' remittances and foreign grants) during the second half of the 1970s and throughout the 1980s, failed in its initial task: to increase and diversify the economy and the labor market.

The sharp rise in the unemployment rate caused the Jordanian authorities to further tighten their controls on foreign workers. In February 1992, the Egyptian Ministry of Labor warned those attempting to work in Jordan without a proper permit that the Jordanian police were combing businesses and companies in order to find illegal workers. Those who were caught would be immediately deported to

Table 13.3 Jordan: GNP per capita, 1976–1993 (US$)

Year	GNP Per Capita
1976	690
1977	780
1978	890
1979	1,120
1980	1,480
1981	1,640
1982	1,720
1983	1,630
1984	1,590
1985	1,890
1986	2,090
1987	2,250
1988	2,220
1989	1,530
1990	1,250
1991	1,060
1992	1,130
1993	1,190

Sources:
1976–84: World Bank, *World Tables*, 1989–90 edn, pp. 332–3.
1985–93: World Bank, *World Tables*, 1995 edn, pp. 4–5.

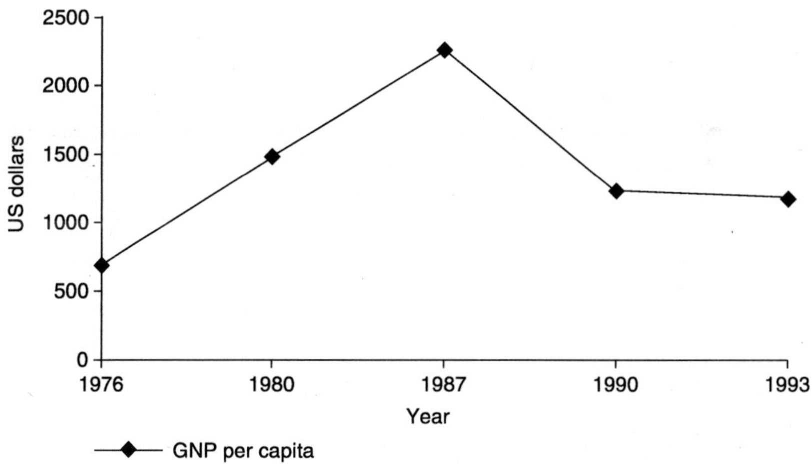

Figure 13.3 Jordan: GNP per capita, 1976–1993 (millions of US$)
Data taken from table 13.3.

their home countries.[45] Such measures, however, did not succeed in reducing the number of illegal migrant workers in Jordan. In mid-1995, it seems that of 250,000 foreign workers employed in the Kingdom, only 42,000 held valid work permits.[46]

Furthermore, substituting local workers for foreign workers proved to be problematic because of the low pay and low occupational status often accepted by the latter.[47] The Minister of Labor, Abdul Hafez Al-Shakhanben, urged Jordanian youth to seek employment in the private sector rather than in the public sector in order to reduce the unemployment rate and the bloated government cadres. The Minister said that:

> "The administrative ranks in the government are highly bloated, as the number of civil servants totals 121,000, whereas in a country like Tunisia where the population is twice as much, the number of government workers is 50 percent less than in Jordan."[48]

Besides the sharp increase in the unemployment level, caused by the return of so many nationals, the cost of absorbing the returnees from the Gulf was also prohibitively high, estimated to be at least $4.5 billion by the Minister of Planning, Ziad Fariz.[49] According to a study conducted by ESCWA, the cost of absorbing the returnees totalled $3.141 billion only for the years 1992–4.[50] In other words, the cost of absorbing the returnees was about 80 percent of the total Jordanian GDP (Gross Domestic Product), which was only $5.5 billion in 1991.

The international economic embargo, which was imposed against Iraq as a result of the invasion of Kuwait, meant that Jordan lost a lucrative export and re-export market, thereby damaging the Jordanian manufacturing sector, which had become heavily dependent on the Iraqi market. Economic activity at the port of Aqaba has been reduced by 50 percent because of the reluctance of shipping lines to use it during the anti-Iraqi blockade.[51] According to official Jordanian sources, Jordan's annual loss as a result of its adherence to the sanctions against Iraq is about $350 million.[52]

5 Increasing External Debt

Another major problem facing Jordan since the late 1980s has been the sharp increase of the external debt.

Like many Middle Eastern countries, Jordan has allocated substantial resources to the military, which, given the narrow base of the economy, is extremely burdensome. In this regard, Abu-Jabarah wrote that: '"With Jordan's very limited resources, the burden of keeping more than 100,000 men in the army is definitely heavy."[53] Until the mid-1980s, Jordan was able to sustain such large military expenditures via foreign grants from the rich Arab oil-exporting countries, as well as low interest rates on public debt, which was significantly below the economic growth rates. However, since 1983 interest payments have been steadily increased in response to the rapid build-up in debt and the sharp rise in interest rates in foreign financial markets.[54]

Table 13.4 Jordan: balance of trade, 1980–1993 (millions of US$)

Year	Import	Export	Balance of Trade
1980	3,318.2	1,781.5	–1,536.7
1981	4,865.2	2,214.6	–2,650.6
1982	4,941.9	2,208.9	–2,733.0
1983	4,042.9	1,930.2	–2,112.7
1984	4,018.4	2,038.4	–1,980.0
1985	3,912.0	2,075.7	–1,836.3
1986	3,566.0	1,903.8	–1,662.2
1987	3,517.0	2,283.0	–1,234.0
1988	4,112.0	2,471.0	–1,641.0
1989	3,657.0	2,390.0	–1,267.0
1990	4,185.0	2,579.3	–1,605.7
1991	3,885.0	2,599.0	–1,286.0
1992	4,633.7	2,778.9	–1,854.8
1993	4,729.8	2,921.0	–1,808.8

Source: World Bank, *World Tables*, 1995 edn, pp. 386–7.

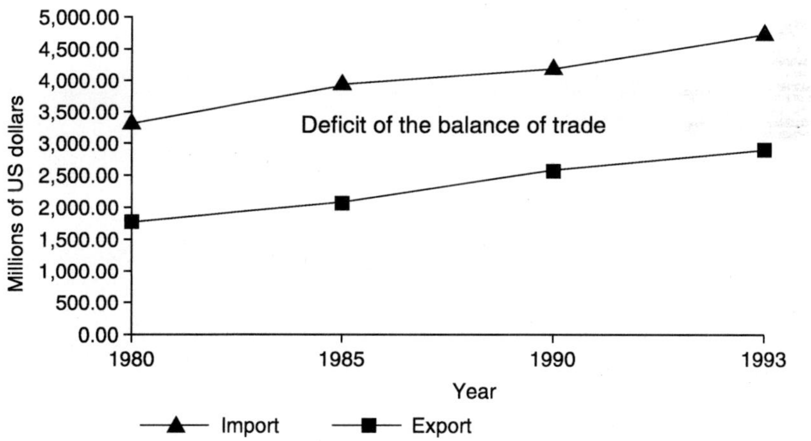

Figure 13.4 Jordan: balance of trade, 1980–1993 (millions of US$)
Data taken from table 13.4.

The net result of these changes was a significant increase in the Jordanian external debt, which reached $7.5 billion by 1989. In addition, due to the King's support of Iraq during the Gulf crisis, overall foreign grants to Jordan declined sharply. Combined with the sharp reduction in workers' remittances, this decline in foreign grants forced the Jordanian authorities to further rely on foreign borrowing. Consequently, Jordan's external debt continued to rise to more than $9 billion in 1991, while the short-term debt was $2.5 billion (see table 13.5).

6 *Social Consequences of Jordan's Economic Crisis*

As the economic situation faltered, the poverty situation deteriorated dramatically in the late 1980s and worsened even further as a result of the Gulf crisis. According to a study conducted by ESCWA in 1994, nearly 30 percent of the total population in Jordan was living below the poverty line, and 5 percent were absolutely poor, meaning that they were unable to afford to satisfy their most basic food and non-food needs.[55] The per capita GNP dropped from $2,200 in 1988 to only $1,060, or less than half, in 1991.[56] Similarly, the per capita income fell from the peak of $2,110 in 1986 to only $840 in 1990.[57] During a press conference conducted at the beginning of 1995, the Minister of Social Development, Muhammad Sqour, stated that 31,800 families in Jordan were living in absolute poverty, and that their monthly income did not exceed JD 60. In addition, there were another 107,800 families with a monthly income of less than JD 120.[58]

Table 13.5 Jordan: external debt, 1988–1994 (millions of US$)

	1988	1989	1990	1991	1992	1993	1994
Long–term debt	4,657	5,556	6,474	6,592	4,803	4,913	..
Short–term debt	1,932	1,267	1,316	2,462	..	.	..
Other unidentified debt	886	618	582	..	..	..	..
Total external debt	7,475	7,441	8,372	9,054	7,805	7,986	6,581

Source: ESCWA, *Survey of Economic and Social Developments in the ESCWA Region, 1994* (New York, 1995), p. 65, Table 38.

The economic crisis has also affected the mortality rates in Jordan. Prior to the Gulf crisis, the rates of infant and child mortality and child malnutrition in Jordan were among the lowest in the Arab world, and epidemic diseases had been more or less eradicated. However, following the Gulf crisis, infant and child mortality rates increased significantly, and malnutrition is now believed to threaten about 20 percent of children under the age of 12. This is due to their families' inability to afford adequate and nutritious food and minimum health care.[59]

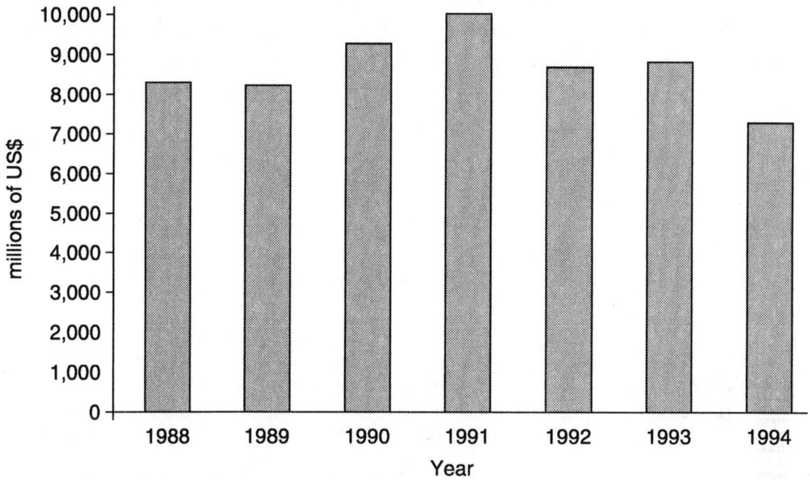

Figure 13.5 Jordan: external debt, 1988–1994 (millions of US$)
Data taken from table 13.5.

All in all, the Gulf crisis undermined the standard of living and drained the government's ability to manage the national economy. This was most profoundly demonstrated by the reduction in per capita GDP and income. By any measure, Jordan's economy was in a severe situation at the beginning of the 1990s. It seems that the Jordanian authorities realized that one of the measures to diminish the economic pressures, caused mainly by rapid population growth and the economic damage of the Gulf crisis, is to end the state of conflict with Israel.

However, in contrast to Egypt, which signed a separate peace treaty with Israel, Jordan could not do the same without the Palestinians, mainly because a high percentage of the Jordanian citizens are of Palestinian origin. Hence, in spite of the socioeconomic pressures affecting Jordan since the late 1980s, the overwhelming political obstacles prevented the Jordanian authorities from attempting separate negotiations for a peace agreement with Israel. However, the Declaration of Principles between Israel and the Palestinians (signed in September 1993) removed the political obstacles, thereby enabling Jordan to sign a peace treaty with Israel.

The Contribution of the Peace Process to the Jordanian Economy

It seems that Jordan's main economic aims from the peace treaty with Israel were: first, a substantial reduction in the size of the external debt, especially the short-term debt; second, a sharp increase of revenues from tourism; third, an alleviation of the severe water shortage; and finally, an increase of foreign aid and investment in order to create a vast number of new work opportunities.

1 Reduction in Foreign Debt

Since the beginning of the peace process between Jordan and Israel, many governments in the world have cancelled on the Jordanian debt. At the beginning of 1995, the US relieved Jordan of $700 million of its debt.[60] During the Amman Summit, the British Minister of Trade, Anthony Nelson, announced that all of Jordan's aid-related debts to Britain, totalling £46 million, had been cancelled. The Minister added that: "this is an important political decision and a vote of confidence in Jordan and the peace process."[61] In addition, Germany has cancelled Jordan's debt of $50 million, Switzerland cancelled $25 million, and France $5 million.[62] By mid-1995, Jordan's total external debt was $5 billion, down from more than $9 billion four years earlier, in 1991.[63] Ziad Fariz, the Governor of the Central Bank of Jordan (CBJ) and the former Minister of Planning, revealed that the external debt, including the military debt, of Jordan amounted to $4.465 billion at the end of 1995.[64]

Furthermore, since the beginning of the peace process, Jordan has been successful in rescheduling parts of its external debt. In 1993, Jordan concluded an agreement with the London Club for debt payment reduction. In June 1994, about $1.2 billion of Jordan's bilateral debt was rescheduled for a period of 20 years with the Paris Club.[65] At the beginning of 1995, $235 million of Jordan's debt to Japan was likewise rescheduled.[66]

2 Development of the Tourism Industry

For Jordan, one of the most important economic benefits of the peace treaty with Israel has been its development of the tourism industry. During the past several decades, tourism has emerged as one of the world's leading industries, exceeding many manufacturing industries and other services, both in terms of employment opportunities and foreign currency earnings. The rapid growth of the tourism industry that has occurred in developed and developing countries alike has propelled it into the position of a major social and economic force worldwide.[67]

Jordan possesses archeological and recreational sites of sufficient interest to attract a large number of tourists. A major attraction is the historic city of Petra which is carved into the cliffs. Aqaba is also a famous tourism site, known for its exquisite stretch of coral reefs located on the northern coast of the Red Sea. Another popular site is the Dead Sea, the lowest point on earth. In addition, Jordan possesses archeological sites in Jarash, Madaba, Karak, Wadi Rum, and Shubak. In terms of cultural and historical interest, it seems that few destinations in the Middle East hold as much interest for tourists as does Jordan.[68]

The Gulf crisis caused a great deal of harm to the Jordanian tourism industry, which started to recover only in 1992.[69] Three years later, in 1995, the total number of tourists in Jordan was 1.07 million, bringing in revenues of $723 million.[70] The tourism industry that year represented the largest foreign exchange earner in Jordan, exceeding the next biggest sector, that of chemicals, by a considerable margin. By 1995, the tourism industry contributed more than 10 percent of Jordan's total GDP. The number of tourists in 1996 was expected to reach 1.3 million, bringing in revenues of about $1 billion, according to sources at the Ministry of Tourism and Antiquities.[71]

The major reason for the rapid development and expansion of the tourism industry in Jordan is the peace process. Since the signing of the peace treaty, the number of tourists in the Kingdom has increased by 35 percent, including more than 150,000 Israeli tourists.[72] The Jordanian Minister of Tourism, Abdul Ilah Al-Khatib, attributed the sharp growth of tourism in Jordan mainly to the stability in the region in the era of peace.[73] However, the continued growth of the tourism industry depends to a great extent on foreign investments.

3 *Attraction of Foreign Investments*

One of the major Jordanian targets in the peace process is the attraction of large-scale foreign investments. Thus, since the beginning of 1994, the Jordanian authorities have invested considerable efforts in establishing measures to reform the Kingdom's tax and investment codes so as to create a more attractive investment environment. The new investment law (as of September 1995) provides many incentives for foreign investors via tax exemptions, which are weighted in favor of less developed areas. The new investment law also contains a commitment that all investment proposals will receive a reply from the Higher Council for Investment within 30 days of application. The law gives equal terms to foreign investors, as specified in article 24 of the law: "The non-Jordanian investor will enjoy equal treatment under this law with the Jordanian investor."[74]

At the Amman Summit in October 1995, the Jordanian government submitted a list of 27 high-priority projects worth an estimated $3.511 billion. The main emphasis for private investment is on the minerals sector, which already has a track record for securing foreign participation. Tourism also has recognized potential, evidenced by the heavy investments already made by local investors. The agreement between the Aqaba Region Authority and a US investor for a $132 million theme park and resort complex in Aqaba three weeks before the Amman Summit was sure to boost investor interest even further.[75]

By the beginning of 1996, hotel construction had become one of the major industries in the country. The reason for this was the confidence of the investors that the Middle East peace process would substantially increase the number of tourists to Jordan. According to the Jordanian Tourism Ministry, 23 new hotels were already under construction in the first months of 1996, another six were undergoing major expansion, and another 12 were on the drawing board. Estimates suggest that about $450 million is being invested in the hotel projects.[76] During the first quarter of 1996, Jordan saw a surge in investment as the result of an improved business climate. According to official Jordanian figures, approvals for projects qualifying for special tax breaks totalled $295 million, of which foreign investors provided $61 million.[77]

4 Soft Loans to Support the Jordanian Economic Reforms

The peace process has created a great willingness on the side of governments and international organizations to support Jordan's economic reforms and to finance new projects in various economic fields. In October 1995, the World Bank gave Jordan an $80 million loan to facilitate the process of implementing these economic reforms. Japan is due to provide a matching loan of $80 million and the Italian government a further $20 million, bringing the total package to $180 million.[78] The total sum of World Bank's loans to Jordan in 1995 was $125 million under co-financing arrangements with other donors, mainly the government of Japan. The Jordanian government was also scheduled to receive World Bank loans worth about $140 million in 1996.[79]

5 Reduction in Unemployment Rates

Perhaps one of the most significant socioeconomic benefits of the peace process is the marked reduction in the unemployment rate. In mid-1995, the unemployment rate in Jordan, as cited by the Minister of Planning, Rima Khalaf, was 15 percent, down from more than 25 percent after the Gulf crisis.[80] The sharp reduction in unemployment rates during the last two years is a reflection of the overall economic development in the Kingdom during this period.

6 Reduction of the Water Shortage

The water shortage has been one of the most acute problems facing Jordan over the last two decades. Since the amount of water for domestic use is increasing steadily as a result of the rapid population growth, agriculture is denied its full potential and the government has to substantially increase the import of food items. The per capita water availability in Jordan in 1990 was 327 cubic metres, as compared with 2,914 in Syria, 5,531 in Iraq, and 1,171 in Qatar. Only in Kuwait, Saudi Arabia, and the United Arab Emirates was the per capita water availability lower than in Jordan.[81] However, these countries are exporting oil in large quantities and thus have the financial resources to implement desalination plans.

The peace treaty with Israel has created the prospect of short-term relief for water shortage. Under the terms of the treaty, Jordan could get over 150 mcm of water from various sources if several dams were to be built. Bilateral technical cooperation programs financed by Germany, the US, and Canada are addressing master planning and institutional development issues through a number of long-term technical assistance projects.[82]

Summary, Conclusions and Projections

In addition to facilitating a simultaneous reduction in military expenditure for Israel and its Arab neighbors, a comprehensive and durable Arab-Israeli peace would involve significant external-related gains. The critical factors determining the economic gains from peace will be the pattern of reallocation of military expenditures; the supportive impact of larger private sector investments and other growth-inducing activities; the response of external savings; and progress toward the regional harmonization of growth-oriented economic, financial and structural policies. It is estimated that Middle Eastern countries would save in the range of about $30 billion per year were their military expenditures (relative to GDP) reduced to the world average.[83]

An additional economic benefit from the peace treaty with Israel is the US obligation to support the Jordanian economy as a part of the peace process. During his March 1995 visit to Jordan, Al Gore, the Vice President of the United States stated that:

> The US is committed to doing everything possible to advance not just the political peace process, but also the process of encouraging free market growth and the expansion of commercial and investment opportunities throughout the [Middle East] region.[84]

The improvement of the Jordanian economy as a result of the peace process is already manifested in key economic indicators. According to official Jordanian sources, the GDP is expected to grow by 6.2 percent in 1995, pushing the total GDP to $6.8–7.0 billion by the end of the year. The current account deficit should decline to 5 percent of GDP, and the budget deficit, excluding grants, to just 4.6 percent. Inflation is being held to less than 4 percent. The trade deficit, reported at $2.1 billion in 1994, is still a major problem for further economic development.[85] Jordan's total exports for 1995 were worth JD 1.0045 billion ($1.4 billion), up by 26.5 percent from the 1994 figure of JD 793.91 million.[86] The structure of imports is also changing, marking a shift from consumer items to raw materials and capital goods for an expanding industrial sector.

In addition, foreign investors are bidding for an estimated $1.2–1.5 billion export-oriented oil refinery to be built in the Red Sea port of Aqaba by the year 2000. The US energy company, Enron Corp, is also moving ahead with plans to spend up to $1.2 billion on a power plant using Qatari gas to generate electricity for Jordan and Israel.[87]

If the political stability in the area continues in the future, Jordan could further expand the tourism industry to the point of becoming the major sector in the Jordanian economy. In this respect, the head of the World Travel and Tourism Council (WTTC), Geoffrey Lippman, may prove to be right in his October 1995 statement to the press:

> This boom [the tourism] can create jobs across the whole economy and a new form of wealth that the region has not experienced before . . . we have enormous faith in this region.[88]

In conclusion, it seems that the economic and demographic pressures facing Jordan since the late 1980s, but particularly after the Gulf crisis, constituted a major factor in forging the Jordanian-Israeli peace treaty. The new economic liberalization and great economic potential of the peace process, accompanied by a substantial reduction in fertility rates and an increase in labor force participation rates, will serve to enhance the Jordanian economy in the coming years.

Notes

1 Said El-Naggar and Mohamed El-Erian, "The Economic Implications of a Comprehensive Peace in the Middle East," in Stanley Fischer, Dani Rodrik, and Elias Tuma (eds), *The Economics of Middle East Peace* (Cambridge and London, 1993), pp. 207–8 [hereafter: Fischer et al., *The Economics of Middle East Peace*].

2 The World Bank, *World Development Report – 1995* (Oxford, 1995), p. 180, table 10 [hereafter: World Bank, *World Development Report*].

3 See Moshe Ma'oz, *Syria and Israel: From War to Peace-Making* (Or-Yehuda, 1996), pp. 168–9 (in Hebrew); Gad G. Gilbar, *The Economic Development of the Middle East in Modern Times* (Tel Aviv, 1990), pp. 203–4 (in Hebrew).

4 Eliyahu Kanovsky, *Economic Development of Jordan* (Tel Aviv University, The David Horovitz Institute for the Research of Developing countries, 1977), p. 63.

5 *MEED* (Middle East Economic Digest), Vol. 39, No. 16 (21 April 1995), p. 9; See also: *Jordan Times* (Amman), 21 November 1995.

6 Peter Gubser, *Jordan – Crossroads of Middle Eastern Events* (Boulder, 1983), p. 12.

7 *Jordan Times*, 30–31 May 1996.

8 Gad G. Gilbar, "Trends in the Demographic Development of the Palestinians, 1870–1987," *Skirot*, (Tel Aviv University – Dayan Center), No. 109 (1989), p. 17 (in Hebrew); Asher Susser, "Demography and Politics in Jordan," in Ami Ayalon and Gad G. Gilbar (eds), *Demography and Politics in the Arab States* (Tel Aviv, 1995), p. 133 (in Hebrew); see also Mousa A. Samha, "The Impact of Migration on Population Changes in Jordan," *Dirasat*, Vol. 15, No. 2 (February 1988), pp. 41–3.

9 Jordan, *Statistical Yearbook – 1994*, p. 21, table 2/5.

10 ESCWA, *Population Situation in the ESCWA Region – 1990* (Amman, May 1992), p. 99, table 5.8 [hereafter: ESCWA, *Population Situation – 1990*].

11 International Labour Office (ILO), *Yearbook of Labour Statistics – 1994* (Geneva, 1995), p. 23, 27, 32, table 1.

12 EIU, *Country Profile – Jordan, 1993/94*, p. 32.

13 *Jordan Times*, 28 May 1996.

14 World Bank, *World Development Report – 1978*, p. 80, table 3.

15 World Bank, *World Development Report – 1995*, p. 166, table 3.

16 ECWA, *Population Bulletin of ECWA*, Special Issue, Nos 10 and 11 (January 1976), p. 17.

17 Jordan, *Statistical Yearbook – 1995*, p. 12, table 2/3.

18 The Hashemite Kingdom of Jordan, Department of Statistics, *1952 Census of Housing* (Amman, 1953), p. 2, table 1.

19 Jordan, *Statistical Yearbook – 1995*, p. 13, table 2/4.

20 Leila Bisharat and Magdy Tewfic, "Housing the Urban Poor in Amman," *TWPR* (Third World Planning Review), Vol. 7, No. 1 (February 1985), p. 7.

21 *MEED*, Vol. 37, No. 21 (28 May 1993), p. 9.

22 *Jordan Times*, 8 April 1996.

23 John M. Wardwell, "Jordan," in William J. Serow et al. (eds), *Handbook of International Migration* (New York and London, 1990), p. 168.

24 World Bank, *World Tables*, 1995 edn, p. 387.

25 *al-Qabas* (Kuwait), 11 September 1989.

26 *al-Ittihad* (Abu Dhabi), 11 December 1989.

27 See Ian J. Seccombe, "Immigrant Workers in an Emigrant Economy: An Examination of Replacement Migration in the Middle East," *International Migration*, Vol. 24, No. 2 (June 1986), pp. 373–8.

28 J. S. Birks et al., "Who is Migrating Where? An Overview of International Labour Migration in the Arab World," in Alan Richards and Philip Martin (eds), *Migration, Mechanization and Agricultural Labor Markets in Egypt* (Boulder and Cairo, 1983), p. 106.
29 J. S. Birks and C.A. Sinclair, *International Migration and Development in the Arab Region* (Geneva, 1980), pp. 137–9, tables 13 and 14.
30 *al-Dustur* (Amman), 17 April 1990.
31 Ahmad A. Hammouda, "Demographic Aspects of Unemployment in Jordan," *Population Studies*, No. 53 (April/June 1980), p. 19, table 2.
32 *Jordan Times* 28 June; 1–2 September; 5–6 October 1989.
33 M. A. J. Share, "Wage Differentials in Jordan: Effects on Integrated Labour Market," *Population Bulletin of ESCWA*, No. 30 (June 1987), p. 66, tables 11 and 12.
34 EIU, *Country Profile – Jordan, 1993/94*, p. 17.
35 World Bank, *World Tables*, 1995 edn, pp. 386–7.
36 Eliyahu Kanovsky, "Jordan's Economy: From Prosperity to Crisis," *Occasional Papers* (Tel Aviv University – Dayan Center, May 1989), p. 41 [hereafter: Kanovsky, "Jordan's Economy"].
37 Hani Abu-Jabarah, "The Economics of Peace: Jordan," in Fischer et al. (eds), *The Economics of Middle East Peace*, p. 182 [hereafter: Abu-Jabarah, "The Economics of Peace: Jordan"].
38 World Bank, *World Tables*, 1995 edn, pp. 4–5; 1989–90 edn, pp. 322–3.
39 IMF, *Jordan Background Information on Selected Aspects of Adjustment and Growth Strategy* (Washington, D.C.: 24 August 1995), p. 68 [hereafter: IMF, *Jordan – Background Information*].
40 Kanovsky, "Jordan's Economy," p. 41.
41 World Bank, *World Tables*, 1995 edn, pp. 386–7.
42 Riad Al-Khouri, "The Political Economy of Jordan: Democratization and the Gulf Crisis," in Dan Teschirgi (ed.), *The Arab World Today* (Boulder and London, 1994), p. 105.
43 *MEED*, Vol. 36, No. 32 (14 August 1992), p. 19.
44 *Jordan Times*, 14 October 1991.
45 *al-Jamhuriyya* (Cairo), 2 September 1992.
46 *Jordan Times*, 26 July 1995.
47 EIU, *Country Profile – Jordan, 1995/96*, p. 17; *Jordan Times*, 8 August 1995.
48 *Jordan Times*, 20 April 1996.
49 *MEED*, Vol. 35, No. 41 (20 September 1991), p. 15.
50 *MEED*, Vol. 35, No. 45 (8 November 1991), p. 17.
51 EIU, *Country Profile – Jordan, 1995/96*, pp. 13–14.
52 *Jordan Times*, 1 October 1995.
53 Abu-Jabarah, "The Economics of Peace: Jordan," p. 189.
54 IMF, Jordan – Background Information, p. 28.
55 *Jordan Times*, 26–27 January 1995.
56 World Bank, *World Tables*, 1995 edn, p. 385.
57 Hani Abu-Jabarah, "The Economics of Peace: Jordan," p. 182, table 7.1.
58 *Jordan Times*, 1–2 January 1995.
59 *Jordan Times*, 26–27 January 1995.
60 *Jordan Times*, 23–24 March 1995.

61 *al-Dustur*, 30 October 1995.
62 *Jordan Times*, 23–24 March 1995.
63 *MEED*, Vol. 39, No. 16 (21 April 1995), p. 9.
64 *Jordan Times*, 18 March 1996.
65 ESCWA, *Survey of Economic and Social Developments in the ESCWA Region, 1994*, p. 64.
66 *Jordan Times*, 23–24 March 1995.
67 M. Thea Sinclair and M. J. Stabler, "New Perspectives on the Tourism Industry," in M. Thea Sinclair and M. J. Stabler (eds), *The Tourism Industry: An International Analysis* (Wallingford, 1993), p. 1; Robert W. McIntosh and Charles R. Geoldner, *Tourism: Principles, Practices, Philosophies* (New York, 1986), p. 18.
68 EIU, "Jordan," *International Tourism Reports*, No. 3 (1992), p. 39.
69 *MEED*, Vol. 39, No. 16 (21 April 1995), p. 16.
70 *Jordan Times*, 6 April 1996.
71 Ibid.
72 *Jordan Times*, 11 May 1996.
73 *Jordan Times*, 27 June, 12 August 1995.
74 *MEED*, Vol. 39, No. 40 (6 October 1995), p. 4; *Jordan Times*, 1 January; 24 April 1996.
75 *MEED*, Vol. 39, No. 43 (27 October 1995), p. 12.
76 *MEED*, Vol. 40, No. 12 (22 March 1996), p. 41.
77 *Jordan Times*, 24 April 1996.
78 *MEED*, Vol. 39, No. 43 (27 October 1995), p. 10; *al-Dustur*, 30 October 1995.
79 *Jordan Times*, 21 January 1996.
80 *Jordan Times*, 18 April; 6–7 July; 28 November 1995.
81 Peter H. Gleick, "Water, War & Peace in the Middle East," *Environment*, Vol. 36, No. 3 (April 1994), p. 37, table 3.
82 *MEED*, Vol. 40, No. 11 (15 March 1996), pp. 14–15; *Jordan Times*, 26 February 1995.
83 El-Naggar and El-Arian, "The Economic Implications," pp. 211–13.
84 *United States Information Agency*, 21 March 1995, p. 8.
85 *MEED*, Vol. 39, No. 43 (27 October 1995), pp. 7–8; *MEED*, Vol. 39, No. 41 (13 October 1995), p. 17; *Jordan Times*, 1 October 1995.
86 *Jordan Times*, 28–29 March; 6–7 June 1996.
87 *Jordan Times*, 3, 24 April 1996.
88 *Jordan Times*, 23 October 1995.

14

The Development of the Jordanian Tourism Industry

Onn Winckler and Gad G. Gilbar

During the past few decades, tourism has emerged as one of the world's major industries, exceeding many manufacturing industries and other services, both in terms of number of employees and foreign currency earning. The rapid growth of the tourism industry that has occurred in both developed and developing countries has propelled it into the position of a major social and economic force worldwide.

For a growing number of countries during the last two decades, tourism has become the largest economic sector, both in terms of trade and number of employees. In many others, it ranks among the top three industries.

One of the most important direct economic benefits derived from the development of the tourism industry is increased governmental revenues, collected through various types of taxation on tourism, which can be used to develop infrastructure facilities and other community services, as well as to assist in overall economic development. An important indirect economic benefit of tourism is that it serves as a catalyst for the development of other economic sectors, such as construction, agriculture, fisheries, transportation and other infrastructure facilities, and certain types of manufacturing insofar as they supply the goods and services used in the tourism industry. In addition, work opportunities in the tourism industry, as compared with other industries and services, are relatively quick and cheap to create. Tourism also provides a wide range of entry points into the labor market, both for skilled and unskilled workers.[1]

The main aims of this chapter are to trace the development of the tourism industry in Jordan as it relates to the overall economic development in the Kingdom, as well as to the peace treaty with Israel signed in October 1994.

The Advantages of the Tourism Industry for the Jordanian Economy

In general, there are a wide variety of direct and indirect economic benefits which provide the impetus for developing tourism in any given area. For the Jordanian economy, in particular, the tourism industry has five main advantages:

(1) Tourism is a heavily labor-intensive field in which it is possible to create a large number of work opportunities in a relatively short period of time, both for skilled and professional workers, as well as for unskilled workers. Since the late 1980s and particularly after the Gulf crisis of 1990/1, one of the main economic problems facing Jordan is a high rate of unemployment. Following the Iraqi invasion of Kuwait in August 1990, about 350,000 Jordanians and Palestinians returned to Jordan from the Gulf countries, most of them from Kuwait.[2] Within a few months (from August 1990 until March 1991), the Jordanian population increased by more than 10 percent, changing the Jordanian labor market dramatically. Jordan, like other major labor-exporting countries in the Middle East (mainly Egypt and Yemen), was not able to absorb hundreds of thousands of returnees in the space of only a few months, especially in the labor market. As a result, within a very short period of time, the unemployment rate in Jordan increased to unprecedented levels.

According to official Jordanian figures, unemployment rose to 22.9 percent of the total work force by October 1991. However, economists and labor analysts believed that the actual figure, including those not registered with the authorities, was closer to 35 percent.[3] This placed Jordan among the countries with the highest rates of unemployment throughout the Middle East region.

It has to be emphasized, however, that such a high unemployment rate is not only a socioeconomic problem, but even more importantly, a severe political problem. High rates of unemployment have the potential to exaggerate opposition activities that are fueled by severe socioeconomic tension. The Middle Eastern regimes, including that of Jordan, are extremely sensitive to the problem of high unemployment rates due to the political structure in these countries.

Thus, creating a large number of work opportunities is one of the most pressing tasks for the Jordanian economy. In this respect, tourism has great potential to become one of the most important sources for creating a large number of work opportunities within a relatively short period of time.

(2) The revenues from tourism are in foreign currency, mainly US dollars and European currencies. Until the Iraqi invasion of Kuwait, the two most important sources for hard currency in Jordan were: (a) the large-scale workers' remittances, which by the early 1980s reached more than $1.2 billion annually,[4] and (b) the large-scale foreign grants, mainly from the rich Arab oil-exporting countries, which reached by 1980 $1.3 billion.[5] However, after the Gulf crisis, as a result of Jordan's support of Iraq, these grants were almost entirely terminated. The result of this, combined with the overwhelming problem of the returnees, was double: first, a sharp increase in the external debt, which by 1991 reached more than $9 billion (of this $2.5 billion was a short-term debt),[6] while the total GDP for that year was only $5.5 billion. The second result was a growing balance of payments deficit, which reached more than $1.5 billion on average during the early 1990s.[7] In this arena as well, the tourism industry has the potential to become a major tool in overcoming the huge external debt and the large-scale balance of payments deficit by absorbing large sums of hard currencies.

(3) Tourism boosts other economic sectors, particularly construction and infrastructure-related industries. As a result of the international economic embargo, which was imposed against Iraq after the invasion of Kuwait, Jordan lost a lucrative export and re-export market, thereby damaging the Jordanian manufacturing sector, which had become heavily dependent on the Iraqi market[8] since the beginning of the Iran–Iraq war. According to Jordanian sources, Jordan's annual loss as a result of its adherence to the sanctions against Iraq is about $350 million.[9] Also in this field, the tourism industry can provide a major impetus for industrial and manufacturing development by replacing the lost Iraqi market with the manufacturing goods demanded by tourism (food and textiles in particular).

(4) Tourism promotes foreign investment, especially in the construction of new hotels and tourism sites.

(5) The tourism industry will generate growth in several regions, such as Aqaba, Amman, the Dead Sea, and Jarash in the north of the Kingdom.

The Tourism Attractions in Jordan

Jordan possesses archeological and recreational sites of sufficient interest to attract large-scale tourism. The major tourist attraction is the historic city of Petra, carved in the sandstone cliffs. Aqaba is another famous tourism site located on the northern coast of the Red Sea. Another popular site is the Dead Sea, the lowest point on earth. In addition, Jordan possesses archeological sites in Jarash, Madaba, Karak, Wadi Rum, and Shubak. In terms of cultural and historical interest, it seems that few destinations in the Middle East hold as much interest for tourists as does Jordan.[10]

Institutional and Regulatory Framework

A number of organizations deal with the tourism industry, in both the public and the private sector. Various governmental institutions coordinate their activities and make decisions through inter-ministerial committees. The principle organizations involved are as follows:

1 *Ministry of Tourism and Antiquities (MOTA)*
The MOTA is the main governmental organization dealing with the tourism industry. Two separate departments are included in the MOTA: the first deals with tourism and the second is the Department of Antiquities. The role of MOTA is to aid the private sector in developing tourism facilities (hotels, tourism agencies, etc.). Accordingly, the marketing and promotion of tourism are implemented by the government in cooperation with the private sector.

2 *Jordan Valley Authority (JVA)*
The JVA is responsible for planning tourism development in the Jordan Rift Valley, including the Dead Sea area. In 1988, the JVA's authority was expanded to include the entire Jordan Rift Valley. The JVA is supervised by the Ministry of Water and Irrigation.

3 *Aqaba Region Authority (ARA)*
Similar to the JVA, the ARA is also responsible for promoting tourism development and planning within its area of jurisdiction. The ARA oversees infrastructure development and investment programs for the proposed South Coast Tourist Master Plan.

4 *Ministry of Planning*
The Tourism Section in the Ministry of Planning is charged with the mission of initiating new projects and overseeing all planning activities within the tourism sector.[11]

The Main Trends in the Development of the Tourism Industry in Jordan

It seems that three main stages can be identified in the development of the tourism industry in Jordan. Similar to other developing countries, modern tourism in Jordan started on a small scale after the World War II. In 1953, there were about 40,000 tourists in Jordan, accounting for less than $4 million in receipts. By 1960, the number of tourists in the Kingdom increased to 131,099 and continued to rise to 616,784 in 1966, accounting for about $35 million.[12] At that time, most of the Jordanian tourism industry was concentrated in the West Bank (East Jerusalem, Ramalla, and Bethlehem), where more than 80 percent of its hotel accommodations were located.

The second stage started after the June 1967 war, when there was an increasing recognition on the part of the Jordanian authorities that the various tourism sites and the potential of the East Bank in this field had been neglected until then. As a result, the Jordanian authorities started to pay more attention to the development of the tourism industry in the East Bank.[13] On the political level, efforts were made to facilitate the movement of tourists between the two banks of the Jordan River, thereby allowing Amman once again to provide access to the tourism sites in the East Bank.

Following the occupation of the West Bank by Israel, it was clear to the Jordanian authorities that there were several main tourism attractions worthy of development in the East Bank to compensate for the loss of tourism sites in the West Bank: first and foremost, the historic city of Petra and the Roman city of Jarash; the crusader castles; and the Aqaba beach. Hence, substantial efforts were made to improve and promote these attractions.[14]

However, the political instability in Jordan during 1970, as a result of the armed struggle between the PLO and the Jordanian authorities, and particularly the clashes in September 1970, known as "Black September," brought about a sharp recession in the Jordanian tourism industry.

By 1972, the third phase started with the sharp recovery of the Jordanian tourism industry. Tourism income in 1975 reached $112 million, as compared with only $32 million in 1966.[15] By 1978, the number of visitors in Jordan rose to 1.2 million, providing an almost unprecedented annual growth rate of more than 30 percent. However, it must be emphasized that a very low proportion of these visitors, only 15 percent, were from Europe and North America, mainly due to the lack of suitable hotels and adequate infrastructure.[16] Moreover, it seems that a large number of these visitors were temporary foreign workers (mainly from Egypt and Syria) replacing the Jordanians who were working at that time in the Persian Gulf oil-exporting countries.

Table 14.1 Jordan: hotels, rest houses and pensions, 1982–1995

Year	Beds	Rooms	Hotels
1982	12,693	6,373	219
1983	14,273	7,168	233
1984	14,042	7,056	226
1985	10,179	5,479	223
1986	13,736	6,929	215
1987	14,229	7,181	220
1988	14,303	7,265	219
1989	15,134	7,458	223
1990	15,302	7,576	224
1991	15,624	7,592	223
1992	16,315	8,083	241
1993	16,791	8,384	254
1994	17,389	8,680	262
1995	17,723	8,848	274

Sources: Jordan, *Statistical Yearbook – 1994*, p. 333, Table 12/2/1;
Jordan, *Statistical Yearbook – 1995*, p. 316, Table 12/2/1.

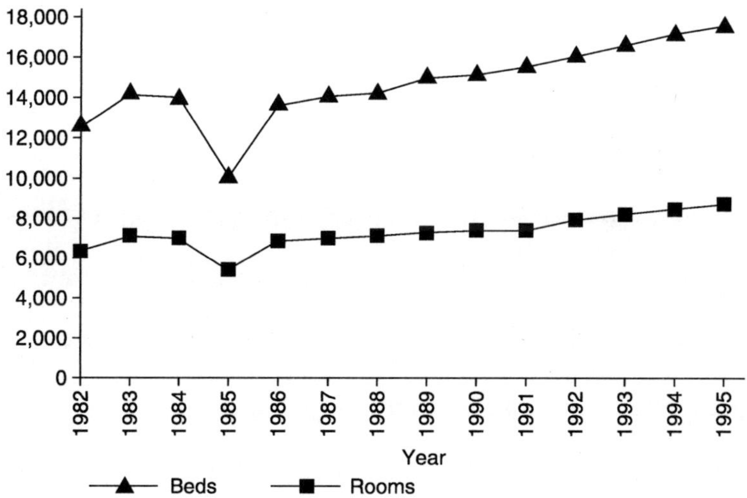

Figure 14.1 Beds and rooms hotel in Jordan, 1982–1995
Data taken from table 14.1

The Five-Year Development Plan for the years 1981–5 had predicted a sharp increase in tourism receipts, reaching over $900 million by 1985.

While there was considerable investment in the construction of hotels, including both expansion and modernization, the subsequent level of tourism activities, especially attraction of a large number of tourists from Western countries, failed to meet expectations. Overall, during the first half of the 1980s, there was a freezing, and even a drop, in the Jordanian tourism industry. In fact, there was a significant decline in tourism activities, and by 1985 the total tourism receipts were only $517 million,[17] as compared with $548 million four years earlier, in 1981 (in current prices).[18]

During the second half of the 1980s, the freezing in Jordanian tourism development continued, and in 1989 the total tourism receipts were $551 million, representing an increase of only 3 percent as compared with the receipts of $535 million in 1986. However, in real terms (measured in constant US dollars), there was even a decrease.[19]

During the Gulf crisis, the number of tourists in Jordan decreased considerably to only 572,000 in 1990, as compared with 639,000 one year earlier, in 1989. The total tourism receipts in 1990 was also very low: only $512 million. This trend continued in 1991 when the total number of tourists was 436,00 with total receipts of only $317 million. However, in 1992, the Jordanian tourism industry started to recover, and the number of tourists that year reached 661,000 with total receipts of $462 million.[20]

The Middle East peace process, and in particular, the peace treaty with Israel in October 1994, boosted the Jordanian tourism industry. By 1994, the tourism activities in Jordan had returned to the pre-war level, with total tourism receipts of $642 million.[21] Since then, the activity level of the Jordanian tourism industry has been increasing by high rates. One year later, in 1995, the number of tourists in Jordan reached 1.07 million, bringing in revenues of $723 million. In that year, the tourism industry constituted 10 percent of the total GDP, representing the largest foreign exchange earner in Jordan and exceeding the next biggest sector, that of chemicals, by a considerable margin.[22] According to the projections of the MOTA, in 1996 the number of tourists in Jordan was expected to reach 1.3 million, bringing in revenues of about $1 billion – almost 30 percent more than in the previous year.[23]

The Development of the Main Tourism Sites in Jordan

1 *Petra*

Petra is the main tourism attraction in Jordan. In 1995, the total number of tourists visiting Petra was about 300,000, an increase of more than 50 percent as compared with the previous year. Recognizing the huge tourism potential of Petra, many countries have offered assistance. Out of a total of $77 million donated to Jordan for tourism projects, more than half is earmarked for Petra.[24] In 1995, there were four classified hotels in Petra with 413 beds. In addition, a 244-bed five-star hotel and a 172-bed four-star hotel were both nearing completion; and another six five-star and four-star hotels with a total of 1,750 beds were under construction.[25]

By 1996, officials in the MOTA estimated that the number of tourists in Petra was nearly double the planned capacity. However, taking into account length of stay reflects Jordan's concern about the growing number of tourists who arrive from Israel on one-day trips, taking up space in the city but spending little. Jordanian officials are now pressing Israel to guarantee that groups from Israel spend at least two nights in the Kingdom.[26]

2 *The Dead Sea*

The Dead Sea area has been identified by both the Ministry of Planning and the JVA as a priority area for tourism development due to its therapeutic attributes, as well as its historical value. Today, the tourism facilities in the area are very limited and include only one hotel. Regarding future tourism development in this area, in December 1994, the JVA adopted the *Dead Sea Tourism Project Master Plan*, identifying three major development sectors in the eastern Dead Sea region: Suweimeh in the north, Zara in the center, and Al-Mazara in the south. The citadel zone, located between Zara and Al-Mazara, will be an additional site for development. The project includes the construction of about 15,000 hotel rooms and 18,000 housing units until the year 2010. The first stage of the plan for the Suweimeh and Zara sectors entails the construction of 5,300 hotel rooms, 5,200 units for rental and holiday homes, and 37,000 square meters for commercial use. The total investment in the infrastructure and tourism facilities in this project is estimated at about $500 million. By late 1995, four hotels with international chains had been approved along the area, costing an estimated $280 million.[27]

3 *Jarash*

The northern region of the Jordan Valley offers a number of tourism attractions, the most important of which is the Roman Decapolis City. The site is well preserved and is still in the process of being excavated. However, despite its attraction, the area lacks adequate infrastructure development, and there are only a few hotels in the area, none of which seem to meet internationally accepted standards.[28]

4 Aqaba

The Red Sea is another major tourism site. However, the Red Sea coastal resort of Aqaba has never attracted more than about 100,000 tourists a year, mainly due to a shortage of suitable hotel accommodations. By 1995, there were only 1,413 hotel beds in Aqaba.[29] As a result of its great tourism potential, the Aqaba area has been attracting foreign tourism companies to invest in this region. The first was France's Club Mediterranee, which started in 1992 to establish a holiday village in Aqaba at a cost of about $20 million. The program was a joint venture with the Royal Jordanian. The French company aimed to attract 20,000–22,000 visitors a year to the village.[30]

Table 14.2 Jordan: tourism statistics, 1990–1995

Particulars	1990	1991	1992	1993	1994	1995
Tourist hotels – rooms	6,373	6,349	6,779	6,931	7,181	7,169
Tourist hotels – beds	12,285	12,525	13,079	13,213	13,719	13,695
Travel agents	212	228	280	298	326	371
Rental car companies	54	54	63	75	100	154
Travel cars	840	840	950	1,100	1,810	2,350
Tourist shops	107	107	112	127	142	153

Sources: Jordan, *Statistical Yearbook – 1994*, p. 334, Table 12/2/2; Jordan, *Statistical Yearbook – 1995*, p. 317, Table 12/2/2.

As for future tourism development in the Aqaba region, by the end of 1995, the Aqaba Region Authority had signed a preliminary agreement with the California-based Magic World Development for the establishment of a $132 million theme park and hotel complex spanning 400 dunams on the southern coast of Aqaba. The focus of the project will be a theme park based on Middle Eastern history and legends and will also include a deluxe 256-room hotel and another 200 cabana suites. This project is the largest tourism venture to have been planned in Jordan in recent years.[31]

Obstacles Facing the Jordanian Tourism Industry

Experts are confident that the Middle East peace process will bring prosperity to the tourism industry throughout the region, including Jordan. However, Jordan will need to expand its tourism capacity in order to benefit from this expected growth. There are various obstacles facing the Jordanian tourism industry which need to be overcome for further expansion, the most important being as follows:

1 *Expanding Tourism Outside Amman*

The major impediment to further expanding tourist attractions outside Amman is the undeveloped infrastructure in the main tourism sites, such as Petra, the Dead Sea area, and Aqaba. For example, the only hotel in the Dead Sea lacks appropriate infrastructure facilities, including sewage treatment and telephone lines. The entire hotel depends on a single cellular telephone. In order to increase the tourism capacity in this area, the Jordanian authorities will have to invest large sums of money in infrastructure development.

2 *Scarcity of Tourism Training and Education*

There is little training available for professionals who are providing tourist services, such as tourist guides, car rental employees, and hotel staff. There is only one hotel management school in Jordan, which was administered by the Ministry of Education until the beginning of June 1996. Following pressure from local investors to transfer the administration of the hotel management school to the private sector,[32] the Ammoun Training Hotel (ATH) was leased to the Jordanian Tourism Hotel Training Company (JTHTC). The lease provides for the introduction of new training courses and curricula approved by the Ministry of Higher Education, as well as for the training of Jordanians in hotel and tourism industry issues. By mid-June 1996, the ATH had already started admitting students for the academic year of 1996/7.[33]

Table 14.3 Jordan: employment in tourist activities, 1990–1995

Field	1990	1991	1992	1993	1994	1995
Classified hotels	5,814	5,880	5,999	4,663	4,828	4,824
Unclassified hotels	360	374	399	444	462	534
Tourist and travel agencies	995	1,059	1,264	1,365	1,472	1,658
Rental car companies	168	168	200	250	400	600
Tourist shops	212	212	220	250	300	335
Tourist guides	111	157	192	240	317	414
Camel and horse guides	377	391	386	385	387	387

Sources: Jordan, *Statistical Yearbook – 1994*, p. 335, Table 12/2/3;
Jordan, *Statistical Yearbook – 1995*, p. 318, Table 12/2/3.

3 Short Length of Stay
Yet despite this relative boom in the number of tourists, the average number of nights spent in Jordan dropped from 5.1 in 1989 to 3.7 in 1995.[34] This is partially due to the relatively large number of tourists who come from Eilat only for a one-day trip to Petra.

Attraction of Foreign Investment to the Jordanian Tourism Industry

Substantial growth of the Jordanian tourism industry depends, to a great extent, on foreign investment. Thus, since the beginning of 1994, the Jordanian authorities have invested a considerable effort in establishing measures to reform the Kingdom's tax codes so as to create a more attractive investment environment. The new law, enacted in September 1995, provides incentives via tax exemptions which are weighted in favor of less developed areas. It also contains a commitment that all investment proposals will receive a reply from the Higher Council for Investment within 30 days of application. Furthermore, the law provides equal terms to foreign investors, as delineated in article 24: "The non-Jordanian investor will enjoy equal treatment under this law with the Jordanian investor."[35]

During the first quarter of 1996, Jordan saw a surge in investment as a result of the improved business climate. According to the Jordanian official figures, approvals for projects qualifying for special tax breaks totalled $295 million, of which foreign investors provided $61 million.[36] By the beginning of 1996, hotel construction had become one of the major industries in Jordan. The reason for this is the confidence of the investors that the Middle East peace process will promote the Jordanian tourism industry. According to the MOTA data, by the beginning of 1996, 23 hotels were under construction all over the Kingdom and another six were undergoing major expansion, while 12 others were on the drawing board. The total investment in these projects was estimated to be $450 million.[37]

Tourism Cooperation Between Jordan and Israel

On 4 April 1995, the Jordanian Minister of Tourism, Abdul Illah Al-Khatib, signed a tourism agreement with his Israeli counterpart, Uzi Bar'am, in the Jordan Valley. The accord calls for broad coordination between the two countries, including marketing of joint tour packages abroad, exchange of tourism information, and cooperation between the two national airlines, Royal Jordanian and El-Al. The two ministers also agreed to set up a joint tourism committee which will meet annually.[38] The full tourism agreement between Jordan and Israel appears in Appendix 1. As a result of this tourism agreement, there are many schemes for cooperation between the two countries, most of which concentrate on cross-border infrastructure projects and joint marketing of tourism in European and North American markets.[39] There is also a relatively large-scale movement of tourists from Israel to Jordan. Since the signing of the peace treaty until May 1996, about 150,000 Israelis visited Jordan;[40] however, a large number of them take only a one day trip, from Eilat to Petra.

Summary, Conclusions, and Projections

The Middle East peace process has raised awareness of the tremendous tourism potential of the Middle East. However, further advances need to be made in the areas of security, infrastructure and services, as well as attraction of large-scale foreign investment. These and other measures will ensure that tourism will become one of the major industries throughout the middle East region.

In this respect, the head of the World Travel and Tourism Council (WTTC), Geoffrey Lippman, paints an optimistic picture:

> This boom [of tourism] can create jobs across the whole economy and a new form of wealth that the region has not experienced before . . . We have enormous faith in this region . . . Peace would allow tours to freely cross borders to visit multiple sites, such as Jerusalem, the pyramids in Egypt, and the ancient city of Petra in Jordan.[41]

In 1995, the Middle East/Mediterranean region accounted for an estimated $78.7 billion of the travel and tourism gross output, representing 2.3 percent of the world total. This share has declined over the past three years from $91.0 billion in 1992, or 2.8 percent, of the world gross output. In that year, the tourism sector in the Middle East/Mediterranean region constituted, both directly and indirectly, 8.7 percent of the total region's GDP, 10.1 percent of all employment, 8.5 percent of capital investment, and 9.8 percent of indirect tax income.

In 1995, an estimated 7.8 million jobs were expected to be created in the Middle East/Mediterranean region, both directly and indirectly, in the tourism industry. This represents about 10 percent of the region's total work force. The tourism sector in the Middle East/Mediterranean region is expected to grow its total direct and indirect output contribution by more than 207 percent (in real terms) over the coming decade to over $332 billion by the year 2005.[42] However, it has to be emphasized that the tourism industry is highly sensitive to geo-political conditions; hence, the regional tourism industry suffered heavily from the effects of the Gulf crisis in 1990/1, particularly in Jordan. However, during the last three years (1994–6), as an outcome of the peace treaty, Jordan has seen a substantial annual increase in international tourism. Today, the tourism industry represents the largest earner of hard currency within the entire Jordanian economy.

There is a general understanding in Jordan and abroad that the increase in the output of the tourism industry is primarily due to the peace process. The Jordanian Tourism Minister, Abdul Ilah Al-Khatib, has attributed the sharp growth of tourism in the Kingdom to many factors, but mainly to the stability in the region in the new era of peace.[43] In August 1995, the Minister stated to reporters that: "Peace has obviously encouraged tourists coming from Israel, the United States, Canada, and Europe to visit Jordan."[44] By December of that year the Minister told Reuters that: "With the peace process we hope that the region, including Jordan, will take a bigger share of world tourism – that reflects its resources and unique heritage."[45]

Freedom of access between the countries in the region, especially between Jordan, Israel, and the areas under control of the Palestinian Authority, has led to an increase of cross-border tourism which is likely to continue at a rapid pace in the coming years. The peace process also brings with it a climate favoring foreign private investors, as well as donor countries and international agencies, both of which are showing increased interest in the Middle East region.[46]

In conclusion, it seems that the tourism industry in Jordan, with proper and wise investments in parallel to the continued stability of peace in the Middle East region, can replace the Gulf oil-exporting countries, not only as a main source of employment, but also as a major source of hard currency for the Jordanian economy in the coming years.

Appendix 1:
Agreement on Tourism between the State of Israel and The Hashemite Kingdom of Jordan

The Government of the State of Israel and the Government of the Hashemite Kingdom of Jordan (hereinafter referred to as "the Parties"); Pursuant to and in the spirit of the Peace Treaty signed between the State of Israel and the Hashemite Kingdom of Jordan on 26 October 1994, (hereinafter referred to as the "Treaty of Peace)", particularly Article 17 therein; Desirous to broaden further the friendly relations between their countries on the basis of equality, for their mutual benefit; and Recognising the importance of tourism, Have agreed as follows:

ARTICLE 1

The Parties shall, within the framework of their laws, regulations and prerogatives, adopt adequate measures to promote and encourage the development of tourism between the two countries and to intensify the cooperation between their tourism organisations, both in the public and private sectors, including their air carriers.

ARTICLE 2

The Parties shall examine possible ways of facilitating and of promoting the tourist movement within the framework of the laws and regulations in each of the two countries.

ARTICLE 3

The Parties agree to facilitate the exchange of information on matters concerning tourism and travel in the two countries, including inter-alia, planned tourism events.

ARTICLE 4

The Parties agree to develop and strengthen technical cooperation in the field of tourism professional training expertise.

ARTICLE 5

The Parties shall encourage tourism from third countries (tourism generating markets). With this aim in mind, both Parties shall give special attention to the cooperation in the field of marketing and promotional activities, especially efforts to bring about the extended stay of tourists, in order to ensure that both Parties shall benefit from this traffic.

ARTICLE 6

The Parties shall make efforts, as appropriate, to further develop their cooperation in international and regional bodies in the field of tourism, and shall exchange information concerning their achievements in this field.

ARTICLE 7

A Joint Commission shall be set up and assigned with the task of studying, agreeing on and following up on measures capable of contributing to the attainment of the above objectives.

ARTICLE 8

The Joint Commission shall consist of two representatives designated by the Ministry of Tourism of the State of Israel and of two representatives designated by the Ministry of Tourism of the Hashemite Kingdom of Jordan, thus constituting national delegations (hereinafter referred to as "National Delegations"). Each National Delegation may be accompanied by their experts, as necessary.

Recognising that governments primarily serve as catalysts for travel and tourism, while private organisations are primarily the providers of goods and services to travellers and tourists, both Parties agree to include private sector representatives from the two countries in all the working groups and committees established in accordance with this Agreement.

ARTICLE 9

The Joint Commission shall meet once a year. The Joint Commission may hold extraordinary meetings if it is deemed necessary, and with the agreement of the Heads of the National Delegations. The Joint Commission shall meet alternately in each of the two countries on a date to be mutually agreed upon by the Heads of the National Delegations. The Head of the National Delegation of the host country shall preside the meeting. The National Delegation acting as host, shall be responsible for the work and expenses of the meeting's secretariat.

ARTICLE 10

The working language of the Joint Commission shall be English.

ARTICLE 11

The Joint Commission shall draw up its program of work and the priority order of the topics and problems to be dealt with, as well as any other matter which may be deemed necessary. The agenda for each meeting shall be jointly established by both heads of the National

Delegations, at least one month before such meeting.

ARTICLE 12

The decisions of the Joint Commission shall be submitted to the appropriate bodies of their respective Governments for approval. Upon approval, the decisions shall be implemented.

ARTICLE 13

Each Party hereby designates its Ministry of Tourism as the agency with the primary long term responsibility for implementing this Agreement.

ARTICLE 14

This Agreement is subject to approval or ratification in accordance with the national legislation and procedures of each Party and shall enter into force on the day following the exchange of notes confirming such approval or ratification.

ARTICLE 15

1. Disputes arising as to the implementation or interpretation of this Agreement shall be resolved by negotiations.
2. If, after a period of six months from the date in which negotiations started, the dispute is still unresolved, Article 29-2 of the Treaty of Peace shall apply.

ARTICLE 16

The present Agreement is concluded for a period of three (3) years, and will be automatically renewed by tacit acquiescence for further periods of three (3) years, unless denounced in writing by one of the Parties by an advance notice of three (3) months.

Acknowledgment

This study is based on research supported by a grant from the Berta Von Suttner Stiftung. Also, we would like to thank Mr M. Benari, the Director of the International Relations Department of the Israeli Ministry of Tourism, who assisted in the task of collecting the material for this research.

Notes

1 M. Thea Sinclair and M. J. Stabler, "New Perspectives on the Tourism Industry," in M. Thea Sinclair and M. J. Stabler (eds), *The Tourism Industry: An International Analysis* (Wallingford, 1993), p. 1; Robert W. McIntosh and

Charles R. Geoldner, *Tourism: Principles, Practices, Philosophies* (New York, 1986), p. 18; Eric Laws, *Tourist Destination Management: Issues, Analysis and Policies* (London and New York, 1995), p. 85.

2 *MEED (Middle East Economic Digest)*, Vol. 36, No. 32 (14 August 1992), p. 19.

3 *Jordan Times* (Amman), 14 October 1991.

4 The World Bank, *World Tables*, 1995 edition (Baltimore and London, 1995), pp. 386–7.

5 Eliyahu Kanovsky, "Jordan's Economy: From Prosperity to Crisis," *Occasional Papers* (Tel Aviv University, Dayan Center, May 1989), p. 41 [hereafter: Kanovsky, "Jordan's Economy"].

6 ESCWA, *Survey of Economic and Social Developments in the ESCWA Region – 1994* (New York, 1995), p. 65, table 38.

7 The World Bank, *World Tables*, 1995 edition, p. 387.

8 EIU, *Country Profile, Jordan, 1995/96*, pp. 13–14.

9 *Jordan Times*, 1 October 1995.

10 EIU, "Jordan," *International Tourism Reports*, No. 3 (1992), p. 39 [hereafter: EIU, "Jordan" (1992)].

11 The Harza JVA Group, *Jordan Rift Valley Integrated Development Study, Sector Profile-Tourism*, April 1996, pp. 3-1, 3-3.

12 EIU, "Jordan," *International Tourism Quarterly*, No. 4 (1979), p. 25.

13 E. Kanovsky, *Economic Development of Jordan*, Report No. 14 (Tel Aviv, 1977), p. 63.

14 EIU, "Jordan," *International Tourism Reports*, No. 138 (1987), pp. 41–2.

15 Kanovsky, "Jordan's Economy," p. 17.

16 EIU, "Jordan" (1979), pp. 25–7.

17 World Tourism Organization, *Yearbook of Tourism Statistics – 1992*, Vol. 1, p. 152.

18 Kanovsky, "Jordan's Economy," p. 17.

19 *Yearbook of Tourism Statistics – 1992*, 44 edition, Vol. 1, p. 112.

20 *Yearbook of Tourism Statistics – 1994*, 46 edition, Vol. 1, pp. 123–5.

21 *MEED*, Vol. 39, No. 16 (21 April 1995), p. 16.

22 *Jordan Rift Valley*, p. 2-4.

23 *Jordan Times*, 6 April 1996; The Hashemite Kingdom of Jordan, Department of Statistics, *Statistical Yearbook-1995* (Amman, 1996), p. 486, table 19/2/1.

24 *Jordan Rift Valley*, p. 8-2.

25 *MEED*, Vol. 39, No. 16 (21 April 1995), p. 16.

26 *Jordan Times*, 13 May 1996.

27 The Government of Israel, Ministry of Foreign Affairs and Ministry of Finance, *Development Options for Cooperation: The Middle East/ Mediterranean Region-1996* (Jerusalem, 1995), p. 7-14; *Jordan Times*, 10 December 1995.

28 *Jordan Rift Valley*, p. 4-1.

29 EIU, "Jordan" (1992), p. 35; *MEED*, Vol. 39, No. 16 (21 April 1995), p. 16.

30 *MEED*, Vol. 36, No. 7 (21 February 1992), p. 14.

31 *MEED*, Vol. 39, No. 42 (20 October 1995), p. 22.

32 The World Bank, *Peace and the Jordanian Economy* (Washington, D.C., 1994), p. 33.

33 *Jordan Times*, 16 June 1996.
34 *Jordan Times*, 13 May 1996.
35 *MEED*, Vol. 39, No. 40 (6 October 1995), p. 4; *Jordan Times*, 1 January; 24 April 1996.
36 *Jordan Times*, 24 April 1996.
37 *MEED*, Vol. 40, No. 12 (22 March 1996), p. 41.
38 *MEED*, Vol. 39, No. 15 (14 April 1995), p. 32.
39 State of Israel, Ministry of Tourism, International Relation Department, *Peace Tourism Update* (Jerusalem, February 1996), p. 4.
40 *Jordan Times*, 11 May 1996.
41 *Jordan Times*, 23 October 1995.
42 World Travel and Tourism Council, *Middle East – Mediterranean* (October 1995), pp. 4–5; *Jordan Times*, 20 March 1996.
43 *Jordan Times*, 27 June 1995.
44 *Jordan Times*, 12 August 1995.
45 *Jordan Times*, 10 December 1995.
46 Patrick Clawson, *Tourism Cooperation in the Levant*, Research Memorandum, No. 16 (Washington, D.C., The Washington Institute, May 1994), p. 17.

15

Opportunities in the Wind: Development and Cooperation in the Triangle

Taisir I. Amre

Almost two years have passed since the holding of the conference co-sponsored by the Institute on Global Conflict and Cooperation, the University of California, the National Center for Human Resources and Development, Amman, and the Jewish-Arab Center, Haifa. A look to the political downs (unfortunately, there are no ups) in the last two years leads to a very gloomy view; nevertheless, one can candidly dip into a methodological analysis of the related issues to diagnose the nature and weight of the interwoven elements which constitute the interests of each party in the Triangle. Those interests will be, and should be, the driving force behind attitudes and strategies of the parties.

To start with, it is regrettable to note that peace is still awaited in the Triangle (let alone Syria and Lebanon). This is so despite the Israeli-Jordanian peace treaty and the Israeli-Palestinian transitional accord.

It is well known that this dramatic political breakthrough brought with it a widespread hope of what has been called a peace dividend in terms of economic cooperation. That is why the parties involved have reinforced the multilateral mechanism by successive economic summits in Casablanca, in October–November 1994; Amman, in October 1995; and Cairo, in November 1996. In addition, there will be the forthcoming controversial conference in Douha, Qatar, in November 1997.

Although the participants agreed in the Casablanca meeting to establish the Middle East Development Bank for the region, it is a truism that the tangible fruits of the multilateral track, as well as the summits, were miserably negligent to the extent of making it not only a priority, but a duty to discuss the pros and cons of this failure and to answer the related causative questions. Since the related issues are not exact science issues, one should not expect an immediate specific answer without digging into the fabric of the region and without emphasizing three principles and five imperatives.

The principles are related to the Palestinians, since they are the weakest member of the Triangle, due to the multitude of factors ranging from denial of their political identity and independence to deprival of control over their land, natural resources and freedom of trade – in short, their economic destiny. Add to that the consensus among regional and international quarters that their cause is the crux of the Middle East problem. Hence, these principles are inevitable and should be as follows:

1 What is involved are rights, not acts of charity.
2 What is involved is not one category of rights, whether human, political, social or economic, but an integrated body of all these categories.
3 What is involved are inalienable rights, that is, rights which are incapable of being alienated, surrendered or transferred. This is the position of the United Nations, the repository of international legitimacy and the guardian of the Palestinian people's rights.

The Five Imperatives

1 Peace First

If, as has been rightly stated on several occasions since the Gulf War of January/February 1991, regional economic cooperation involving Israel as one of the parties will be a "peace dividend," then surely peace must be achieved. Yet such peace within the region as a whole is inconceivable without a political (therefore peaceful) settlement having been achieved between Israel and the Palestinians.

I recognize that criticism might be leveled at this essay because it introduces a political note into a discussion which is economic in nature. In anticipation, it can be stated that there is very little that can be achieved in the way of cooperation among parties unless they have normal relations with each other within a framework of peace and mutual confidence.

2 The Interface between Cooperation and Development

Cooperation is a positive value in itself, but in the context of this essay, which is meant to discuss it with the "hot" Triangle, it has four additional merits: *First*, it makes possible the pursuit and achievement of objectives that could not be achieved if the parties acted separately, or, if at all achieved, then the returns would be more limited and/or more costly, as cooperation is bound to create both internal and external economies. *Second*, cooperation, seriously and rationally pursued, can be conducive to a sharing of experience and a better allocation of resources, thus evening out shortages and surpluses. *Third*, cooperation enhances the process of development. Cooperation and development are but a twin that can interchangeably play the role of cause and effect, as development will provide a firmer base for cooperation, and cooperation, in return, will broaden opportunities of development. The *fourth* merit of cooperation, which is the most important and the outcome of the three points made above is that cooperation, following the establishment of a just and generally accepted peace, and the generation of mutual confidence, will consolidate the peace and enrich and boost the confidence level.

3 Cooperation is not Dependence

The intensity of the present dependence by the Palestinian economy should not be taken as a perpetual fate to which Palestinians must gear themselves. Rather, it should be taken as a trial of other parties' intentions to lend a helping hand to the Palestinian economy to gain a sufficient degree of independence, as this is the logical threshold of having a meaningful cooperation, which replaces dependence with independence. This, however, does not mean to attempt autocracy or complete "de-linkage"; it is to seek genuine cooperation based on voluntarism, reciprocity and equity.

4 Fair Implementation of Projects

This is to imply that parties to the regional economic cooperation in the Triangle should take into account when implementing projects the necessity of reducing economic disparities among them.

5 The Premise of Palestinian Control Over Natural Resources

The most important imperative to record is the exercise by the Palestinians of full control over their natural resources. Such control, arising from the inalienable right of ownership, is not merely a right explicitly declared and confirmed by the long-standing instruments of international law. It has also been stated, without equivocation, in a number of United Nations' resolutions on the right of states and of the Palestinian people to economic self-determination (in addition to political self-determination), and to unhampered control over their natural resources. The return to Palestinian control and use of the land and water resources expropriated by Israel since its occupation in 1967 is essential for the development of many sectors and programs which have so far been shelved in the concerned ministries of the Palestinian National Authority.

A Bird's-Eye View of the Actual Situation

Now, after having discussed the necessary and indispensable political foundations of any sound regional economic cooperation in the Triangle, one would certainly like to examine the actual situation on the ground. Palestinian laborers have been required to obtain work permits to enter Israel from 1991 onward, and since March 1993, Palestinians of the West Bank and Gaza Strip have been denied entry to Israel and Jerusalem, unless they have an Israeli-issued permit. Fixed roadblocks have been set up by the Israeli army at the major crossing points between the West Bank and the Gaza Strip (WBGS) on the one hand, and Israel (including Arab Jerusalem), on the other hand, to enforce these restrictions. While the permit policy has prevented the majority of Palestinians from casual entry into Jerusalem and Israel, it was not necessarily effective – at least initially – against the entry of workers seeking jobs, particularly in the West Bank, where the borders with Israel are long and porous. Moreover, there is no effective enforcement for compliance on the Israeli side (e.g., construction site or farm). The actual number of Palestinians working in Israel at any one time has often deviated substantially from the number of work permits issued. For example, in 1992 the number of issued work permits was around 70,000, while the actual number of Palestinians working in Israel was around 116,000 workers. However, this situation has been reversed with the increased intensity and policing of the borders.

The introduction and enforcement of the permit policy in March 1993 heralded a new era of controlling Palestinian access to Jerusalem and the Israeli labor market. In the period of border closure, even Palestinians with valid work permits are denied entry into Israel.

Limitations on Movement of Goods

The limitations on Palestinian mobility during closures largely constrain the mobility of goods and factors of production. Vehicles owned by and registered in the WBGS are generally denied entry into Jerusalem and Israel. During periods of closure, permits are largely rendered invalid. Thus, a border closure inhibits the movement of individuals and prevents Palestinians cars and trucks from crossing the border into Israel. Such limitations interrupt Palestinian trade substantially, whether it is with or through Israel, internal trade between the West Bank and Gaza Strip, or even between different parts of the West Bank.

These limitations result in a decline in total trade, with or through Israel. Generally, during closures Israeli exports to the Palestinian areas decline, but Palestinian exports decline much faster. Not only this, but a new concept of "internal" border closure emerged following the implementation of the Oslo II agreement, when authority over the main cities of the West Bank was transferred to the Palestinian National Authority in the fall of 1995. This means that during a period of internal closures, Palestinians cannot move from one urban center to another within the West Bank, or even to and from the surrounding villages to the urban centers.

As a result, West Bank urban centers have become small isolated islands, surrounded by the Israeli army, with no mobility in or out of these towns. Internal closures were applied when a sequence of suicide bombs occurred in February–March 1996, though there is no single piece of evidence capable of showing any relationship between collective punishment, such as closures, and the improvement of the security situation; on the contrary, there are many signs pointing to the opposite direction.

Low Level of Investment

The border closure policy can largely explain the difference between the substantial interest of local and diaspora Palestinians in investing in the economy and the actual low levels of investment that have materialized to date. First, the strong interest is based on a rosy scenario of long-run economic development, but the demand for investment has been reduced by the closure policy due to an overall decline in aggregate demand. Second, closure generally interrupts sales and increases operating costs, thus reducing overall profitability and reducing the incentive for new investment. Third, investment is deterred by the increased risk arising from uncertainty in the timing, duration and intensity of closures, an uncertainty which is over and above the strategic uncertainty resulting from the interim status of the political situation and the lack of clarity on the permanent status of the WBGS, particularly after the current Israeli government has opted to virtually paralyze the Oslo accord. Fourth, border closures have reduced public investment due to the diversions of donor funds allocated for projects that are largely aimed at income maintenance and budgetary support to cushion the impact of closures.

In addition to the above factors, closure reduces the supply of funds available for investment and increases the cost of such funds. Within an environment of closure, commercial banks have become much more conservative in their lending practices than they otherwise might be, leading to lower debt-financed investment levels. From another perspective, what is more obvious is the impact of border closure on increasing the expenditures of the Palestinian National Authority (PNA), such as on welfare to mitigate increasing levels of poverty. A significant part of the increased public expenditure is due to the substantial increase in public sector employment (some of which is accounted for by the desire to alleviate the impact of high unemployment).

Opportunities

Since the Palestinian National Authority has the power to make its own economic decisions, it will undoubtedly be a healthy member in the Triangle and the region as a whole. It will definitely launch an energetic drive for development, which will comprise infrastructure, housing, and the various goods and services-producing sectors of its economy. The dynamics of such a drive will necessarily strengthen the Palestinian economy, as it will facilitate the creation of jobs to absorb the expanding labor force. Hence, the nearly total dependence on the Israeli labor market should be reduced. However, this drive should not be confused with the concept of "de-linkage"; rather, it should be taken as a remedy to the security pretexts which result in an endless series of closures. If this remedy is taken, then it will improve the security atmosphere in the region in a manner which also reinforces the development prospects that necessitate one form or another of regional cooperation. The overall guiding principle regarding trade in goods and services among the parties of the Triangle should be that of unhampered free trade. This is an important principle because in the recent years trade has fallen dramatically as a result of repeated closures and transaction costs at the borders. The recent cut-off from Israel leaves the Palestinian economy caught in a predicament. Starting with the occupation in 1967, a one-sided customs union resulted in a preponderance of trade with Israel at the expense of other partners. The resulting unbalanced structure of trade is proving to be costly in the face of repeated border closures, while also creating a difficult policy dilemma, since any sudden redirection of trade away from Israel will be costly in the short run.

Water, Infrastructure, Environment, Food Production, and Tourism

The control, management, and use of water resources in the Triangle should be discussed and agreed upon by all parties. In this context, it is worth noting that Israel currently controls and confiscates more than 80 percent of the Palestinian water resources.

Much of the physical infrastructure in the WBGS is linked to or integrated with that of Israel. Hence, it is feasible to rehabilitate and join it with that of Jordan at a low level of cost.

Cooperation between Triangle parties in the environmental matters is important, as it implies the cleansing, purification, protection, and, to whatever extent possible, the shared heritage of and interest among three peoples living side by side in a relatively small piece of land, sharing the same sea line (Palestine and Israel), the same gulf (i.e., Aqaba when it relates to Israel and Jordan), adjoining the same river, and having an economic stake in the mineral resources of the Dead Sea.

The parties should not underestimate the fact that it is in their vital interests to look after the environment which they share. Not one party of the Triangle is self-sufficient in food production. This brings out the need for cooperation in the production of food products.

The parties of the Triangle, and indeed the region as a whole, enjoy excellent attractions for tourism, vacationing, and visits for more serious purposes. In the context of the last category, I refer to pilgrims, historians, archeologists, and scientists interested in the flora and fauna of the region. The tourist industry can be expected to expand considerably in the Triangle and the region. Adequate preparation will have to be made for the large influx of all categories of tourists and visitors. Such preparation involves infrastructural facilities and services, hotels, restaurants, sports and entertainment facilities, expanded transport and telecommunication facilities, and the training of many more guides and other workers skilled in the tourist and catering business and related activities.

In closing, I would like to point out what Professor Shimon Shamir, the former Israeli ambassador to Jordan, said at the opening of this conference: "The zero-sum approach is not any more valid or workable; hence, it should be replaced by the win–win approach." The meaning of this statement is nothing but a direct call to compromise, as this is the only way to a just and lasting peace in order to make regional cooperation in general, and within the Triangle in particular, both possible and desirable.

Part IV

Concluding Remarks

16

The Importance of Timing and Momentum

Dale F. Eickelman

I came to the conference after having spent three months in Morocco. When there, I mentioned to Moroccan colleagues that I was going to Jordan and Israel for the first conference by Palestinian, Jordanian, and Israeli academics held in their own lands. I was cautioned to expect mutual recriminations, in which people would talk past one another for at least the first day or two.

This did not happen. From the beginning, discussions were civil, and the hard issues were confronted directly: Palestinian refugees, water rights, the holy places, and historical memory – the experiences through which people of different generations have lived and which shape how they interpret contemporary events. The conference was ordinary in its conduct, but extraordinary in achievement.

The first issue emphasized by many of the speakers – Israeli, Palestinian, and Jordanian – was that the peace agreement, formulated at the highest levels of government, needs to be practically translated so that it is understood and has an effect at all levels of society. These include "ordinary people," those often without a direct political voice, people of different generations, and people from different religious and ethnic groups.

Our task as educators is to pay attention to the timing and sequencing of events intended to demonstrate that the peace agreement has practical and immediate implications. The issues raised in these concluding remarks are first steps in promoting a momentum to build upon the initial political steps toward peace.

A second issue is the practical steps through which progress toward peace can be made at levels below the apex of society and the state. Such steps should include textbooks, the mass media, and, as one of our Jordanian colleagues said, not waiting for committees and committees of committees to get things done. Since most of us here are educators who will soon return to our student constituencies in Jordan, in the Palestinian Authority, Israel and elsewhere, let us especially think about what is learned in school.

We must also recognize that the elite and the spokespersons of an older generation may not necessarily speak for their followers or for a younger generation, whether the group in question is *Hamas*, an Israeli political party, or a religious party or sect. In the Israeli–Palestinian–Jordanian "triangle," as in North Africa and the Arabian peninsula, there is often a major divergence between the voices of the leaders and those they claim to lead, just as there are major differences between school curriculums and what is learned in school.

As educators, we quickly learn that perhaps one-third of education relates to the formal curriculum. Peer learning accounts for the rest: "Don't take a course from Professor X, he is a tough grader; take a course instead from Professor Y. S/he grades easy and all you have to do is look at two or three books from a long reading list." Or, "don't pay much attention to religion course; it is out of date and everyone is going to get an A." Peer learning overshadows the formal curriculum, and it suggests where we must begin to effect significant change.

One essential point of departure is to figure out what youth are thinking. In Amman, for instance, Nasser Tahboub spoke about current political thinking among Jordanian university youth. Paradoxically, we know more about the political thinking of university students in Gaza and the West Bank, where universities have often been closed and disrupted, than we do about those in Jordan, where studies are subject to fewer interruptions. We need to know more about the stereotypes and popular understandings which have to be overcome. This includes the perception and attitude of many youth that the elite do not recognize issues which concern them. This is not a problem unique to the Middle East, but the political implications for the Middle East are more direct.

We must also pay more attention to the majority of moderate voices rather than those of extremists alone. There is a mini-industry in the United States fixated on questions of Islamic fundamentalism, and Yitzhak Rabin's assassination poignantly reminds us of the dangers of radicalism among Israeli Jews. At the same time, there are basic changes going on throughout the entire region. In the last thirty or so years, for example, higher education has spread to the masses and is no longer confined to the elite alone.

In Morocco, the commitment to universal education only followed independence in 1956. While the potential is not yet fully realized, the number of people educated, especially in higher levels of education, has multiplied far beyond anything envisaged in the years of French and Spanish colonial domination. Although the education of women still lags behind that of men, the gap is narrowing. For the Arab world, secondary and higher education also develops the formal language skills needed to talk back to the government and to religious leaders.

In Egypt, the massification of education at higher levels took off in the 1960s and 1970s, creating new communities of readers. The beneficiaries of mass higher education do not possess the same skills as the elite of an earlier generation, but they read and write, and it behooves us to find out what they are reading. If they are not reading Nobel laureates, such as Nagib Mahfuz, then we must ask what they are reading: we need to know about their "sidewalk" style books and what habits of thought these books inculcate. Why are certain books, with their colloquialisms, capturing such a wide audience? What need do these books address? Rather than just deplore the lowering of educational standards, we should ask what the consequences are of mass higher education and who are the new audiences created by it.

Mass higher education has reconfigured how people think about religion and politics. One of its important consequences has been to fragment religious and political authority. No state can speak for all of its people anymore, even if it says so. Fax, photocopies, cassettes, and other means allow different kinds of voices to be heard.

Books such as Syrian Muhammad Shahrur's *Al-Kitab wa-l-Qur'an,* an 800-page book arguing for new ways of reinterpreting the Qur'an, explain that Muslims must reinterpret the Prophet's message as if it was delivered only yesterday. This means exercising a direct access to the Qur'an, freeing believers from the shackles of medieval interpretation.

Even though the book was banned in Saudi Arabia, Saudis estimate that 10,000 or so photocopies were circulated anyway. In Egypt, another 10,000 photocopies were circulated until the book was finally published (in a pirated edition) after the assassination of Faraj Foda. Shahrur's book is only one of many, but with the exception of novels, 800-page books do not sell in the United States in significant numbers. Why do such books appeal to so many people and who are they? Who is interested in a radical reinterpretation of Islamic tradition which appeals directly to the reasoning skills of individual readers?

In Kuwait, in 1993, I tried to buy a copy of Shahrur's book in a religious bookstore. I was told that I should not read it because it was a book worse than Salman Rushdie's *Satanic Verses,* worse because Shahrur says that he is a Muslim, while Rushdie never emphasizes this claim. I finally found the book in a scientific and technical bookstore, itself a clue as to readership. Even books less intellectual than Shahrur's point to the growing fragmentation of religious authority and the influence of changing patterns of education. Radicalism is a significant threat to civil society in both the Islamic and Jewish religious traditions, but in both religious communities, albeit in not necessarily parallel ways, ideas of religious and political authority are rapidly changing.

In order to understand how to translate ideas from the elite to the general populace, we must recognize how shifting and flexible are concepts that we often take for granted, such as "ethnicity". The *Oxford English Dictionary*, which illuminates the archeology of words, indicates that the word "ethnicity" was not used in its modern meaning until about 1953. Now such identities are foregrounded in the consciousness of large numbers of people.

In Amman, for example, Asher Susser spoke about how the question of what it means to be a Jew has become a major issue in the debate over national and religious identity. Twenty years ago, Shlomo Deshen asked a profound question in one of his writings on Israeli society: Why is it that orthodox Jews have a political influence in Israel far beyond their numbers? If only one in twenty people are orthodox Jews in Israel, then why do they have such a dominant political voice?

Deshen's answer to these questions related to ongoing issues of Israeli national identity, issues unlikely to be resolved in the near future. Similarly, in Jordan, there are ongoing struggles over national identity between those of Palestinian and tribal origin. In the regions of the Palestinian Authority, one of which has inherited an Egyptian-dominated curriculum, and the other a Jordanian-dominated one, educators must work out the practical implications of what it means to be a Palestinian. As Abass Shiblak has said, this issue must be translated into curricular detail.

Alan Richards notes that the issues of implementing the peace process depend less on a complete resolution than a managerial one of process, of sustaining a sense of momentum. Learning to speak of sensitive issues in a civil manner in public and away from the partial secrecy of negotiating tables is a major accomplishment in itself.

Let me suggest a comparison with the Arabian peninsula which relates to timing. In the immediate aftermath of the discovery of oil in commercial quantities in Oman, for example, many people tried to persuade the former ruler to implement reforms so that people would perceive a direct benefit from the oil. Far from being a mere economic operator, the oil company recognized that a failure by the government to deliver tangible and immediate benefits would contribute significantly to creating a politically unstable condition.

The analogy with the Israeli–Palestinian–Jordanian triangle is imperfect, but timing, a sense of momentum, and steady progress are essential. As some participants have suggested, small changes in border-crossing procedures could contribute more to a sense of momentum than any number of solemn government pronouncements.

A greater accessibility of local governments might be another step, as might be textbooks which clearly and adequately represent the claims of religion and territory made by the "opposite" side. Recognition of the volatile and changing notions of religiosity and ethnic identity might be a way to begin talking openly about competing claims.

I am familiar with the Jordanian-designed curriculum for one of the Gulf states and the way in which it talks about Israelis. It is a more open and objective curriculum than that prevailing in other countries in the area. I do not know the Israeli curriculum in Hebrew as well, but it has been suggested that there is room for dramatic improvement in how Arab groups are represented. It will be a special challenge for the Palestinian Authority to find non-volatile ways of representing different groups, religions, and senses of identity. Can it be done? Yes! In Morocco, for example, after independence, a French and Moroccan team got together and worked out a shared curriculum representing the colonial past. The result was not a perfect solution, but the key textbook included original documents, even formerly incendiary ones.

Mass communication is another issue. One can mock American and French attempts to show "diversity" in portraying children on the ethnically-neutral representations of prime-time television. But the lack of any such initiative is a worse alternative. Only in the cinema can one hear ethnic and racial language in the United States. Television dramas, with their mass audiences, are significantly constrained in what they can say. This is an area where the investment of foundations and the cooperation of recalcitrant broadcasting authorities to show other people's religious traditions and children's programming is necessary and vital. Textbooks, like media representations, must be seen as urgent tasks which need not come out perfect on the first try, but which can be launched in the short term and rapidly improved. Such initiatives must be started now so that all parties concerned can see practical effects and benefits within a reasonable period of time.

Contributors

Musallam Abu-Helu is Assistant Professor of Political Geography at Al-Quds Open University, and a Director of Refugee Studies and Research Center. Dr Abu-Helu specializes in Palestinian refugees and housing policies for low-income people.

Taisir I. Amre is, since 1994, Director General – Ministry of Economics and Trade – Palestinian National Authority. Formerly he was Director of the Department of Foreign Affairs – Asia and Australia Division – PLO during the years 1990–1, and a member of the Palestinian delegation to the Refugee Working Group in the multilateral track of the peace process in the Middle East. Dr Amre also served as a member of the Palestinian delegation to the Palestinian–Egyptian–Jordanian–Israeli Quadripartite committee concerning the Palestinian displaced issue.

Fredrik Barth is a social anthropologist, and currently a research scholar under the Norwegian Ministry of Culture. Professor Barth has done fieldwork in the Middle East (Iraq, Iran, Oman, and Pakistan), in Indonesia, in New Guinea, and currently in Bhutan. His books include: *Political Leadership among Swat Pathans* (1959); *Nomads of South Persia* (1961); *Ethnic Groups and Boundaries* (1969); *Cosmologies in the Making* (1987); and *Balinese Worlds* (1994).

Aaron Ben-Ze'ev is Professor of Philosophy and Dean of Research at the University of Haifa. His research focuses on the philosophy of mind – particularly sense perception and the emotions, and on moral psychology and epistemology. His publications include: *Aristotle on the Soul* (Tel Aviv, 1989, in Hebrew); *The Perceptual System* (Peter Lang, 1993); *The Subtlety of Emotions* (MIT Press, forthcoming); and a co-edited volume of *Good Gossip* (University Press of Kansas, 1994).

Dale F. Eickelman is Ralph and Richard Lazarus Professor of Anthropology and Human Relations at Dartmouth College. Since 1968 he has traveled extensively in the Middle East, including long-term field research in Morocco and the Sultanate of Oman. His publications include: *Moroccan Islam (1976); Knowledge and Power in Morocco (1985); Muslim Travelers: Pilgrimage, Migration and the Religious Imagination* (co-edited, 1990); *Russia's Muslim Frontiers: New Directions in Cross-Cultural Analysis* (edited, 1993); *Muslim Politics* (co-authored with James Piscatori, 1996); *The Middle East and Central Asia: An Anthropological Approach*, 3rd edn (1988); and numerous scholarly articles and contributions to edited books. He was 1991 President of the Middle East Studies Association of North America, a 1992 Guggenheim Fellow, and a 1996–7 Fellow at the Woodrow Wilson International Center for Scholars (Washington, D.C.).

Gad G. Gilbar is Rector of the University of Haifa. His fields of specialization are economic and demographic history of the modern Middle East. His previous publications include: *Economic Development of the Middle East in Modern Times* (Tel Aviv, 1990, in Hebrew); *Population Dilemmas in the Middle East* (London, 1997); and *The Middle East Oil Decade and Beyond* (London, 1997). He is editor of *Ottoman Palestine 1800–1914, Studies in Economic and Social History* (Leiden, 1990); and co-editor of *Demography and Politics in the Arab States* (Tel Aviv, 1995, in Hebrew).

Joseph Ginat is Professor of Social and Cultural Anthropology and former head of the Jewish-Arab Center at the University of Haifa. He served as adviser to the Cabinet and the Prime Minister on Arab affairs and as personal adviser to Moshe Dayan. He was formerly head of the Israeli Academic Center in Cairo. His previous publications include: *Women in Muslim Rural Society: Status and Role in Family and Community* (New Brunswick, 1982); *Blood Revenge: Family Honor, Mediation and Outcasting* (Brighton, 1996); and *Polygamous Families in Contemporary Society* (co-author Irwin Altman, Cambridge, 1996).

Menachem Klein is a Research Fellow at the Jerusalem Institute for Israel Studies and lecturer in the Department of Political Studies at Bar-Ilan University. His book *Doves Over Jerusalem Sky: Jerusalem in the Israeli-Arab Peace Negotiations 1977–1997* is forthcoming. His publications in the field of Palestinian politics include: "Competing Brothers: the Web of Hamas-PLO Relations," in *Terrorism and Political Violence* (Summer 1996); "Quo-Vadis: Palestinian Dilemmas of Ruling Authority Building Since 1993," in *Middle Eastern Studies* (April 1997); and "Between Right and Realization: The PLO Dialectics of 'The Right of Return'," in *Journal of Refugee Studies* (forthcoming).

Uri M. Kupferschmidt is a Senior Lecturer in the Department of Middle Eastern History at the University of Haifa. His major field of specialization is the social history of the modern Middle East. His previous publications include: *The Supreme Muslim Council, Islam under the British Mandate for Palestine* (Leiden, 1987); a co-edited volume with Gabriel R. Warburg, *Islam, Nationalism, and Radicalism in Egypt and the Sudan* (New York, 1983); and several articles in scholarly journals on twentieth-century political Islamic movements. In addition, he has for over two decades served as a frequent commentator for Dutch and Belgian radio stations, *inter alia*, covering the fluctuations between war and peace in the Middle East region.

Moshe Ma'oz is Professor in the Department of Middle Eastern History at the Hebrew University in Jerusalem, and the Director of the Harry S. Truman Research Institute for the Advancement of Peace. His major field of specialization is modern Syria and Palestine. His previous publications include: *Ottoman Reform in Syria and Palestine, 1849–61* (Oxford, 1968); *Palestinian Leadership on the West Bank* (London, 1984); *Asad. The Sphinx of Damascus: A Political Biography* (London and New York, 1988); *Syria and Israel: From War to Peace-Making* (Oxford, 1995).

Mary E. Morris is a partner in Morris & Morris. She is also the Vice President of Programs, at the Los Angeles World Affairs Council. Previously, she was Associate Director of the Greater Middle East Studies Center at RAND in Santa Monica, as well as a senior researcher and Associate Director of the Strategy and Doctrine Program in RAND's Arroyo Center. She is an instructor in international conflict resolution at California State University, Dominguez Hills. Ms Morris is the author of reports, monographs, and journal articles on the Middle East, including: *New Concepts for Middle East Alliances* (Hebrew University of Jerusalem, 1996); *The Post-Peace Agenda for the Middle East: Coping with Demographic Stresses* (RAND, 1995); *Where Environmental Concerns and Security Strategies Meet: Green Conflict in Asia and the Middle East* (RAND, 1995); *The Persistence of External Interest in the Middle East* (RAND, 1994); "Poisoned Wells: The Politics of Water in the Middle East," in *Middle East Insight* (1993); and "The Pivotal Player: Jordan's Geostrategic Role in the Middle East," in *Al-Nadwa*, the Jordanian World Affairs Council, 1992.

Joseph Nevo is Professor in the Department of Middle Eastern History at the University of Haifa. He has published extensively on the modern history of Jordan, Saudi Arabia and the Arab society in pre-1948 Palestine. His recent book, *King Abdallah and Palestine: A Territorial*

Ambition, was published in 1996 by Macmillan and St Antony's College, Oxford.

Moshe Shemesh is a Senior Lecturer on Middle Eastern studies at the Ben-Gurion University, Beer-Sheva, and a Senior Research associate at the Ben-Gurion Research Center, Sede-Boker. In 1988–9 he was Visiting Fellow at St Antony's College, Oxford University. His previous publications include: *The Palestinian Entity 1959–1974: Arab Politics and the PLO* (1988); *The Suez-Sinai Crisis 1956, Retrospective and Reappraisal* (co-editor, 1990); as well as articles on Palestinian politics and the PLO, the Arab-Israeli conflict, the Lebanon crisis, Egypt and inter-Arab relations.

Steven L. Spiegel is Professor of Political Science at the University of California, Los Angeles. He specializes in the analysis of world politics, American foreign policy, and American foreign policy in the Middle East. Professor Spiegel has published extensively. His books include: *The Other Arab-Israeli Conflict: Making American's Middle East Policy, from Truman to Reagan* (University of Chicago Press, 1985); *World Politics in a New Era* (Harcourt Brace, 1995); *Dominance and Diversity: The International Hierarchy* (Little, Brown and Company, 1972); and *The International Politics of Regions* (Prentice-Hall, Inc., 1970), written with Louis Cantori. His most recent edited volumes are: *Conflict Management in the Middle East* (Westview Press, 1992); *The Arab-Israeli Search for Peace* (L. Rienner Publishers, 1992); and two volumes of *Practical Peacekeeping in the Middle East* (Garland Publishing, 1995), with David Pervin. He is now working on a volume about the Middle East in the post Cold War era.

Asher Susser is a Senior Fellow at the Moshe Dayan Center for Middle Eastern Studies at Tel Aviv University, and former head of the Center (1989–95). He is also Professor in the Department of Middle Eastern History at Tel Aviv University. Professor Susser's research and teaching has focused on modern Middle Eastern history, religion and state in the Middle East and Arab-Israeli issues, with particular reference to Jordan and the Palestinians. He has been a Fulbright Fellow, a Visiting Professor at Cornell University and at the University of Chicago, as well as a Visiting Fellow at the Washington Institute for Near East Policy. He is the author and editor of a number of books and monographs, including: *Between Jordan and Palestine; On Both Banks of the Jordan; At the Core of the Conflict: The Intifada; Jordan's Disengagement and the Middle East Peace Process;* and *The Hashemites in the Modern Arab World.*

Unni Wikan is Professor of Anthropology at the University of Oslo. She has published extensively in the field of anthropology in the Middle East, including: *Life Among the Poor in Cairo* (London, 1980); *Behind the Veil in Arabia: Women in Oman* (Baltimore, 1982 and new edition, Chicago, 1991); *Managing Turbulent Hearts: A Balinese Formula for Living* (Chicago, 1990); and *Tomorrow, God Willing: Self-Made Destinies in Cairo* (Chicago, 1996).

Onn Winckler is a Lecturer in the Department of Middle Eastern History at the University of Haifa. His major field of specialization is the demographic and economic history of the modern Middle East. His previous publications include: *Syria: Population Growth and Its Consequences, 1960–1990* (Tel Aviv, 1995, in Hebrew); *Population Growth and Migration in Jordan, 1950–1994* (Brighton, 1997); "Syria: Population Growth and Family Planning, 1960–1990," in *Orient*, Vol. 36, No. 4 (1995); "Syrian Migration to the Arab Oil-Producing Countries," in *Middle Eastern Studies*, Vol. 33, No. 1 (1997).

Index

[redacted]